The Translocal Island of Okinawa

SOAS Studies in Modern and Contemporary Japan

SERIES EDITOR:
Christopher Gerteis (SOAS, University of London, UK)

EDITORIAL BOARD:
Stephen Dodd (SOAS, University of London, UK)
Andrew Gerstle (SOAS, University of London, UK)
Janet Hunter (London School of Economics, UK)
Barak Kushner (University of Cambridge, UK)
Helen Macnaughtan (SOAS, University of London, UK)
Aaron W. Moore (University of Edinburgh, UK)
Timon Screech (SOAS, University of London, UK)
Naoko Shimazu (NUS-Yale College, Singapore)

Published in association with the Japan Research Centre at the School of Oriental and African Studies, University of London, UK.

SOAS Studies in Modern and Contemporary Japan features scholarly books on modern and contemporary Japan, showcasing new research monographs as well as translations of scholarship not previously available in English. Its goal is to ensure that current, high-quality research on Japan, its history, politics and culture, is made available to an English speaking audience.

Published:
Women and Democracy in Cold War Japan, Jan Bardsley
Christianity and Imperialism in Modern Japan, Emily Anderson
The China Problem in Postwar Japan, Robert Hoppens
Media, Propaganda and Politics in 20th Century Japan,
The Asahi Shimbun Company (translated by Barak Kushner)
Contemporary Sino-Japanese Relations on Screen, Griseldis Kirsch
Debating Otaku in Contemporary Japan, Patrick W. Galbraith,
Thiam Huat Kam and Björn-Ole Kamm (eds.)
Politics and Power in 20th-Century Japan, Mikuriya Takashi and
Nakamura Takafusa (translated by Timothy S. George)
Japanese Taiwan, Andrew Morris (ed.)
Japan's Postwar Military and Civil Society, Tomoyuki Sasaki

The History of Japanese Psychology, Brian J. McVeigh
Postwar Emigration to South America from Japan and the Ryukyu Islands,
Pedro Iacobelli
The Uses of Literature in Modern Japan, Sari Kawana
Post-Fascist Japan, Laura Hein
Mass Media, Consumerism and National Identity in Postwar Japan,
Martyn David Smith
Japan's Occupation of Java in the Second World War, Ethan Mark
Gathering for Tea in Modern Japan, Taka Oshikiri
Engineering Asia, Hiromi Mizuno, Aaron S. Moore and John DiMoia
Automobility and the City in Japan and Britain, c. 1955–1990,
Simon Gunn and Susan Townsend
The Origins of Modern Japanese Bureaucracy,
Yuichiro Shimizu (translated by Amin Ghadimi)
Kenkoku University and the Experience of Pan-Asianism,
Yuka Hiruma Kishida
Overcoming Empire in Post-Imperial East Asia,
Barak Kushner and Sherzod Muminov
Imperial Japan and Defeat in the Second World War, Peter Wetzler
Gender, Culture, and Disaster in Post-3.11 Japan, Mire Koikari
Empire and Constitution in Modern Japan,
Junji Banno (translated by Arthur Stockwin)
A History of Economic Thought in Japan, Hiroshi Kawaguchi and
Sumiyo Ishii (translated by Ayuko Tanaka and Tadashi Anno)
Transwar Asia, Reto Hoffman and Max Ward (eds.)
Haruki Murakami and the Search for Self-Therapy, Jonathan Dil
Japan's Empire of Birds, Annika A. Culver
Chronicling Westerners in Nineteenth-Century East Asia,
Robert S. G. Fletcher and Robert Hellyer (eds.)
The Tale of Genji through Contemporary Manga: Challenging Gender and Sexuality in Japan, Lynne K. Miyake
Contesting Memorial Spaces of Japan's Empire,
Edward Boyle and Steven Ivings (eds.)

The Translocal Island of Okinawa

Anti-Base Activism and Grassroots Regionalism

Shinnosuke Takahashi

BLOOMSBURY ACADEMIC
LONDON • NEW YORK • OXFORD • NEW DELHI • SYDNEY

BLOOMSBURY ACADEMIC

Bloomsbury Publishing Plc, 50 Bedford Square, London, WC1B 3DP, UK
Bloomsbury Publishing Inc, 1359 Broadway, New York, NY 10018, USA
Bloomsbury Publishing Ireland, 29 Earlsfort Terrace, Dublin 2, D02 AY28, Ireland

BLOOMSBURY, BLOOMSBURY ACADEMIC and the Diana logo are trademarks of Bloomsbury Publishing Plc

First published in Great Britain 2024
Paperback edition published 2026

Copyright © Shinnosuke Takahashi, 2024

Shinnosuke Takahashi has asserted his right under the Copyright, Designs and Patents Act, 1988, to be identified as Author of this work.

For legal purposes the Acknowledgements on pp. viii–ix constitute an extension of this copyright page.

Cover image: KAZUHIRO NOGI/AFP via Getty Images

All rights reserved. No part of this publication may be: i) reproduced or transmitted in any form, electronic or mechanical, including photocopying, recording or by means of any information storage or retrieval system without prior permission in writing from the publishers; or ii) used or reproduced in any way for the training, development or operation of artificial intelligence (AI) technologies, including generative AI technologies. The rights holders expressly reserve this publication from the text and data mining exception as per Article 4(3) of the Digital Single Market Directive (EU) 2019/790.

Bloomsbury Publishing Plc does not have any control over, or responsibility for, any third-party websites referred to or in this book. All internet addresses given in this book were correct at the time of going to press. The author and publisher regret any inconvenience caused if addresses have changed or sites have ceased to exist, but can accept no responsibility for any such changes.

A catalogue record for this book is available from the British Library.

A catalog record for this book is available from the Library of Congress.

ISBN: HB: 978-1-3504-1153-1
       PB: 978-1-3504-1156-2
       ePDF: 978-1-3504-1154-8
       eBook: 978-1-3504-1152-4

Series: SOAS Studies in Modern and Contemporary Japan

Typeset by Integra Software Services Pvt. Ltd.

For product safety related questions contact productsafety@bloomsbury.com.

To find out more about our authors and books visit www.bloomsbury.com and sign up for our newsletters.

Contents

Acknowledgements		viii
Explanatory notes		x
List of acronyms		xi
1	Imagining the islands against the grain	1
2	Struggles in the US-occupied Okinawa	21
3	Remaking the site of struggle	45
4	Shimao Toshio's cultural resistance	65
5	From Okinawa to Asia	89
6	Translocal lives in anti-base activism	113
7	Invisible threads of regionalism	139
Notes		147
Selected bibliography		164
Index		168

Acknowledgements

Writing this book would have been impossible without support from innumerable individuals. Although I cannot refer to all of them individually here, I do wish to single out some names.

First and foremost, I want to thank Professor Tessa Morris-Suzuki for her tireless support and encouragement, which has literally saved me countless times. I am confident that I was never an 'easy' student to supervise. But her patient guidance helped me tremendously to formulate my messy thoughts throughout my doctoral research. Her excellence and dedication as a scholar and educator are still my main source of inspiration, and I am still learning from her ethics as an academic. The support of the late Professor Brij V. Lal was also irreplaceable. Brij, who was a renowned expert of modern Pacific history, taught me the power of writing the history of individuals who otherwise hardly receive scholarly attention. The influence of these two scholars has been decisive for my approach to the field of historical research in terms of perspective, style and ideas.

My biggest thanks go to the members of Okinawa-Korea People's Solidarity, including Takahashi Toshio, Nishio Ichirō, Yu Yeongja and Tomiyama Masahiro for providing me with their life histories. I am also hugely indebted to academics and activists in or from Okinawa, including Arasaki Moriteru, Wakabayashi Chiyo, Abe Kosuzu, Shinjō Ikuo, Mori Keisuke, Tokuda Masashi, Doi Tomoyoshi, Tasaki Masami, Taira Osamu, Makishi Yoshikazu, Itokazu Keiko, Okamoto Yukiko, Takazato Suzuyo, Yamashiro Hiroji, Ashimine Gentasu, Isa Masatsugu and Takahashi Masahiro.

I am also grateful to my colleagues and friends in Australia and New Zealand for their company along the way, namely: Alexander Brown, Yasuko Hassall Kobayashi, Simon Avenell, Pedro Iacobelli, Danton Leary, Dario Di Rosa, Lauren Richardson, Vera Mackie, Ruth Barraclough, Rowena Ward, Hyaeweol Choi, Narangoa Li, Chris H. Park, Lina Koleilat, Yonjae Paik, Gavan McCormack, Nori Onuki, Shun Ikeda, Miyume Tanji, Julia Yonetani, Markus

Bell, Keiko Tamura, Catherine Churchman, Justin Tutty, Dougal McNeill, Stephen Epstein, Dennitza Gabrakova, Yoko Yonezawa, Yoshie Nishikawa, Yiyan Wang, Alexander Bukh, Grant Jun Otsuki, Courtney Powell, Joshua Jeffery, Ju Eok and Yuri Cerqueira dos Anjos. Also, the students who took my undergraduate courses (i.e. JAPA 213 and JAPA 322) over the past four years gave me a great motivation to complete this book.

Many other individuals in Japan, South Korea and elsewhere also helped me at different stages of this project directly or indirectly. This includes Karashima Masato, Daniel Joachim, Andy Wang, Chen Kuan Hsing, Sun Ge, Baik Yeong-seo, Kim Kyongmook, Shiobara Yoshikazu, Kawabata Kōhei, Ogasawara Hiroki, Park Sara, Yasui Daisuke, Heonik Kwon, John Brown Childs, Hiroshi Fukurai, Kim Yeonghwan, Modjtaba Sadria, David Ewick, Claudia Kim, Inazu Hideki, Takahara Taichi, Tanabe Juichirō, Joshua Rickard, Keida Katsuhiko, Umeya Kiyoshi, Fukada Yūko, Ishiwata Hiroshi, Wolfram Manzenreiter, Jimmy Yamauchi, Tabuchi Yoshihide and Takeuchi Masatoshi.

This book would not have been possible without support from a number of institutions in Australia, New Zealand and Japan, including the ANU Japan Alumni PhD Scholarship, CHL Fieldwork Grant, Grant-in-Aid for Young Scientists by the Japan Society for Promotion of Science (Grant No. 18K12930), Victoria University's Research Establishment Grant and the Faculty Strategic Research Grant, and Asian Collection Room of the National Library of Australia. I want to thank some individuals who kindly guided me along the way, in particular Mayumi Shinozaki and Jo Bushby.

This book is dedicated to my family in Japan, South Korea, the United States and Australia, especially my parents, Yang Kuy-young and Takahashi Ichirō. My deepest gratitude goes to my partner, Melissa Ahlefeldt, and two boys, Kai and Dan. I appreciate your company, love and support on sunny and rainy days across three countries.

Explanatory notes

In this book, the names of Japanese and Koreans are written in the East Asian order, except in the case of scholars writing mainly in English. Therefore, the surname comes first, followed by the given name.

For romanization of Japanese and Okinawan pronunciation, this book generally uses macrons when necessary (e.g. Satō Eisaku).

This book generally uses 'Okinawa', but 'Ryūkyū' or 'Ryukyu' is also used to describe particular nouns of institutions (e.g. the University of the Ryukyus), places (the Ryūkyū Arc) and the polity (the Ryūkyū Kingdom).

A previous version of Chapter 4 was published in *Transpacific Visions: Connected Histories across North and South* (Lexington Books, 2021) as 'The Journey to the Archipelago: Shimao Toshio, Southern Localism, and the Dream of *Japanesia*'. An early version of Chapter 5 was published in *Rethinking Postwar Okinawa: Beyond American Occupation* (Lexington 2017) as 'Beyond Minority History: Okinawa Korea People's Solidarity and Internationalization of the Okinawa Struggle'. Part of Chapter 6 was published in *PORTAL: Journal of Multidisciplinary International Studies* 16(1).

Acronyms

ACSA	The Action Committee for Solidarity with Asia (Ajia to Rentai-suru Jikkō Īnkai)
ARC	Activism by the Residents of the Ryūkyū Arc (Ryūkyū-ko no Jūmin Undō)
CROHC	The Council for the Return of Okinawa to the Home Country (Sokoku Fukki Kyōgi-kai)
GRI	Government of the Ryukyu Islands (Ryūkyū Seifu)
IRS	Institute of Regional Studies (Chiiki Kenkyūjo)
NOF	New Okinawa Forum (Shin Okinawa Fōramu)
ODA	Okinawa Democratic Alliance (Okinawa Minshu Dōmei)
OKPS	Okinawa-Korea People's Solidarity (Okinawa Kankoku Minshū Rentai)
OLDP	Okinawa Liberal Democratic Party (Okinawa Jimin-tō)
OPP	Okinawa People's Party (Okinawa Jinmin-tō)
OSMP	Okinawa Social Mass Party (Okinawa Shakai Taishū-tō)
OTGSA	Okinawa Teachers and General Staff Association (Okinawa Kyōshokuin-kai)
RDP	Ryūkyū Democratic Party (Ryūkyū Minshu-tō)
SACO	Special Action Committee on Okinawa
SPKB	Society for the Protection of Kin Bay (Kin Wan wo Mamoru-kai)
USCAR	The United States Civil Administration of the Ryukyu Islands

1

Imagining the islands against the grain

The northern part of Okinawa Island is a highland covered with a massive forest, called *yanbaru*, which means 'a mountainous field' in the local language. This is a home for a diverse range of endangered indigenous species such as the Okinawan rail and Okinawan woodpecker. Deep in this lush and verdant forest, there is a sparsely populated community, Takae, which is also known as 'a village embraced by the forest'. However, in recent years, this peripheral community has also been described as 'a targeted village' (*hyōteki no mura*) because the Japanese Ministry of Defense and local contractors started a military helipad construction project in summer 2007 for the use of the US Marines.[1] Fearing the possible natural and cultural catastrophe, some of the concerned villagers and their supporters began to organize protest campaigns. Their activism includes protest marches, public meetings, petitions, publishing media articles and lobbying in the local and national assemblies, etc. But the core of their activism is direct action, trying to physically interrupt further construction work. The prime site of confrontation was the gates of the construction sites. The protesters occupied the areas through sit-ins and human chains. People also used their cars as a blockage, parking the vehicles neatly in a parallel line.

This is a snapshot of the little-known world of civic activism in Okinawa, or Okinawa's so-called anti-US base movement, whose roots date to the grassroots land rights movement in the early 1950s. As a result of the Battle of Okinawa, one of the hardest-fought battles in the Pacific theatre towards the end of the Second World War from March to June 1945, the US military incorporated Japan's south-western island region under its direct occupational rule.[2] The first ten years of the occupation were crucial as it was during this period that the US occupation authority transformed a significant part of Okinawa Island and its neighbouring smaller islands, such as Ie Island, into land for the bases, training areas and other military facilities.[3] Washington considered this region to be strategically crucial as it is located at the heart of the East Asian region between the Chinese continent, the Korean Peninsula and mainland Japan. After the founding of the People's Republic of China in October 1949, the US occupation administration rushed to extend military facilities that were already constructed by the Japanese army prior to the war and created new bases. The construction process often involved coercive eviction of the original local residents, threatening them with arms and destroying their houses and spaces of livelihood. Upon his visit to Okinawa in January 1957, Yanaihara Tadao, then President of the University of Tokyo, described Okinawa as America's 'military colony', comparing it with Singapore, Malta and Gibraltar under the British rule.[4]

Confronted by the violent evictions and subsequent loss of means of life, some of the community leaders gradually organized petitions, direct negotiations and sit-ins at the front of the headquarters of the US Civil Administration of the Ryukyus (USCAR), demanding decent payment of land fees and no new land requisition. Yet, the response from the US government, which was issued as the Price Recommendation in June 1956, only fanned local frustration, which led to the first mass protest across Okinawa Island, or the so-called first 'whole-island struggle' (*shimagurumi tōsō*). Almost seven decades have passed since then. In the meantime, numerous large and small political actions have taken place at parliament, courts and in the streets to redress social injustice, including different forms of human rights violations and political and military violence against individuals and communities. Through various forms of activism, Okinawans have been crying out for the dignity of local inhabitants and for administrative, political, economic and social rights that are continuously neglected and deprived of under the shadow of the US-Japan bilateral security alliance system, which some critics call the 'structural discrimination' against Okinawa.[5]

However, Okinawa's subordinated status did not just start during the American occupation. Rather, there is a deeper and longer historical root. One of the critical moments arrived in 1609 when the Shimazu clan, a feudal lord based in the Satsuma domain, invaded the Ryūkyū Kingdom. Shimazu's intention was at least twofold – extension of their southern territory to as far as Amami-Ōshima and monopolization of the maritime trade between the Ryūkyū and their southern counterparts, particularly Ming China. This invasion resulted in the incorporation of the northern Ryūkyū islands as Satsuma's penal colonies and sugarcane plantations. Also, Shimazu succeeded in placing the Ryūkyūans' trade business under its control. Together with white and black porcelains produced by ethnic Korean potters who were forcibly taken to Satsuma during Toyotomi Hideyoshi's invasion of Korea (1592–3 and 1597–8) and their descendants, Shimazu became a major economic player with rare trading items and one of the wealthiest domains in Japan under the Tokugawa Shogunate (1603–1867). Thus, the invasion of Ryūkyū brought a significant advantage to Satsuma, as it resultantly prepared a ground for the Shimazu clan not only to be a powerful domain but also to take off as one of the earliest domains with modern warfare technology in the mid-nineteenth century with which they, with Chōshū and other domains, eventually toppled the Tokugawa regime in 1869.

The end of the Tokugawa period and the subsequent opening of modern Meiji Japanese government brought another challenge to the Ryūkyūans. In 1879, the Ryūkyū Kingdom was fully incorporated by the Japanese government and the islands were transformed into Okinawa Prefecture. The Japanese government executed the incorporation of the Ryūkyū by referring to it as 'disposal' or 'punishment' (*shobun*). The use of those terms clearly suggests a firm conviction among the Japanese leaders about the rationale behind the abolishment of the Ryūkyū Kingdom, which was to 'civilise' the people of Ryūkyū. The territorial integration of the islands was executed in order to establish Japan's political influence in the southwestern seas. Thus, it was pursued in tandem with Japan's invasion of Taiwan. Yet, as reflected in the very notion of *shobun*, the abolishment of the Ryūkyū Kingdom was part of the punitive measures towards the Ryūkyūan leaders who otherwise would persist with the old or previous customs (*kyūkan*), which translated into 'backwardness' vis-à-vis modern Japan, including their diplomatic relationship with Qing China.

Japan's imperialist desire entailed in the notion of time lag was expressed in entrenching the logic of differences between mainland Japanese and Okinawans, such as the Human Pavilion in the Osaka National Industrial Exhibition in 1903, a traumatic embodiment of the racialization of Japan's colonial others. As such, while Okinawans were officially regarded as people from mainland Japan (*naichi*), as opposed to overseas colonial and occupied territories (*gaichi*), they were still subjected to various social, cultural and racial discriminations based on the logic of the lag and the civility, which is also compellingly depicted in a number of literary works such as Kushi Fusako's 'Memoir of a Declining Ryūkyūan Woman'.

The Battle of Okinawa in 1945 was, in many respects, regarded as one of the most excruciating culminations of Okinawa's modern experience. The forcible incorporation of the Ryūkyū Kingdom with military forces in the 1870s took place in an early stage of Japan's colonization of the neighbouring territories. However, what differentiates Okinawa and other colonized territories is, as Uemura Naoki points out, that Okinawa was one of Japan's *internal* colonies along with Hokkaido.[6] This logic of ethnic and racial difference reflected in the ambiguous formation of 'Japanese national identity' among Okinawans became a deep cause of numerous tragedies. In the war, Japan's Imperial General Headquarters saw Okinawa as a sacrificial lamb to buy some time before the war on the mainland. This decision led Okinawa to become one of the worst battlegrounds in the Pacific, with over one hundred-thousand civilians were being killed, including uncountable deplorable stories that have been revealed or still kept in memory of individuals or a local community, such as the forced suicide in Kerama Islands that happened in March on the eve of the US invasion of Okinawa Island as well as all the other stories that follow.

What this history suggests is that today's political and social situation in Okinawa did not start in 1945 but is another segment of a deeper experience endured in the island community on the edge of the Japanese archipelago. Therefore, their challenges would not be fully understood without acknowledging the layers of grievance that are entailed in the people's struggles in Okinawa. It is precisely because of this reason that we need to understand that 'Okinawan anti-base movement' is a general term which refers to numerous different de-imperial and de-colonial activisms in the past and the present. Thus, the local activism is not self-apparent and homogeneous, contrary to the view that is widely shared outside of the island. In other words, Okinawa's anti-base struggle is an aggregation of different civic activism and a multitude of individuals with ideas, resources and networks that are not unitary. Also, the type of activism varies depending on the context and the actors involved. It ranges from institutional actions such as lawsuits, lobbying and parliamentary debates at both local and national scales and grassroots activism such as direct actions and protest gatherings. Even if these might not be categorized as 'activism' in a strict sense, other platforms to learn and exchange knowledge and experiences such as seminars, study groups and casual meetings are also integral parts for constructing a sense of community and shared understanding among participants in the anti-base movement across social, cultural and territorial boundaries. This complex, and sometimes internally contradictory, representation of locality compels me to ask myself about what it means to be 'the local', although we often use this concept without scrutiny of its meaning, and how are these concepts manifested in the development of Okinawa's anti-base struggle?

In this book, I examine the meaning of locality in the context of Okinawan activism by considering the historical processes, conflicts and negotiations involved in presenting and representing the collectivity of their activism. It is true that, in general, locality is understood as a concept that is characterized by various attributes of place, culture and inhabitants. In geology, for example, locality might indicate a particular bioregional territory that is characterized by specific types of flora and fauna. In anthropology and sociology, locality could mean a bounded social or cultural community in which the members share a particular system of values and social reality. Yet, from a constructivist perspective, this very notion of community or society might be seen differently as it involves labour, resource, discourse and practice to constitute the system of value or social reality. As those approaches suggest, locality is not a single-layered entity but is structured by material and discursive conditions.

In a political context, however, such as Okinawa's base politics, this intricate structure of locality tends to be sidelined and subsumed into oversimplified monolithic images, often highlighting the most conspicuous traits, such as people with placards or activists taking confrontational political actions. Even for the last ten years or so, public media, high government officials and even academics misconceive Okinawan activists in one way or the other, portraying them as people acting upon their 'egoism'. Kevin Maher, the former Director of the Office of Japan Affairs at the US State Department, for example, once described the local protesters as the 'master of extortion'.[7] In a similar vein, Mark Ramseyer, a Harvard law professor, recently writes that 'Okinawan elites obtain higher subsidies from the national government' by instigating the local population to protest.[8] Also, within Japan, too, the current affairs program *News Joshi* (News Girls) on Tokyo MX TV depicts the local protest movement even further along the line by calling the activists 'terrorists'.[9]

In this context, the local protesters are framed as a minor fraction of 'angry dissidents' who do not speak on behalf of the majority of 'normal citizens'. This is a taxonomical understanding of the local population that is exercised to categorize people as to whether they are 'real local or non-local', 'local elite or mass', or 'locals who think rationally or emotionally'. Therefore, this framing is not only partial but also divisive and manipulative, which does not reflect the entirety of the anti-base movement, nor does it help us have nuanced insight into the 'local' activism.

This taxonomical understanding of the local population has been a core instrument that constitutes modern government. The census, through which people, lands, cultures and beliefs are characterized and classified as an object and registered centrally, is a great invention in this regard. As Michel Foucault elucidates, the concept of population is in itself a means, exercised directly and indirectly, through which the multitude of people become both subject and object of governance to 'improve' their society and living conditions.[10] So, the taxonomical understanding of the 'locals' such as those I mentioned above is not merely a partial or misconceived representation of the actual scene. The more serious and imminent issue here is that those divisive and manipulative discourses also have generative power over or can reconfigure the form of space, life and culture of a place that is called 'Okinawa' at our cognitive level.

This kind of discursive manipulation of local reality is not new in the history of Okinawan anti-base politics. Like anti-authoritarian movements in post-colonial nations in East Asia during the Cold War, such as South Korea and Taiwan, the political bipolarization through the trope of the 'pro-government' and 'anti-government' forces is so deeply entrenched in the society that this antagonistic Cold War rhetoric is felt as if it still 'haunt[s] the physical and mental alleyways of significant parts' of Okinawa's political life.[11] Also, this kind of binary logic reformulates the meaning of the place, most typically as a 'troubled land', so that Okinawa's base politics is often called the 'Okinawan problem' (*Okinawa mondai*).[12] Therefore, what I tentatively call *Cold War geopolitical reductionism* plays a crucial role in the affirmation of this divisive rhetoric to be employed, structured and ultimately felt real at the societal level.

Against the grain of this manoeuvring technique of space, people and culture, I argue that Cold War geopolitical reductionism is detrimental for us in fostering a reasonable understanding not only of local activism but also *what locals are*. It sees, at the epistemological level, territoriality and social and cultural relations that constitute Okinawa in a paternalistic manner by regarding the local lives as 'petitioning subjects' who need to be cared for, guided and protected from internal and external threats by more powerful others.[13] In this sense, the project that I undertake in this book goes beyond a purely academic concern. This book serves to counter the paternalistic discourse and the political economy that marginalizes, or *minoritizes*, local politics. Put differently, this is a project to recuperate our social imagination on Okinawa's anti-base politics in light of anti-colonial/anti-imperial struggles in the context of Japan, East Asia and beyond.

This book examines the local world of Okinawa's anti-base activism in terms of the complexity of the geopolitical scale and social relations. While I am against Cold War geopolitical reductionism, this does not mean that I reject the entire discussion on geopolitics. On the contrary, it has been a profound source of inspiration to engage in critical analysis of Okinawa's political constraints and subjectivity. The series of pioneering works by Arasaki Moriteru (1936–2018) are one of the great examples in this sense. From the early days of his career in the 1960s, Arasaki's analyses of Okinawan politics for over half a century were continuously centred around the question of how to interpret Okinawa's geopolitical position in Japan and Asia in terms of anti-imperialist politics.[14] For example, in his speech delivered in 1988 at the graduation ceremony of Okinawa University, Arasaki, who was then President of the University, said to the attendees that Okinawa's locational advantage enables [us] to be diagnostic about the limits and problems of the postwar Japanese politics, particularly in relation to the United States, while at the same time it allows us to see the similarities between Okinawa's postwar path and that of other post-colonial nations in Asia. Okinawa's distinct characteristic not shared by the rest of the country means, he argues, that Okinawa has the 'privilege of standpoint' (*ninshiki no yūisei*) vis-à-vis Japan in understanding the regional relations.[15]

Yet, Okinawa's geopolitically advantageous or privileged position does not just derive from its topographical whereabouts but rather it comes from

Okinawa's modern experience, that is, the atrocities of war, the occupation period under the US military and unending legacies of those periods as embodied in the local military bases. In other words, Arasaki's standpoint is formulated through the devastation and deprivation of the land and placed-based life and through the history that is shaped by people's struggles for the recovery and reconstitution of their livelihood space. Therefore, Arasaki's standpoint indicates an alternative way to conceive geopolitics in Okinawa, which is built around people's political control over their own lands and lives and bounded by the 'memories of wounds', as Shinjō Ikuo describes it.[16]

Here, the 'wounds' suggest not only the catastrophe experienced by the dead and injured in the long gone past, but the ones that are felt in the present and that speak to the living as ethical imperatives. These wounds are repeatedly remembered through experiencing direct and structural violence. This could be crime, harassment or other forms of unnerving actions such as the explosive noise of the fighter jets, the sight of camouflage-patterned jeeps, the leakage of water contaminated with fluorine compound and the remains of war dead which are still discovered in the ground. Thus, the wounds are felt presently, as they are embedded in many corners of everyday scenes, and those implicit and explicit traces of the past appear through the 'cracks' (*sakeme*) of the landscape.[17] It is 'the material aspects of traces', which some historical theorists such as Ewa Domanska call 'presence', that sends the voice of the dead to the living, and the texture of the past to the present. Presence can sometimes conjoin semiotics, discourse theory or representation theory, and yet it has its own specific realm as a concept. As Domanska points out, through sensing presence, we are able to discern the 'traces on an aspect that is marginalized or neglected by traditional notions of the source.'[18] Therefore, the memories of wounds as recalled mnemonically through material embodiment will never cease sending signals of the past and speaking to the living.

The memories of wounds do not belong exclusively to the war dead and other types of immediate victims of military violence, but also to those who are related personally, communally or contextually. Feeling the pain of others enables us to have a sense of our historical being that is multi-nodal, compounded by manifold contexts and points of connectivity. Or, it reminds us that we are living in what Tessa Morris-Suzuki calls the 'implication' of the past, even if it is the past of a distant period and place.[19] As such, we are embedded in multiple scales of locality, and for this reason, Okinawa's memories of wounds can be a 'channel' (*kairo*) that connects us with the others who endure personal and social predicaments in the face of direct and indirect military violence. It can take us beyond the narrowly defined 'I' or 'We', as the power structured upon the US-Japan Security Treaty is exercised not only in Okinawa but also in other parts of Japan, which, on a broader scale, is also linked with other US-led bilateral security alliances in Asia and the Pacific such as that with South Korea, the Philippines and Australia. Therefore, Okinawa's place-based politics is qualitatively different from the strategic use of geopolitics, and its significance cannot be fully grasped without knowledge of the social struggles in the region across local and national borders.[20]

The translocal island of Okinawa

Rearticulating Okinawa's geopolitical disposition enables us to imagine the form of Okinawa's anti-base politics that entails dynamic and extensive social relations within its collective representation. My argument draws upon some of the existing studies by scholars such as Abe Kosuzu and Mori Keisuke. Their ethnographic research, based upon long-term participation and observation of the direct actions against the helipad construction in Takae, shows that the space of protest action is a dynamic construct through physical and discursive labours by individual actors who are involved in making the activism and that the activism cannot be subsumed into a single cultural identity. Their studies similarly show that the protest community is a complex aggregation of different agents, actions, rationales and networks that are related to each other.[21] This means terms such as 'uniqueness', often used to characterize the collective representation of Okinawan base-politics, are not self-evident.[22]

Yet, I am not suggesting abandoning our focus on the identity of the local activism in praise of the individualistic approach as an alternative analytical concept. Instead, what I suggest is to focus on interactive aspects that foreground the processes involved in the making of collective identity. Historian and critic Yakabi Osamu argues that the form of the local activism in places such as Henoko, especially the participation of individuals of diverse origin, shows us that 'Okinawan' could be something that one 'becomes' (*ni naru koto*) as well as 'is' (*de aru koto*). Through 'becoming', Yakabi brings to the fore a mode of 'the locals' that is not reducible to cultural heritage. Compared to 'being-an-Okinawan', 'becoming-an-Okinawan' stresses the importance of consciousness towards the problems Okinawa is facing and action to address the problems. Therefore, the 'becoming' model understands the nature of activism slightly differently from the 'being' model in the sense that the former model allows us to see the space and community as the construct of enculturation, not as a result of acculturation. By doing so, his argument provides an alternative mode and layer of Okinawanness that is not necessarily bounded by the logic of one's ancestry.

Yakabi's imaginative conceptualization of Okinawa's locality appears as a space, community and radical subjectivity on the sites of the protest movement in places such as Takae, Henoko, Naha and most recently in other islands of the Arc of Ryūkyū where the military bases and facilities not only of the United States but also Japan's Self Defense Forces are installed such as Amami in the north and Yonaguni in the southwest of the archipelago.[23] This alternative mode of locality, or localities, is what I call *the translocal island*. The value of this actor-based approach is that it shows the change and continuity of Okinawa's anti-base struggle in terms of activists' diverse ways of articulation of Okinawa's locality. Also, by highlighting the multiplicity of meaning and actors entailed in the Okinawan struggle, the translocal island intervenes in the monolithic representation of local activism as portrayed by the culturalist account. Centring human activities as the core force in making history, this concept uncovers how different kinds of social practices and ideas are woven into the social fabric of the local protest movement. As a result, the translocal perspective allows us to *recontextualize* the ways in which Okinawa's anti-base politics have been organized and practised across the cultural and territorial boundaries by those who have been involved in this historical struggle from as early as the early 1950s.

The concept of the 'translocal island' is my own yet it is built upon the lineage of scholarship on the local anti-base struggle, which, in my view, has shown a significant development particularly in the last two decades. One of the key issues scholars have been addressing is how to articulate the complexity of actors and extensive scale of space and contexts entailed in the local activism. These scholars of Okinawan activism try to present the world of the local struggle that has been continuously simplified and overlooked by Cold War geopolitical reductionism. For example, Miyume Tanji's *Myth, Protest and Struggle in Okinawa* and Masamichi S. Inoue's *Okinawa and the U.S. Military* are some of the most important works in this regard. Based on their fieldwork from the late 1990s until early 2000s, both scholars similarly address the issue of collective identity, including different perceptions of and motivations for the Okinawan anti-base movement. Tanji's conception of 'protest community' and Inoue's 'civic identity' echo one another and reveal the differences of identities within what is often represented as the 'Okinawan' anti-base movement.

Julia Yonetani and Kelly Dietz raise another issue with cultural reductionists' view on locality in terms of both geographical and social scales. Yonetani and Dietz take into account 'locality' not as a marker of cultural uniqueness but as a basis upon which a particular mode of activism is constructed. Their works enable us to see not only Okinawa's distinctiveness but its relevance to local activism as part of anti-colonial struggles against the presence of the United States in other parts of the Asia and Pacific region and beyond.[24]

While the above-mentioned scholarship is focused on the contemporary situation, historical research shows earlier cross-border encounters between Okinawans and activists from overseas. For example, Yuichiro Onishi's work delves into the transpacific solidarity movements that took place around the same period in the form of anti-imperialism/anti-racism struggles in Okinawa, Japan and the United States.[25] Similarly, Abe Kosuzu has written an article in which she examines the interaction between the anti-Vietnam War Black GIs and Okinawans by focusing on the local situation in Okinawa.[26] Uehara Kozue's research shows the interaction between Chamorro activists in Guam and Okinawans who were involved in the protest movement against the construction of the central terminal station of petroleum in Kin Bay during the 1980s. Those studies are crucial as they show a way to frame Okinawan activism in the past and the present in terms of interconnections with extra-local actors whose presence might otherwise be sidelined or neglected at the corners of the mainstream narrative. In other words, those studies have shown a new horizon, which allows us to revisit and conduct more nuanced examination of the very notion of locality as something that is constituted through regional social forces, connectivity and convergence. As such, the translocal perspective on the culture and history of Okinawan anti-base activism helps us see its radical political subjectivity in terms of *links* and *flows* with other communities in the past and present, instead of uniqueness of cultural identity.

Put differently, this relational approach conjures up a form of locality that is enmeshed within, not isolated from, the web of interconnections. The image of locality presented here is best exemplified by the metaphor of 'vortex', which Tessa Morris-Suzuki described as a place where 'multiple flows meet'.[27] Seen through the prism of vortex, we can conceive of the alternative version of locality that may take various forms. It may appear as 'a series of linked dots far removed from one another in space' instead of a large block of land or an administrative territory.[28] Or, it could take form of the livelihood space of people whose stories are normally underrepresented yet contain extensive networks beyond territorial boundary. Ultimately, the fluidal articulation of locality as a vortex indicates that things like cultural cohesion offer no ground for us to assume that there is a unchangeable demarcation that separates the 'inside' from the 'outside' of the borders for a long period of time. In other words, what Morris-Suzuki suggests is to *unfocus* the institutional borders and to try to see underrepresented relationships that are more flexible and multidirectional and have often unexpected ways in which space and borders are articulated on the ground level.

Grassroots regionalism and the question of 'postwar' in Okinawa

So, what kind of radical subjectivity of Okinawa does the translocal perspective help us see? In other words, what are the reasons for us to take into account the links and interconnections in understanding the history of the Okinawan anti-base struggle? Before we wrap up this introduction, I want to consider this question. Here, we need to come back to an earlier discussion on Okinawa's historical, cultural and geopolitical disposition in the region.

As discussed earlier, what differentiates Okinawa's political criticality derives from the experience of and consciousness towards the recent past after the Second World War, or the period that is called 'postwar', as well as the discrete history and memory of colonization in the 1870s. The issue is that, unlike mainland Japan, the definition of postwar (or *sengo*) has yet to be settled in Okinawa. The controversies can be summed up in the following question: When was or is the 'postwar' period in Okinawa? In the rest of Japan, August 1945 is often referred to as the beginning of Japan's long postwar given its acceptance of the Potsdam Declaration. The common historical narrative around this period normally traces the occupation of the Japanese archipelago by the Allied powers until Japan recovered its territorial sovereignty in May 1952 (and December 1953 for the southern island region of Amami). At school in Japan, students learn that those early days of the postwar period are the start of 'contemporary' history, the past that is directly relevant to 'now'. Yet, we cannot automatically assume that this applies to Okinawa's experience as its 'postwar' period was radically different from the rest of Japan.

In his book, *The Postwar History of Okinawa* (*Okinawa Sengo-shi*), Arasaki points out two characteristics that define the condition of Okinawa's early postwar experience. The first point he raises is Okinawa's separation from the other regions of Japan in terms of its political administration as the direct result of the Battle of Okinawa, where a quarter of local population were killed. Incorporated under the direct rule of the US military administration, Okinawa's war was not felt by the local population to have 'ended' but rather it appeared that the wartime continued in the form of occupation by the victor of the brutal war. The second feature concerns the ways in which the local economy and society were developed in the early 1950s. In mainland Japan, this was the period when the special procurement demand from the US occupation forces due to the outbreak of the Korean War boosted the Japanese economy. However, in the US-occupied Okinawa, this was the time when the US occupation forces reinforced the extension of the airbases and other military facilities.[29]

The contrasting trajectories of history in Okinawa and Japan inscribed a critical gap in terms of the beginning of postwar, which became even deeper in the following decades. After the Korean War, Okinawa, together with the US bases in the Philippines and northern Thailand, was involved in US anti-communist warfare in Vietnam. Yet, throughout the 1960s until the early 1970s, the rest of Japan experienced a transformative period in terms of economic growth. The administration handover in May 1972 could have been an opportunity to fill in this gap.[30] However, this controversial 'reversion' of Okinawa to Japan resulted in an even higher density of the US bases in Okinawa, as some of the bases in mainland Japan were relocated to Okinawa. This situation saw little change even after the collapse of the Berlin Wall and dissolution of the Soviet Union as Okinawa was incorporated into a new regional and global security politics of the United States and its Japanese counterpart. Given this context, Abe Kosuzu published a short essay in which she says that 'we cannot find the "postwar"', and this sense of incompleteness of the 'postwar' era is a reason for the locals to question, and disagree on, the assumption that the Second World War was the last major warfare Okinawans were involved in.[31]

Although Okinawa's postwar experience is not easily comparable with that of mainland Japan, its experience should not be subsumed into the discourse of mere provinciality. Rather, the difficulties in marking the beginning of the postwar era in Okinawa should be also examined in the regional as well as Japanese contexts. The case I make here is that Okinawa's historical experience during, and after, the occupation period is not necessarily a peculiar case in light of the local experience of the Cold War in East Asia. As Heonik Kwon points out, it was the Japanese experience of the Cold War which was radically different from most other communities in the region.[32] In the time when many parts of East (and Southeast) Asia suffered the pain of political struggles for the establishment of post-colonial nation-states, which were in many cases interrupted by Cold War politics, Japan was one of the very few parts of the region where both the significant economic growth and stable parliamentary system were achieved. Therefore, in Japan, it is inferable that the Cold War tends to be regarded and remembered as something akin to that of the North-Atlantic world. In this context, Okinawa's local experience is a crucial case to understand the significant costs that were paid on the other side of Japan's 'long peace' in the regional terms.

Nevertheless, I am not naively suggesting subsuming Okinawa's postwar experience into that of the rest of post-colonial East Asian countries. The political conflicts experienced in many parts of the former colonial territories were in essence struggles for post-colonial nation building. Also, the borders that are drawn between the Thirty-Eighth Parallel between North and South Koreas and the Taiwan Strait between China and Taiwan are based upon competitive rivalry, which defines not only political system but also the ideal model of human progress, whereas the administrative separation of Okinawa from mainland Japan reflected the strategic and political decision made in Tokyo and Washington to have Okinawa as the vanguard of the pro-US camp. In this context, Okinawa's position and the meaning of the anti-base struggle require careful consideration when they are compared with other parts of the region.

However, it can also be said that Okinawa's position and experience as a military colony between postwar Japan, post-colonial Cold War in East Asia and Pax Americana complicates the regional experience of this period, which allows us to see a more ambiguous form of governance, sovereignty and resistance in the region.[33] In fact, this ambiguity involved in Okinawa's disposition in the national and regional political contexts is a strong reason for Okinawan activists to be able to create links with other anti-colonial/ imperial movements not only in Japan but also in the United States, East Asia and beyond. By actively mobilizing their past and present in reference to the struggles of regional others, Okinawan activists continuously seek and create the language that articulates and translates violence, discrimination, destruction and deprivation of local rights and any other forms of social injustice experienced by others. This effort also made it possible for Okinawans to establish solidarity movements with their regional neighbours. I argue that the translocal perspective foregrounds people's individual and collective efforts, consciousness and actions to regionalize activists' mindset, or what I call *grassroots regionalism*.

The very early seeds of regionalism can be seen already in the 1950s. Students at the University of Ryukyus such as Arakawa Akira, who later became a renowned journalist and critic, saw the meaning of their resistance in the context of the Third World movement in Asia.[34] This precedent was followed by other cases such as the solidarity movements with anti-Vietnam War, anti-racism, indigenous activism in the Pacific and others. Aside from that, the joint projects for discovering and commemorating the memories of Korean conscripted workers as labourers and military prostitutes (or the so-called comfort women) in various parts of Okinawa Prefecture in the 1980s created a momentum among scholars and concerned citizens for re-examining and reconstructing their wartime history in the region through the eyes of the colonial others. The direct interactions with anti-base activists in Asia and the Pacific such as the Philippines and South Korea in the 1990s are one of the examples which show how regional solidarity of the anti-base politics was achieved at the inter-communal level.

The accumulation of sporadic exchanges has progressed to yield collaborations with regional counterparts in a more institutionalized and sustainable way in recent years. One of the important turning points for Okinawan activists and scholars came around 2010. Prompted by the increase in the interests in Okinawa in places such as South Korea, Taiwan and China, one of Arasaki Moriteru's seminal texts, *The Contemporary History of Okinawa* (*Okinawa Gendai-shi*), was translated into Korean in 2008 and in Chinese in 2010. This was followed by a major book launch conference at Okinawa University in Naha and the East Asia Critical Journals Conference held in Quemoy in Taiwan in 2010. These projects had laid the foundation in furthering interest in the role of such historically marginalized islands as Quemoy and Okinawa in regional political relations in the past and the present.[35]

It was in this context that Arasaki Moriteru presented a paper titled 'Can Okinawa Be a Catalyst for the Peace in East Asia?' at the Asian Circle of Thought 2012 Shanghai Summit in October 2012. The event was large in scale, with participation by scholars, artists, curators and publishers across the region such as India, South Korea, Okinawa, Japan, Taiwan, Malaysia, Indonesia and Hong Kong to discuss and find common challenges in each locale from regional perspectives. One of the main hosts of the conference, Kuan-Hsing Chen recalls that while the issues that were raised by the participants are rooted deeply in the social and cultural conditions in different locales, 'the dimensions of observation, explanation, and critical thinking usually go beyond the single matter itself, to coalesce, in time, into diverse modes of thought, characteristic to either specific thinkers or intellectual groupings'.[36] Along with other distinguished scholars including Paik Nak Chung, Ashis Nandy, Partha Chatterjee, Itagaki Yūzo, Hilmar Farid and Jomo Kwame Sundaram, Arasaki represented Okinawa, discussing its particular local challenges, especially on the people's struggles, which he regards as the primary driving force of post-Second World War Okinawa. While explaining the development of the anti-base politics in the postwar Japanese context, he also insists on the need to consider Okinawa's geo-historical location from a regional perspective. So, the second half of his discussion was about the history of political relations around

Okinawa in the region in terms of the experience and history of people making their lives on the borderlands in the East China Sea, including Okinawa. In it, he coins the concept of 'the sphere of living' (or *seikatsu-ken*), where he argued that it is important to shift our focus on the map of the region, which is strictly and strongly defined by 'domain' or 'territory', to a more flexible and liquefied world such as that of local fishermen.[37] Presented in plain language, Arasaki's argument was yet compelling as it reminds us of the presence of alternative communal relations in the region that have always been regarded as too trivial to take into account. The sphere of living, as opposed to militaristic concepts such as 'sphere of influence', highlights a shared space that is fluid, as it is shaped by the currents of the sea and directions of the wind and human interactions. Yet, it has been a way to maintain the common space by the inhabitants of the borderland communities. Arasaki's thesis on Okinawa as a 'catalyst' for peace in the region, therefore, was his critical intervention in the concept of areas that has predominantly been defined by Cold War geopolitical reductionism.

The Translocal Island of Okinawa unravels the stories of communities and individuals whose actions weave the history and the social fabric of Okinawa's anti-base movement. Those stories, which tend to be neglected in the shadow of geopolitical reductionism, bring to the fore the memories of people who play a crucial role in making, unmaking and remaking local activism.

Structure of the book

This book consists of seven chapters, including the introduction and the concluding essay. All are centred around the question: how has grassroots regionalism been playing a constitutive part in the enactment of local activism?

In Chapter 1 I have discussed the meaning of the translocal islands, a concept which enables us to examine the political and cultural conditions that are involved in making 'locality' from a trans-border perspective.

Chapter 2 focuses on the early period of Okinawa after the 'end' of the Second World War, from the late 1940s until mid-1950s. One of the key issues addressed in this chapter is how Okinawans, especially city dwellers in the central and southern regions of Okinawa Island and farmers in Ie Island, coordinated the early protest movement. Drawing upon both primary and secondary sources, this chapter unveils the origin of the anti-base community, which was not necessarily ideologically organized but emerged as grassroots politics after a series of negotiation failures with the US military government over land rights and other everyday concerns. The accumulated frustration led to the eruption of the first island-wide protest campaign in the summer of 1956. This mass protest campaign attracted several hundred thousand islanders across Okinawa Island, which laid the foundation for the history of Okinawa's anti-base movement. This chapter discusses the roots of Okinawa's struggles and how the protest culture was created.[38]

Chapter 3 examines Okinawa's challenge around the period of its return to Japan in the late 1960s and the 1970s. This was another crucial period in that the island-wide campaign for the return to Japan, or the second island-wide mass campaign led by local progressive leaders, ended in the reinforcement of Okinawa's subordinated status in the subsequent post-reversion era under the US-Japan security system. This failure of party-led progressive politics, however, became a reason for the local villagers of Kin area to challenge their leaders over the plan to construct a major petroleum repository facility on the shores of the nearby bay where they fished. Their activism gave a new meaning to Okinawa's radical subjectivity, which was grassroots and non-partisan.

The deep sense of locality that emanated from the Kin Bay struggle created an opportunity among activists to wonder about the situations of other locales not only within Okinawa Island but also the entire southern islands, some of which had been incorporated as part of Kagoshima Prefecture. Their concern gave a momentum to start a new form of activism, which is dedicated to creating a network beyond their site of struggles. This chapter highlights the stories around the activists, academics, journalists and other concerned citizens who established the Society for Promoting the Anti-CTS Struggle. The Society's promotional activities urged the activists to have a common language to describe their action with people from different island communities, which gave rise to a regionalism as *Ryūkyū-ko* (or the Ryūkyū Arc). Activists perceived and used this geological concept as a socio-cultural concept in expressing their sense of unity as one people who live in the area which was formerly the Ryūkyū state. Therefore, the Society was later renamed *Ryūkyū-ko no Jūmin Undō* (the Residents Movements in the Ryūkyū Arc). By examining their central concept, *chiiki*, which can be translated into both 'location' and 'region', this chapter delves into the challenge of this early form of grassroots regionalism.

Chapter 4 examines the dynamics of this region in the 1960s and 1970s from a slightly different perspective. Instead of discussing activism *per se*, this chapter elucidates ideological background of those activists through examining the concept of the Ryūkyū Arc or *Ryūkyū-ko*. The idea of *Ryūkyū-ko* had a significant impact on Okinawan students and young critics, such as Arakawa Akira, Kawamitsu Shin'ichi and Okamoto Keitoku, who later organized the Society for Promoting the Anti-CTS Struggle in the mid-1970s about the way they define their radical regionalism. Therefore, it is not unreasonable to say that their activism would not be fully understood without the knowledge of *Ryūkyū-ko* as a cultural and political concept.

For this reason, this chapter examines the thoughts and activities of Shimao Toshio, a novelist, essayist and a leader of the local historical society in Amami Island, who is regarded as the main advocate of *Ryūkyū-ko* throughout the 1960s and early 1970s. Especially, this chapter focuses on the way that he described Amami and the southern islands, including Okinawa, as Japan's 'sugarcane plantation' by comparing Puerto Rico and Hawaii, where he stayed prior to his first visit to Okinawa in the early 1960s. Through closely examining his journey and texts, this chapter argues that Shimao's concept of 'sugarcane plantation' should be read as his critique of Japanese colonization and his liberatory cultural politics advocating for the southern island region to decentre or to dislocate the centrality of Japanese influence, which was rapidly spreading in the southern islands and reincorporating the region into its political economy.

Chapter 5 examines another form of grassroots regionalism by delving into the history around the founding and development of Okinawa-Korea People's Solidarity, an activist community which was started with the aim to build and reinforce the anti-base solidarity with South Korean activism. While the 1980s and 1990s saw creation of various forms of non-partisan civic activism, it was also the time when the activists were concerned about the future directions, especially how to expand the networks of their activism under limited material, cultural and financial resources. Despite multiple structural constraints, it was in this context that some of them conceived of starting international solidarity with people who would also experience similar struggles. Some activists who later founded the Association for Solidarity with Asian People were those who were inspired by the historic success of popular politics against the authoritarian regime in the Philippines and South Korea in the late 1980s. They saw those events not as the fire across the river but regarded them as an event with much for Okinawans to learn about in galvanizing their own activism. This momentum led to the founding of Okinawa-Korea People's Solidarity movement in 1998. This chapter unravels a micro-history of internationalization of Okinawan activism.

Chapter 6 addresses the origin of the Okinawa-Korea People's Solidarity through the life history of some of its key members. Through examining their lived experiences as well as relevant historical events, this chapter revisits what it means to be 'local activists' in the context of Okinawan anti-base politics beyond a culturalist account. The lives of those individuals and the ways they engage in Okinawan activism show that what we often call bluntly 'the locals' is a heavily bordered concept and a subject of negotiation and contestation. By tracing the footsteps of the three key individuals, this chapter allows us to understand how different social contexts such as student activism in the 1960s and the 1970s, civil rights struggles of the ethnic Korean population, religious activism and engagement in the South Korean anti-authoritarian movement are intricately intertwined in making an invisible layer in the social fabric of the Okinawan anti-base community.

The last chapter is an autoethnographic essay that centres around my journey over the past ten years. In conceiving and writing this book, I had the great privilege of being in different parts of the South Pacific as a resident or as a sojourner, including Darwin in Australia's Northern Territory which has become one of the key stations, together with Okinawa and Guam, for the US Marine Corps who serve in the containment operation of China since 2012. Building upon my personal experience, particularly in Australia, this essay invites us to conceive of Okinawa and Okinawa's base politics as relevant to the life in their South Pacific region in terms of political context and structure, and to address how Okinawa can be a crucial reference for us to critically engage in insular nationalism in those countries. I argue that this translocal interpretation of homeland politics in Australia is imperative in the time when the regional political relations are increasingly polarized and severed due to rivalry rather than cooperation.

2

Struggles in the US-occupied Okinawa

Life in the ashes of the war

On 26 March 1945, the Allied powers landed in the Kerama Islands region, to the west of Okinawa Island. Prior to this campaign, the Allies issued Proclamation No. 1 under the Commander in Chief of the US Pacific Fleet, Admiral Chester Nimitz, declaring the establishment of the Military Government in the occupied lands and adjacent waters, while suspending the influence of the Japanese government. This was the beginning of the Battle of Okinawa, which was fought over the period of the next two months, followed by the subsequent occupation of Okinawa Prefecture by the US military forces until May 1972. This period was also remembered as the formative period of the long-lasting struggle in Okinawa, known as 'the Okinawan anti-base movement' or 'the Okinawan struggle'. This chapter investigates actors, institutions and some of the key historical events involved in making the anti-base movement in the early period of US-occupied Okinawa. It examines the political and social processes by which the local protest communities were formed.

The Ryūkyū Islands region, including Amami Islands (which are currently part of Kagoshima Prefecture), had been administered under the US Military Government of the Ryūkyū Islands for the first five years of the occupation period. Yet, as the strategic significance of the region increased, reflecting on the founding of the communist countries in continental Asia, it was replaced by the US Civil Administration of the Ryukyu Islands (USCAR) in December 1950. Although USCAR was established with the intention to implement 'civil administration' in the region, in a practical sense, it was still an administration led by the US troops under the directive of the Far Eastern Command of the US Forces.[1]

In the early period, USCAR was represented by the Governor, the position held by the Supreme Commander of the Allied Powers (SCAP) based in Tokyo. Therefore, it was the Deputy Governor, an army general, who was responsible for the local administration of the region. This system was maintained until in 1957, when the US Far East Command was integrated into the Pacific Command based in Hawaii. Upon this change, the Deputy Governor was replaced by the High Commissioner, who had greater influence than the Deputy Governor on the local governance, including the civil affairs.[2] Therefore, with mixed feelings of awe and hostility, the local people called him 'the Emperor of Okinawa'.[3]

A renowned historian Prasenjit Duara once described one of the characteristics of the US influence in overseas territories as 'imperialism without colonialism'.[4] Of course, Duara is fully aware that this principle does not apply to some places such as the Philippines. Yet, his remark is still useful in understanding the ambiguity around the position and policies of the US military government in Okinawa since Washington did not intend to establish colonial rule in Okinawa for trade, farming or other economic purposes as we saw in British and other European and Japanese colonial administration in their overseas territories.[5] The US President Dwight D. Eisenhower, for example, stated that one of the seminal missions of the military government was 'to encourage the development of an effective and responsible Ryukyuan government based on democratic principles' according to the Executive Order signed in June 1957.[6]

The US occupation policy was built on this principle from the outset. Bringing together former local senior politicians, the Okinawa Advisory Council (*Okinawa shijun-kai*) was established in a displaced persons' camp in 1945, which was subsequently transformed into the Okinawa Civilian Government (*Okinawa Minseifu*) to implement local administration of Okinawa Island and neighbouring islands in 1946. The same kind of administration was established to govern other regions in the Ryukyu Islands such as Miyako Islands region, Yaeyama Islands region and Amami Islands region. These administrative groups formed the four regional governments

(*Guntō Seifu*) in 1950, where the Governors and the members of the assembly for each region were chosen locally by election.

However, the level of local administrative and political autonomy was limited. The US Military Government Special Proclamation Number 37 stipulates that the resolutions by the local assembly were inferior to the decisions made by the US military government. Therefore, the US military government was able to refuse, overturn or invalidate the decisions made by the local representatives. The regional government system was dissolved and integrated into a single governing body, which is called the Government of Ryukyu Islands or GRI (*Ryūkyū Seifu*) in 1952, which comprises the Legislature and the administrative agencies. This integration in part took place as the US occupation authority felt the need to conduct more effective and direct control of the Ryūkyū Islands, reflecting on the increasing local demand for Okinawa's return to Japan, led by the Governor of the Okinawa Islands Regional Government, Taira Tatsuo. As Historian Ōta Masahide states, local autonomy was tolerated as long as it did not threaten the US authority.[7]

The position of the US military administration was, therefore, ambivalent. It is true that the US did not have a plan to establish a colonial government, yet it was still a colonial power of some kind. In this sense, Yanaihara Tadao's analogy of military colony by comparing Okinawa with Singapore and Malta would still be important, and the very reason why Washington granted USCAR such strong power was a purely strategic motive for establishing America's influence in East Asia and the north-western Pacific.

The long-term US occupation of the Ryūkyū Islands was already deemed necessary in the late 1940s given the precarity of the regional politics. In the declassified document titled 'The Ryukyu Islands and Their Significance', dated August 1948, Washington considered the location of the Ryūkyū Islands 'one of the most controversial issues in any settlement of Far Eastern problems.' Also, it says that control of this region would enable the occupying country to gain benefits in both 'offensive and defensive operations' in Asia and the Pacific regions, which would also be effective 'to discourage any revival of military aggression on the part of the Japanese.'[8] The document also reports the potential risk, if the US withdrew from the Ryukyu Islands, that Chinese communist forces would take over the region. One year later, this concern had become more imminent for the United States when the People's Republic of China was established in 1949.

Along with Okinawa's geopolitical location, the military facilities that had already been constructed by the Japanese Imperial Army also gave a strong reason for the United States to settle on the island. The above-mentioned document states that there were overall 'twenty-two airplane bases and sea plane bases, eleven of which were constructed on Okinawa [Island] during the war'. Also, it says that six of the eleven airbases on the island were capable of accommodating the heavy bomber B-29 *Superfortress*, which they deem possible to 'bring within range of the interior of China, any part of Japan and Korea, portions of eastern Siberia including Vladivostok, the whole Philippine Islands, Guam and Marinas, and portions of Southeast Asia and the Netherlands East Indies.'[9]

However, the problem for the US occupation authority was how to justify their occupation of Okinawa. While Okinawa had experienced six years of US occupation under SCAP as a former 'enemy territory', Washington had to resolve the issues around Okinawa's sovereignty to keep its camps in the soil on the island. This was because there was no statement in either the Cairo Communique or the Potsdam Declaration which defined the treatment of Okinawa after the war. It was the San Francisco Peace Treaty, signed in 1951, where Okinawa's status had been clarified.

Although this Peace Treaty allowed for the recovery of Japan's territorial sovereignty, in the Article Three of the Treaty, Okinawa was decided to be incorporated under the control of the United States while it still remained as part of Japanese territory. Situated in this ambiguous position, Japan was allowed to execute its administrative power on only 'residual' matters, whereas USCAR would have 'exclusive authority' over the Okinawa Islands region and the other three regions of the Ryūkyū Islands (i.e. Miyako Islands, Yaeyama Islands and Amami Islands) and Bonin Islands for an 'indefinite' period.[10] This political process shows the degree of complexity in establishing the legitimacy of the US occupation in Okinawa as something akin to a military colony, which still complicates the interpretation of Okinawa's historical position until today.

The war and occupation had significant impact on a number of aspects of civic life, such as dislocation. In this sense, we should look at how the local populations experienced the end of the war and thereafter. While approximately one-fourth of the local residents, including civilians and military personnel, were killed during the Battle of Okinawa, those who were captured by the Allied troops were taken to sixteen different camps, eleven of which were established on Okinawa Island. Camps in places such as Ishikawa, Kin, Kushi, Taira and Ginoza were allocated to civilians, whereas former military soldiers, officers and personnel, including mainland Japanese, Okinawans and Koreans, were kept in Yomitan, Chatan, Urazoe and Yaka as Prisoners of War (PoW). The largest camp for civilians was in Ginoza, which occupied almost the entire village. At one point this camp contained over two hundred thousand Okinawan residents, which was almost one-third of the civilian population who managed to survive the warfare.[11] Although there were camps in the southern part of Okinawa Island, such as Ōnoyama, most of them were later closed due to the construction of the military bases in that region.[12]

Upon Japan's acceptance of the Potsdam Declaration in August 1945, the local civilians and Okinawan PoWs were gradually allowed to return to their homes.[13] However, while some returned to their local land, as Wakabayashi Chiyo points out, many chose to settle in or around the camps instead of returning to the southern region.[14] This can be attributed to the fact that they could not identify the areas where they used to live due to the devastation of the land. To make matters worse, military facilities for the US troops were constructed in the former residential areas. Along with Ōnoyama, places such as Mawashi, Urazoe, Ginowan and Futenma had been confiscated to build residential areas for US military personnel, storage and power plants, the military hospital and the large aircraft landing zone.[15] In most of these cases, the original owners had no choice but to give up their lands.[16]

These radical changes caused not only displacement but also the transformation of the local economy and other aspects of civic life. Prior to the war, the main industry in Okinawa was agriculture, which accounted for more than 60 per cent of its entire economy.[17] However, towards the late 1940s, farmers were increasingly leaving their jobs due to the decline in price for agricultural products and the prohibition on using the land around the bases for farming, as well as the loss of private property.[18] These factors made it difficult to continue businesses such as agriculture, which requires a high labour intensity. Furthermore, another factor that changed Okinawa's industrial structure was the decline of the US military personnel in Okinawa after the war and the subsequent labour shortage for base-related jobs. As of August 1945, the US military had more than two hundred fifty thousand personnel in Okinawa. However, the number declined to twenty thousand in 1946, and ten thousand in 1948.[19] This radical decrease in military personnel inevitably created a high labour demand as the US military government planned to fill in the insufficiency of base workers with local Okinawans.

Social and political landscape of Okinawa before the 'anti-base' movement

How did the unprecedented scale of social transformation and the life under occupation urge the local population to conduct the protest campaign and why did they choose to do so? These issues are crucial to address when we try to understand today's anti-base activism which is built upon the legacies of the past.

In July 1955, a group of men and women, both young and old, walked along Kokusai Dōri, one of the main streets running in the middle of Naha, the capital city of Okinawa. Starting from the building of the Government of the Ryukyu Islands, they headed slowly in the direction of Cape Hedo, the northern tip of Okinawa Island. Some of them were carrying placards with messages addressed to the rest of the islanders, one of them read, 'We have no homes, no jobs and no food. What should we farmers from Ie Island do?'

This was the start of what was later called, 'the beggars' march' (*kojiki kōshin*). This march was organized by farmers and their families from the Maja community of Ie Island. In his memoir, one of the group leaders, Ahagon Shōkō, recalls that participants in the march thought that becoming beggars was shameful not just for themselves but also for other community members. 'Nevertheless', he says 'what is really shameful is the [US] Government and its inhumane behaviour in forcibly appropriating people's land, making them jobless, starving, and eventually turning them into beggars.'[20] This long march attracted the attention of other fellow citizens. Many of those who witnessed it sympathized with the farmers. Ahagon writes 'some women were shedding tears while listening to us. Those who didn't have wallets went back to their homes to grab money for us. Sympathetic police officers hesitated about giving us donations but instead asked some women to pass these on to us.'[21] Even for strangers, it was obvious why the Ie farmers had to walk on.

In April 1953, USCAR announced the commencement of land requisition under Ordinance Number 109.[22] This directive allowed the US military government to confiscate privately owned lands in order to build various kinds of US military facilities. USCAR justified the legitimacy of the land acquisition by saying 'the United States has certain requirements concerning the use and possession of land in the Ryukyu Islands' in which 'there are no provisions of Ryukyuan law whereby such requirements may be satisfied'.[23] For this reason, they argued that it is 'appropriate and necessary' to introduce a decent procedure for the land acquisition including 'just compensation' in the Ryukyu Islands.[24] However, in many cases, the process of acquisition was exercised forcibly upon the Okinawan villagers without their consent.[25] Furthermore, farmers not only lost their land but also did not receive even a decent amount of financial compensation.

During this period, there were small-scale protests against the US military authority's land requisition. In places such as Oroku and Isahama, the villagers and their supporters, such as students from the University of the Ryukyus and local school teachers, conducted sit-ins, denouncing the intolerable way of requisitioning the land. However, winning against the armed military personnel was impossible to achieve. In Maja, for example, about three hundred armed soldiers arrived on 11 March 1955, and used tear gas in order to evict protesters. Many of those who refused to hand over their land were beaten, arrested or chased by trained military dogs. Houses were burnt down or demolished by bulldozers, and residents were forced to move into tents which were designated as 'the shelters for evacuees'. Some villagers were forced to receive a bag of money as 'compensation' and as a sign of 'consent' between the occupation authority and the villagers.[26]

While the story of the Ie farmers shows us one instance of early popular resistance, the cases of various other local societies reveal other types of local protests. The Okinawa Teachers and General Staff Association (OTGSA) is a notable case as it reveals how teachers and schools played a crucial role in mobilizing and consolidating the local communities across Okinawa Island to organize the collective actions. This society, joined by local school teachers and general staff, was established in 1947. It was initially called the Okinawa

Education Consortium (*Okinawa Kyōiku Rengō-kai* or *Kyōren*) and was started under the initiative of the Department of Education of the Okinawa Civilian Government. Its primary mission was to set up a basic schooling system in each local district, including supplying textbooks and building schools. In April 1952, the Okinawa Education Consortium became the Okinawa Teachers and General School Staff Association and they became a network organization of the local community as they were able to reach out different households. However, the OTGSA was not a mere successive body of its predecessor. While the Okinawa Education Consortium was primarily involved with the establishment of educational infrastructure, the OTGSA was more politically engaged. As such, by raising *jichi* (self-governance) and *fukkō* (reconstruction) as a slogan, the OTGSA became one of the main social forces which led the so-called reversion-to-Japan movement or Okinawa's reversion movement, especially during the 1960s and the early 1970s.

The political influence of OTGSA is primarily attributed to the roles that school teachers played in and out of the classroom. Although many of them were newly appointed young teachers to fill in the work shortage as a result of the war where around six hundred school teachers had been killed, they were still respected as educated leaders in the local community.[27] These young ardent teachers responded to that social expectation by actively engaging with various community services. For example, some of them had participated in the protest actions with farmers. To do so, they even took leave from teaching duties.[28] Also, as Okinawa Island experienced rapid urbanization with the increase in the number of city dwellers who sought jobs related to the bases such as the 'entertainment' industry, the range of duties teachers engaged in also became more extensive, including the activities that were related to monitoring public safety in the growing new cities and towns.[29] In this context, along with members of other local societies such as Okinawa Youth Association and Okinawa Women's Association, teachers were also concerned about and took active roles in protecting their communities from potential moral deterioration.

The local schools also played an important role in connecting the members of the community and upholding integrity. So, schools were not just for pupils but they were also a place where various community activities took place, such as meetings where both elders and juniors gathered for drinks or to exchange recent updates about their community. Furthermore, school buildings were used as a place for local community members who were acting as civilian police to stay.[30] Usually, this role was assigned to young male teachers, and they were dispatched whenever troubles such as theft and other sorts of crime occurred in their neighbourhoods. Reportedly, they sometimes even had to intervene in the domestic problems of other households such as marital disputes.[31]

Yet, what they were most concerned about was the troubles and crimes committed by the US military personnel. It was not uncommon for locals to be victims of crimes and accidents caused by American soldiers in that period, including rape, theft, car accidents and so forth. Approximately one thousand crimes were reported as being committed by the US military personnel in 1964 alone on Okinawa Island.[32] In those cases, teachers collaborated with the Ryūkyū Police to investigate the criminal cases, although much of the cases went beyond their control due to the extraterritoriality of the military personnel. Therefore, it is reasonable to infer that the presence of school teachers was significant in the community and their commitments allowed them to become community leaders.

Last, we need to examine the roles of political parties to understand the social and political dynamics of Okinawa under the US occupation. The first political party in the post-Second World War Okinawa was the Okinawa Democratic Alliance (ODA, *Okinawa Minshu Dōmei*). It was established by local leaders, such as Nakasone Genwa, in June 1947 in Ishikawa, a city located in the central region of Okinawa Island. Nakasone had been one of the earliest members of the Japanese Communist Party when it was established in 1922. However, after he was arrested in 1923, he gradually withdrew from communism and eventually became an anti-communist politician when he was later elected as a member of the Okinawan Prefectural Assembly.[33] Along with his colleagues such as Yamashiro Zenkō and Miyazato Eiki, Nakasone played a pivotal role in founding the ODA while crying for 'democratisation of Okinawa' and 'independence and reformation of Okinawa'. Particularly, the ODA stressed the importance of 'the liberation of Okinawa by the people of Okinawa'.[34] With this principle, the ultimate political goal raised by the ODA was to create a republican state independent from Japan.

The establishment of the ODA was problematic for the US military government, because this was the first home-grown political party in postwar Okinawa to be critical of the Okinawan Civilian Government and the US authority. In that period, the Governor and other senior members of the Okinawan Civilian Government were all appointed by the US military government. Also, political activism in public places, especially criticism of the Civilian Government, was prohibited. In such an environment, local leaders such as Nakasone conducted a political campaign calling for the election of their representatives.

A month after the establishment of the ODA, in July 1947, another political party, the Okinawa People's Party (OPP, *Okinawa Jinmin-tō*), was established. The founders were a group of local journalists, including Senaga Kamejirō, Kaneshi Saichi and Ikemiyagi Shūi. Some key figures such as Senaga and Kaneshi were already known for their political careers as communists prior to 1945. Although the OPP was later identified as the political party most threatening to the US authority, that was not the case in the late 1940s. Senaga and his OPP colleagues saw and welcomed the US military government as the liberation forces for the people of Okinawa from Japanese imperial oppression.

Like the ODA, the OPP also took a critical stance towards the Civilian Government by arguing that the leaders of the Civilian Government were formerly involved with the Imperial Rule Assistance Association (*Taisei Yokusan-kai*) during the war. When the OPP organized its first congress in July 1947, it presented a political manifesto that included a call to purge those wartime local political leaders as well as the establishment of an independent government by Okinawa's people.[35]

The establishment of the ODA and the OPP reflected the frustration among the local elites with their leaders who were selected by the occupation authority. The momentum for creating various political parties increased to represent the alternative local voices to the politics in the early days of the US occupation. In December 1947, the members of the ODA submitted a petition to the US military government with signatures of ten thousand people calling for public elections. Also, the ODA, the OPP and even the pro-American party called the Okinawa Social Party (OSP, *Okinawa Shakai-tō*, established in September 1947) organized a joint campaign, calling for the positions of Governor and members of the Government to be elected by the Okinawan people, rather than appointed by the US authority.

However, despite the strong local demand, the US military government was reluctant to take actions towards running the election. The military government used the still undecided status of Okinawa as a reason to justify its direct control over the region. Yet, the movement and expectations for the election were becoming so intense that the US military government could no longer ignore them. Particularly, the local US authority was concerned about the local perception of themselves. In this political environment, the US authorities decided to dissolve the Civilian Government and hold a public election for the Governors and the Members of the Assemblies of the four newly established regional governments in Okinawa, Miyako, Yaeyama and Amami in September 1950.

However, it turns out that political parties such as the ODA and the OPP could bring little influence in the first election. As Higa Mikio points out, the ODA, OPP and the Okinawa Social Party were all organized by social elites whose political and social philosophies were not regarded as important for the majority of the voters who considered personal influence and connections to be more relevant in deciding their leaders. Therefore, this election presented an opportunity for many non-partisan politicians to enter politics.[36] In this context, the Okinawa Social Mass Party (OSMP, *Okinawa Shakai Taishū-tō*) was established under the leadership of Taira Tatsuo, a former mayor of Taira City. He was one of many who ran in the election campaign as an independent candidate. With popular support, he was elected as the Governor of the Okinawa Regional Government. After the election, Taira and his supporters established the OSMP in October 1950. The OSMP was joined by people from all political backgrounds, including Kaneshi Saichi, one of the founding members of the OPP and Higa Shūhei, a former English teacher at a local high school, who later became one of the most trusted counterparts for the US military government. By incorporating other small parties which came into power in other regional governments, the OSMP became an all-Okinawan party which involved diverse political interests.

With a clear majority position in local politics, the OSMP was the most powerful political party when the Government of the Ryukyu Islands (GRI) was established as the result of integration of four regional governments in 1952. Prior to this, in late 1951, the Governors and the Members of Assemblies in four regional governments requested the establishment of a single governing body responsible for all regions. Based on this request, the USCAR issued Proclamation Number 13 in which the US authority approved the establishment of the GRI.³⁷ It consisted of independent executive, legislative and judicial powers, where the Chief Executive of the Ryukyu Government was to be appointed by the Legislature. Although this was still defined as a 'Provisional Central Government' under the USCAR's initiative, Okinawa's political struggle came to have a more effective influence over its territory compared to the previous system.

Although the large popular support enabled the OSPM to have its senior member, Higa Shūhei, as the first Chief Executive, Higa and his supporters decided to leave the OSMP to start a more conservative and pro-America party called the Ryūkyū Democratic Party (RDP, *Ryūkyū Minshu-tō*) in August 1952. In addition to former members of the OSMP, the RDP absorbed former members of the ODA, which was dissolved after the first election and became the Republican Party (*Kyōwa-tō*), and other non-partisan politicians.

Not only conservative political leaders but progressive politicians also left the OSMP, such as Kaneshi Saichi who was a co-founder of the OPP. He left the OPP in protest towards Senaga Kamejirō, who was elected as the leader of the party in 1949 and joined the OSMP as a co-founder with Taira Tatsuo. During the election campaign for the mayorship of Naha City in 1957, however, the leaders of the OSMP had decided to support Taira as the official candidate. This conflict split the party, followed by Kaneshi's resignation from the OSMP. Despite experiencing a difficult campaign as an independent candidate, Kaneshi managed to win the majority of votes and was elected as the new mayor of Naha in January 1958.³⁸ After the victory, he and his supporters started the Okinawa Socialist Party (*Okinawa Shakai-tō*). This is how the major political landscape in post-1945 Okinawa was created under the four major parties (i.e. the Ryūkyū Democratic Party, the Okinawa Social Mass Party, the Okinawa People's Party and the Okinawa Socialist Party).

The whole-island struggle

In June 1955, six Okinawan delegates visited Washington, DC. They were representatives from the Ryukyu Legislature, the Government of the Ryukyu Islands, the Okinawan Mayors' Association and the Association of the Okinawan Landlords. One of the primary missions of these delegates was to negotiate directly with the US government on the newly planned land requisition policy. Prior to their departure, in March 1954, USCAR had proposed a plan which enabled the US military government to pay lump-sum rental fees for the use of the privately owned land over the period of sixteen and a half years. The Chief Executive of GRI, Higa Shūhei, and the majority party in the Legislature of the Ryukyu Islands, the Ryukyu Democratic Party, accepted this proposal. However, two opposition parties, the Okinawa People's Party and the Okinawa Social Mass Party, were strongly opposed to this plan. On 30 April 1954, the proposal was rejected by the Legislature. Reflecting on this decision, the local political leaders decided to visit the US House of Representatives in order to discuss the issue with the Armed Services Committee in the Senate.

In response to the request by the Okinawans, delegates from the Committee arrived at Kadena Airbase on 23 October 1955. The team comprised over ten members including Charles Melvyn Price, a member of the US House of Representatives who was also appointed chairperson of the delegates. Their visit was organized to investigate the issues regarding the military bases, particularly the land requisition, on Okinawa Island. However, they stayed only for a few days. After their rather short stint, the US delegates submitted a report to the US House of Representatives in June 1956. In this report, which is known as the Price Report, the American delegates endorsed the proposal for lump-sum payments for land leases. They also confirmed that USCAR needed to continue acquiring more land to fulfil its mission. As 'an essential part of our worldwide defenses', the report stated, 'our base tenure is dependent upon the continued existence of friendly governments.'[39] Noting 'the absence of a belligerent nationalistic movement', the delegates also insisted on the necessity of 'long-term use of a forward military base in the offshore island chain of the Far East-Pacific area, subject, of course to our own national policy.'[40] Furthermore, the report not only asserted the importance of the presence of its own troops in Okinawa but also stated that Okinawa did not have any 'restrictions imposed by a foreign government on our rights to store or to employ atomic weapons.'[41]

The Price Report fanned the fury among the local islanders, including pro-US politicians and social elites. They saw it as clear evidence showing that the US authority had ignored their demands, summarized into 'four principles to protect local land', which were unanimously endorsed by the members of the Ryūkyū Legislature. These four principles were: (1) refusal of lump-sum payment of land rental fees; (2) decent compensation for the confiscated lands; (3) decent compensation for the affected landowners who lost their lands; and (4) objection to new land requisition by the US occupation authority. Furthermore, until that period, collaboration with USCAR had been believed to be one of the best ways for Okinawans to achieve self-governance and socio-economic recovery from the war. However, what historian Toriyama Atsushi calls 'the decade of cooperation' resulted in an enormous sense of disappointment and betrayal for most of those who had put their faith in the United States.[42] On top of these events, the rape and murder of a six-year-old girl in Kadena in September 1955 further angered the locals.[43] The only remaining option, the locals thought, was to express their strong disagreement with the United States. This was how what is called the first 'whole-island struggle' was created.

On 15 June 1956, the representatives of the four local authorities – the Ryukyu Legislature, the Government of the Ryukyu Islands, the Okinawan Mayors' Association and the Association of the Okinawan Landlords – decided to dissolve the coalition body in charge of land problems. Dissolution of the coalition authority was to prevent the policy from becoming effective. On 18 June, the Okinawa Teachers and General Staff Association, the Okinawa Youths Association, political parties and other civic groups decided to organize a joint protest campaign, which involved all corners of Okinawan societies, crying for the 'Four Principles' to be accepted. In this process, the key stakeholders established the Council for the Promotion for the Resolution of the Military Land Problem (or *Gunyōchi Mondai Kaiketsu Sokushin Renraku Kyōgikai* or *Renkyō*). On 20 June, there were large protest meetings in fifty-six towns, villages and cities in Okinawa out of sixty-four municipalities, where over several hundred thousand people participated in total. This scale of popular mobilization was unprecedented in the modern history of Okinawa, and this was literally an island-wide protest, regardless of ideology, against the US occupation.[44]

Although USCAR witnessed the mass protest with surprise, it showed little sympathy for the protesters. On the contrary, it took a hardline approach to subdue the protest. For example, USCAR demanded the University of the Ryukyus take punitive measures towards its university students who participated in the public protest campaign. Also, USCAR placed pressure on the executive committee of the university by threatening a possible suspension of financial support to the university. In August 1956, USCAR declared the central region of Okinawa Island off-limits to US military personnel for an indefinite period. In this region, a large part of the local economy depended on the bases. Therefore, the withdrawal of the military personnel from this region meant critical damage for the local economy. USCAR's hardline approach soon yielded desirable outcomes for them. For example, reflecting on this policy by USCAR, the mayors of the central region decided to ban political meetings in public places given the economic damage caused to the local communities.[45]

Nevertheless, this island-wide protest was historic as it made the US authorities compromise on its governing policy of Okinawa for the first time after the Second World War. In April 1957, the High Commissioner of USCAR, James Moore, announced a temporary suspension of the lump-sum payment system. A few days later, the Secretary of State John Foster Dulles announced that the US government was considering a revision of the existing military land policy in Okinawa. In May, six Okinawan leaders, including the new Chief Executive of GRI, Tōma Jūgō, were invited to visit Washington, DC, to have a meeting with the senior government officials and politicians on the renewal of land compensation. On 7 July, the two sides issued a joint communique in which the leadership of the US government and the GRI undertook a promise to make an effort to build a more harmonious relationship in relation to the US bases in Okinawa. Following their statement, on 13 October, two proposals on the land problem were passed with support from the majority of the Ryukyu Legislature. With this new legislation, the land price for leases for the US military was increased at a rate six times higher compared to the level prior to the protest. Also, lump sum payments became optional instead of mandatory. From this perspective, the land struggle during the 1950s appeared to end in the Okinawan locals' victory.[46] However, it is important to note that Okinawa's victory was only partial, given the range of problems that they had with the US military. This sense of unfulfillment generated further struggle at both political and grassroots levels, which eventuated in the demand for Okinawa's return to Japan in the next decade.

The reversion-to-Japan movement

The energy of the 1950s popular struggle prepared the basis for further mass social movements in Okinawa in the next decade and thereafter. In this very sense, the first whole-island protest was the hallmark in the history of the Okinawan struggle. The heated atmosphere that was born out of the 1950s led to the demand for Okinawa's return to Japanese administration, or the so-called reversion-to-Japan movement, which historian Arasaki Moriteru calls 'the second wave' of the whole-island protest movement against the US occupation regime. People's fears, anxieties and the unending base-inflicted problems fuelled the local desire to recover its full status as part of Japan, which was believed to be the best, and almost the only, way to leave the subordination under the US domination.

One of the key elements in understanding the nature of the reversion movement in the 1960s is the rise of Japanese nationalism in Okinawa. While there were pro-US groups, the majority of Okinawan society supported the reversion movement back to Japanese administration. So, it was not only progressive parties such as the Okinawa People's Party but also conservative forces, including the newly established Democratic Party, which was led by those who split the pro-US conservative party, the Okinawa Liberal Democratic Party, that led the campaign. However, it was the Okinawa Teacher and General Staff Association which played the central role in terms of popular mobilization. With charismatic leaders such as Nakasone Seizen and Yara Chōbyō, the OTGSA was the leading social force, actively involving grassroots communities such as the Parent Teacher Association.

Yet, the reversion movement did not appear for the first time in the 1960s. The origin of this movement dates to as late as the early 1950s. In 1951, the Association for the Return of Okinawa to Japan (*Nihon Fukki Sokushin Kiseikai* or AROJ) was founded jointly by the Okinawa Communist Party and the Okinawa Social Mass Party. Taira Tatsuo, who was then leader of the OSMP was known as an ardent advocate for Okinawa's reversion to Japan. A former mayor of Shuri City, Nakayoshi Ryōkō, was another influential politician who was involved in the founding of the AROJ. Working together with the Association of People from Okinawa Prefecture in mainland Japan, the AROJ petitioned for the revision of Article Three of the San Francisco Peace Treaty, which defined the US military administration in Okinawa. Yet, their campaign could not succeed in changing the Treaty. After the petition failed, in January 1953, the AROJ was transformed into the Association for the Return of Okinawa Islands to the Home Country (AROIHC, *Okinawa Shotō Sokoku Fukki Kisei-kai*) with new leadership. One of the prominent leaders of this renewed reversion campaign was a former high school chemistry teacher and then representative of the OTGSA, Yara Chyōbyō.

USCAR vigilantly watched the growing presence of the OTGSA and its leader, Yara, in Okinawa's progressive circles. In February 1954, USCAR sent a letter to the OTGSA and warned against teachers' involvement with activities other than the education of students. Also, in April, USCAR did not issue a visa for Yara to visit Tokyo and other parts of mainland Japan for collecting donations for school buildings due to his political activism in Okinawa. Furthermore, the USCAR demanded Yara's resignation as leader of the AROIHC. Reflecting on this order, Yara chose to resign as the representative of the AROIHC, which was subsequently followed by the dissolution of the organization.[47] However, this hard measure had little influence on reducing people's support for Yara and his strong leadership among pro-reversion communities. Although he was no longer the representative of the pro-reversion movement, he still remained the leader of the OTGSA.

Yara's strong community-wide leadership was demonstrated in the following year. In September 1955, a six-year-old schoolgirl, Nagayama Yumiko, was found dead on a rubbish dump in Kadena Airbase. A US serviceman was arrested for the rape and murder of the girl. This incident, the so-called Yumiko-chan Incident, was widely reported around Okinawa amid increasingly intense negative local sentiment towards the US bases. A week after the tragic murder, a nine-year-old girl was raped by another US military serviceman. The Ryukyu Legislature expressed dismay with the strongest terms in condemning the criminals. USCAR was concerned about the local reaction. So, it indicated the possibility of imposing severe punishment on the criminals. However, Okinawa's local judiciary could not interfere in the rape and murder cases due to Section 10 of USCAR Proclamation Number 13, which guaranteed the superior status of the Governor and the Deputy Governor of USCAR over the local Okinawan jurisdiction, including criminal cases.[48] This extraterritoriality triggered wide anger against the US authority.

Concerned parents and teachers, the Okinawa Women's Association and the OTGSA established the Association for Protection of Okinawan Children (APOC), and Yara, who was already the leader of OTGSA, was chosen as the representative of the Association. The APOC organized a series of actions including petitions, protests and negotiations with USCAR for the just treatment of the victims and their families. Not long after these events, in June 1959, an American military plane crashed at a local school, Miyanomori Elementary School, killing seventeen people, including eleven schoolchildren, and injuring more than two hundred people in and out of the school. The ineffective local jurisdiction over the base-related crimes generated a strong sentiment of distrust in the US and local authorities in Okinawa.

On 28 April 1960, the Council for the Return of Okinawa to the Home Country (CROHC, *Fukki-kyō*) was founded as a successive organization of the Association for the Return of Okinawa Islands to the Home Country.[49] The CROHC was organized as an umbrella society for a bipartisan island-wide reversion movement. Although the conservative Okinawa Liberal Democratic Party did not participate, the Council still secured a wide range of local support on Okinawa Island with the involvement of progressive political parties such as the OPP and the OSMP, workers' unions such as the Okinawa Prefectural Government Employees Union (*Kenrōkyō*) and local communities such as the Okinawa Youth Association along with the Parent and Teacher Association among many others. Supported by many organizations and groups, Okinawa's reversion movement was rapidly growing as a whole-island campaign.

Towards the late 1960s, Okinawa's reversion to Japan became a crucial issue not only in Okinawa but also between the Japanese and US governments. In 1965, Japanese Prime Minister Satō Eisaku had the first official meeting with US President Lyndon B. Johnson on Okinawa's status. Two years later in 1967, the two leaders presented a joint communique in which a possible plan for Okinawa's return to Japan in the following three years was mentioned for the first time. Also in this year, the Satō government established the advisory council on the treatment of Okinawa. Directly accountable to the Prime Minister, it was led by the former President of Waseda University, Ōhama Nobumoto. Ōhama originated from Ishigaki Island, one of the southwestern islands of the Ryūkyū Islands and had been a highly respected leader of the Okinawan community in Tokyo. The anti-Vietnam War movement in

Japan also urged the Japanese government to take action on the treatment of Okinawa's reversion. Knowing that bombers were sent from Okinawa along with the Philippines and Thailand to Vietnam, progressive Japanese, particularly university students, were critical of Japan's involvement with the war and the US occupation of Okinawa.[50] In November 1969, Prime Minister Satō presented a joint communique with the new President of the US, Richard Nixon, in which it was announced that both governments would strive for Okinawa's return to be realized by 1972.

Amid the growing demand for Okinawa's return to Japan, on 31 October 1968, USCAR announced that it had decided to hold a popular election of the chief executive of GRI. This announcement excited not only conservative and progressive parties but also the local population.[51] The conservative coalition nominated the President of the Okinawa Liberal Democratic Party (OLDP, *Okinawa Jiyū Minshu-tō*), Nishime Junji, whereas the progressive coalition joined by the Okinawa People's Party, Okinawa Socialist Party and Okinawa Social Mass Party chose Yara Chōbyō as their candidate. For his background and career, Yara's supporters comprised primarily educational societies and workers' unions, and Nishime was supported by business owners and economic elites. This ideological difference was expressed in slogans for the election campaign. While the conservative side appealed to voters by asking whether Okinawan people would choose 'to eat potatoes by voting for Yara, or to be prosperous with young Nishime (*Yara wo erande imo wo kūka, wakai Nishime de sakaeruka?*)', the progressive side raised the base problems as the most imminent issue to resolve. While the conservatives claimed that the gradual removal of the bases was taking economic concerns into consideration, the progressive coalition insisted on the complete clearance of the bases when Okinawa was returned to Japan.[52]

While the progressive coalition was leading the campaign, the Japanese government did not welcome them due to their radical take on the bases that could potentially unsettle the governmental negotiation over Okinawa's return between Tokyo and Washington. Although Okinawa's return had become one of the chief agendas for the US and Japanese governments, both governments had not come to terms with a roadmap with a clear timeline for the return of Okinawa. Therefore, the Japanese Liberal Democratic Party supported Nishime and his conservative coalition by sending ministers of the cabinet and other executive members of the party. The Japanese LDP also mobilized nationally popular people including the award-winning writer and MP, who later became the Governor of Tokyo, Ishihara Shintarō, and the national female volleyball team, which won the gold medal at the Tokyo Olympics.

Despite the significant investments the Japanese LDP made in their support for Nishime, it was Yara who won this historic election. The reason for the conservative coalition's defeat is not simple. Yet, one clear factor was that the Japanese LDP did not really understand or even consider carefully the political emotions of the local society. For example, the Secretary-General of the Party, Fukuda Takeo, who later became Prime Minister during the 1970s, stated that reversion would be delayed if Yara won the election. This attitude was regarded not only as the lack of sensitivity but also as the ignorance and arrogance in Okinawa. What they had to understand was that the reversion to Japan was not the goal but a means for Okinawans to be liberated from the colonial conditions under foreign occupation.

The anti-reversion movement

Towards the end of the 1960s, a small fraction of Okinawans started a counter-movement against the reversion to Japan, which later became a crucial hallmark in the history of Okinawan radicals in the post-reversion era. This protest campaign was called 'the struggle for prevention of ratification [of Okinawa's return to Japan]' (*hijun soshi tōsō*) or later 'anti-reversion struggle' (*hanfukki tōsō*). The protest campaign was conducted by diverse social forces. Students from the local universities and high schools, also workers from the local unions such as the All-Base Workers Union (*Zengunrō*), some groups and individuals from the Okinawa Teachers and General Staff Unions, public servants and others organized and participated in street marches and public forums, demanding the local leaders not to make hasty moves towards the ratification of Okinawa's immediate return to Japan.

One of the critical issues felt among the anti-reversion activists was the fact that local communities had lost control over the direction of the reversion movement, particularly after the Satō-Nixon communique was released, promising the return of Okinawa in 1972. The whole discussion about Okinawa's return between Tokyo and Washington seemed as if the only problem was the ways in which Okinawa was returned and the extent to which the Japanese government would regain its administrative, political and economic powers over Okinawa. However, the political and legal issues pertaining to the US bases never appeared to be a serious concern to consider. Also, there was a rumour that nuclear weapons were brought in and kept at the local bases.[53] The social anxiety about nuclear weapons became acute when a B-52 bomber exploded in Kadena Airbase on 19 November 1968. Anti-reversion campaigners were concerned whether the exploded plane contained nuclear weapons and others immediately thought that the war had started again.[54]

Their voices increasingly drew the public's attention as Okinawa's return began to materialize. A week prior to Okinawa's return being approved by the National Diet of Japan on 17 November 1971, union workers, students and other concerned Okinawan citizens conducted a protest campaign and general strike, while holding a protest march in the middle of Naha. This general strike was preceded by the ones that were organized in February and May in the same year. In total, nearly a hundred and fifty thousand people participated in the protest across Okinawa Island against the immediate return of Okinawa to Japan. Even so, the general strikes could not overturn the course of direction that seemed to have been fixed.

Although the anti-reversion movement was a minority movement compared with the pro-reversion campaign, its significance cannot be underestimated, especially its influence on students and critics in the period that followed. Its significance lies in the fact that it established a new language for Okinawans and on the meaning of peoplehood for critics and students in a time where the mainstream social struggle had already been encroached and appropriated by widespread fervent Japanese nationalism. Therefore, the impact brought by this critical genealogy, which is later called 'the philosophy of anti-reversion' (*han-fukki no shisō*), cannot be belittled just because it held barely any political influence during the reversion era.

One of the key intellectuals involved in the anti-reversion movement was a journalist and critic, Arakawa Akira, who published works such as *Okinawa: Antithesis to the Nation State* (*Hankokka no Kyōku*). In the book, which was published only a year prior to Okinawa's return to Japan, he criticized the utopian imageries of Japan shared by the pro-reversion camp, a particularly rosy delusion of the postwar Japanese 'peace constitution'. By combining ideas related to class conflict and the anti-Vietnam war movement, Arakawa became a prominent advocate for anti-reversion in Okinawa along with his colleagues and friends such as Kawamitsu Shin'ichi, Okamoto Keitoku, Nakazato Yūgo, Irei Takashi, etc. Although the anti-reversion thinkers did not refuse to become 'Japanese nationals', people such as Irei Takashi thought that solidarity between Japanese and Okinawan would only be possible if citizens from both regions collaboratively struggled against the expansion of not the base or the American imperialism but further infiltration of Japanese capitalism in Okinawa.[55] As such, it is fair to say that the very criticality of anti-reversion movement was that it shed light on various problems entailed in the political process of Okinawa's reversion to Japan in which critical voices were sidelined for the benefit of the old and new imperial powers.

Conclusion

On 15 May 1972, the administration of Okinawa was handed over to the Japanese government after twenty-seven years of occupation under the US military government. This was the event that necessitated the integration of Okinawa's political economy, society and culture into the Japanese system. In politics, the major parties except for the OSMP (i.e. the Okinawa Liberal Democratic Party, the Okinawan People's Party and the Okinawan Socialist Party) were incorporated as a local branch of the Liberal Democratic Party, the Japan Communist Party and the Japan Socialist Party, respectively. This had happened in the business industry as well, particularly construction firms, many of which became sub-contractors of major Japanese companies. While systemic integration progressed, Okinawa's base problems and the situation around the US military personnel and camps remain unchanged, if not worsened. For those reasons, although Okinawa's return to Japan was a historic event, Okinawans were left with ambiguity about the result of their campaigns.

That said, however, it is also true that the island-wide campaigns had taken an important part in bending the territorial politics of the world's most powerful nation, however partial it was. For this reason, the popular protest movements in US-occupied Okinawa are regarded as the 'origin' of local anti-base politics. Yet, it should be clear by now that there is no such thing as the 'origin' of this long-lasting history of resistance. What I intend to argue here is that, while some of us are often tempted to identify the single most important event that played a decisive role in establishing Okinawa's anti-base struggle, the Okinawan resistance was shaped by a series of events and major and minor actions taken by elites and non-elites. The same goes for the sort of question about who the 'central figure' was in creating the anti-base struggle. There is no 'single most important' leader in establishing the protest movement as far as those events were created by a multitude of individuals. Overall, the 'identity' of the Okinawan anti-base activism was constructed through numerous efforts and social and political processes.

While the search for 'the origin', 'the leader' and 'the identity' appear to be crucial in analysing and clarifying the complex nature of local activism, sometimes it can be counterproductive as those ways of identification could cast aside actors, events and peripheral social contexts which are not 'representative' in making the anti-base politics in its early period. It is precisely because of this reason that this chapter highlights actors, associations, events and actions involved in making the 'local' anti-base struggle. In other words, 'Okinawan-ness' within the Okinawan anti-base struggle would not have been conceived without these actions. Therefore, this chapter tries to emphasize political dynamics which *shaped* Okinawa's anti-base activism in its early days. In the next chapter, we will look into the social and political processes by which Okinawan activism was developed after Okinawa's administrative hand-over to Japan, and how the discourse of 'locality' was articulated in this new context.

3

Remaking the site of struggle

'Constructing peaceful Okinawa'

On 15 May 1972, the administration of Okinawa was handed over from the United States to Japan. Through this event, Okinawa recovered its full status as one of Japan's forty-seven prefectures. In this context, as we saw in the previous chapter, the reversion movement of the 1960s was a crucial historical event, which still occupies a special place in the history of modern Okinawa. The last Governor of the Ryukyu Government, Yara Chōbyō, who subsequently became the first Governor of Okinawa Prefecture, is remembered as one of the most iconic political leaders in this context.

Prior to the administration handover, Yara raised five principles for the new Okinawa: (1) construction of a peaceful Okinawa; (2) resolution of the US base problems; (3) redevelopment of the Okinawan economy; (4) improvement of social welfare and (5) enhancement of self-governance of the cities, towns and villages. However, Yara's optimism was soon hammered down by Japan's ruling party, the Liberal Democratic Party (LDP), which supported Yara's opponent, Nishime Junji, and the Okinawa Liberal Democratic Party during the last election for Governor. As such, this twist between the prefectural and national politics caused to create challenges for Okinawa throughout Yara's administration. The LDP simply considered Yara's policy manifesto 'unrealistic' and Nishime, who was then a Member of the National Diet, was also still active as the leader in local conservative politics.

Also, the political and social situation around the US military in Okinawa Prefecture showed no sign of change. Instead of taking back the territory, the Japanese government allowed the US military to keep on using the land in

Okinawa, and so did the extraterritorial status of the US military personnel under the Status of Forces Agreement. Contrary to popular expectation, the proportion of US military bases in Okinawa gradually increased compared to the pro-reversion period. This increase was due to the closure of some bases and military facilities in the Japanese mainland, which were instead transferred to Okinawa. As such, by 1978, over 70 per cent of all US troops in the country were stationed on Okinawa and adjacent islands, which accounted for less than 1 per cent of the national territory. Although territorial sovereignty was recovered, the reversion was felt only partially and people still had to endure the continued presence of the US military bases.

However, Yara's political choices were limited because of Okinawa's weak economy and the shortage of industrial and public infrastructure, which were a critical disadvantage at the negotiation table with Tokyo. Although he sought politically progressive policies to ensure strong, self-reliant governance of Okinawa, the reality was that Okinawa Prefecture had few options to choose vis-à-vis the LDP Government. While being cautious of the base issues, Okinawan leaders both in mainland Japan and in Okinawa placed higher policy priority on the economic development and improvement of social infrastructure. Especially, Ōhama Nobumoto, who served as the main organizer for Prime Minister Satō's brain trust on Okinawa's reversion, was a strong advocate for this economy-first policy. Therefore, prior to Okinawa's reversion, the Japanese Diet prepared the roadmap and policy platform to achieve 'the same economic standard as mainland Japan' (or '*hondo nami*').

On 31 December 1971, the Government passed the bill, and the Act on Special Measures for the Promotion and Development of Okinawa (*Okinawa Shinkō Kaihatsu Tokubetsu Sochi-hō*) was enacted. Subsequently, the Satō administration passed another bill, which was the Act to Establish the Okinawa Development Agency (*Okinawa Kaihatsu-chō Secchi-hō*) a few days before Okinawa's reversion on 13 May 1972. Based on those legislations, the Japanese government implemented the first ten-year master plan for Okinawa's socioeconomic development for the next ten years (*Daiichiji Okinawa Shinkō Kaihatsu Keikaku*).[1] Covering the whole range of fields related to the improvement of the Okinawan economy and civic infrastructure, this was truly the master plan which designed and shaped Okinawa's economic and social development. However, it also functioned as a major factor that limited Okinawa's political agency and autonomy. So, the fundamental political issue at stake in the early post-reversion Okinawa was: What does it mean to 'construct peaceful Okinawa'?

Also, this was a period in which we see a qualitative change in the Okinawan struggle. While the base issues remained a major problem, activists and concerned citizens began to address environmental degradation due to the mass industrial development of mountains and seas, as well as other social and economic issues such as poor average household income, the relatively high unemployment rate and discrimination towards social minorities such as women and the disabled. Therefore, one of the key characteristics of post-reversion Okinawan activism we need to take into account was the diversification of the struggle in terms of the site, the issues and the ways in which the activists organized the protest politics.

This chapter examines the grassroots activism that emerged during the 1970s and 1980s. Those civic actions played a significant role in advocating for the need to address a diverse range of social issues as well as the base problems. What is notable is that the activism during this period introduced an extensive connectivity among activists across local boundaries. This new mode of connectivity was built upon the concept of 'region' that encapsulates multiple flora and fauna and cultural lives.

Starting with the case of villagers' protest action in Kin, a town located in the mid-eastern part of Okinawa Island, I investigate the impact that this pioneering environmental activism in post-reversion Okinawa had on other corners of society. Particularly, I delve into the establishment of a support network, the Society for the Promotion of the Kin Bay Struggle (*Kin-wan Tōsō wo Hirogeru-kai*), joined by journalists, academics, teachers and other sorts of concerned citizens from Naha and other parts of Okinawa and beyond, with the aim of extensive support for the Kin villagers.

The Society was later renamed the Activism by the Residents of the Ryūkyū Arc (ARC, *Ryūkyū-ko no Jūmin Undō*) to be the main networking group amongst individuals and collectives dedicated to environmental activism and other civic activism in the Ryūkyū Islands region. Organizing activities such as study tours and publishing pamphlets, the ARC played a significant role in linking the Kin Bay struggle to localized environmental activism from Amami on the northern fringe of Ryūkyū Islands to the southernmost islands such as Yonaguni Island. As such, the ARC played a vital role in enacting a shared sense of communal identity as a region among the people of the Ryūkyū Arc.

Aqua-polis and predicament of 'development'

My fellow Japanese citizens, we must learn the lesson of our valuable history, and reaffirm our determination for peace, and strive to build a peaceful and wealthy Okinawa as a bridge of friendship and cooperation with our neighbours in Asia and the Pacific.[2]

On 15 May 1972, then Japanese Prime Minister, Satō Eisaku, spoke the above statement in his speech at the ceremony to celebrate Okinawa's return to Japan. Satō, who had become the longest-serving Prime Minister, must have been contented with his achievement, which he had publicly promised as one of the chief political agendas during his first term. However, Satō was probably not really prepared for how to design Okinawa's course of development. That is to say, what made him proud at the podium at the ceremony was not so much the fact that Okinawa had been returned. That matter was already an issue of the past. What was more important then, was that he had a firm *vision* about the way in which he could navigate his country with this newly returned prefecture, which was clearly expressed in the statement above: 'a bridge' between Japan, Asia and the Pacific.

His vision was embodied in massive financial investment and the reconstruction of Okinawa as a popular tourist destination. By doing so, the Japanese government intended to create industries and employment, particularly in the northern half of Okinawa Island, where only an imperceptible amount of investment had been made to develop the area until then. In some parts of the region, drainage systems were still uncommon and roads and public transport systems also remained far less developed than in the southern half of Okinawa Island. In such circumstances, the modernization of the infrastructure was an imminent issue. Put differently, the northern region of Okinawa Island was deemed as the key site of not only economic but also political investment.

Yet, this ten-year development plan was not just a relevant matter to Okinawa. Rather, it was part of Japan's nationwide redevelopment policy, called the New Master Plan for the National Land Development (*Shin Zenkoku Sōgō Kaihatsu Keikaku* or *Dai-niji Shin Zensō*), which was drafted in 1969 and had been implemented during the 1970s. The first Master Plan of Land Development (*Dai-ichiji Zensō*) was developed and implemented under the initiative of former Prime Minister Ikeda Hayato during the 1960s, as part of his famous 'Income-doubling Plan'. Taking 'the balanced development of the national land' as its slogan, this master plan provided a grand design for equitable social improvement in postwar Japan.

In the earlier plan of the 1960s, the Ikeda administration had two aims to achieve: (1) significantly increasing the annual income per capita and (2) the creation of regional industrial centres between major cities to avoid further congestion of the population. Although the average annual income per capita dramatically increased by up to four times compared with the previous decade, the high concentration of the population and socioeconomic capital in urban centres failed to be resolved. Therefore, in the new nationwide land development plan, the Satō administration was eager to fill in the gap of socioeconomic development between the major cities such as Tokyo and the regional areas by distributing social investment more extensively around the country.[3] One of the major tasks was to establish efficient and modern transport networks. This included not only constructing roads but also building ports and airports in order to connect regional areas and major cities.

In this context, Okinawa was deemed as one of the frontiers, not of national security politics, but for investment firms. The report on the second master plan (first published in 1967, and the revised version published in 1969) stated that Okinawan society had been constrained in its development compared to the rest of Japan because of its 'isolation from the mainland', 'the bases that occupy massive areas of the land' and 'small and scattered islands and the impact of typhoons.'[4] However, the report also said 'its location between Japan and Southeast Asia, unique nature as the only subtropical region in Japan, abundant marine resources and many different kinds of resources for tourism make this region a culturally and naturally distinctive place.'[5] Therefore, the report concluded that 'the whole of Okinawa needs to be developed to the standard of the mainland in order to depart from the base-dependent economy and transit to a peaceful economy.'⁶ In order to achieve Okinawa's development, the Satō administration emphasized that it was essential to establish 'communication infrastructure' (i.e. roads, ports and airports) in Okinawa and adjacent islands.⁷

What characterized Tokyo's vision for Okinawa's development was its emphasis on 'the South' and turning this region into a major leisure resort destination like Hawai'i in the United States. Yet, there had already been test cases of this way of regional development in Japan such as Chiba, a peninsular prefecture, immediately east of Tokyo, and Miyazaki, one of the southwestern prefectures in Kyūshū Island. Especially, Miyazaki's case set a precedent in this context. Located in mainland Japan, which enabled relatively easier access to people, Miyazaki's industrialization as the southern quasi-tropical region was built upon the two problematic cultural legacies of pre-war Japan: the 'Orientalist' gaze to the South Sea (or *nanyō*), which was actively promoted as Imperial Japan's south-ward advance, and the myths as the place where the Goddess of the Sun, Amaterasu, was conceived according to one of the oldest Japanese myths, *Kojiki*. Yet, by rendering those historical and cultural legacies into commercial capital, local banks and other businesses, with the endorsement of the prefectural and the national government, invested in making it a leisure destination in the 1960s.⁸ As such, Miyzakai as Japan's 'exotic South' was successful in attracting a wide range of the urban middle-class population across Japan such as young couples for their honeymoon trip and sports teams for their winter training.

In this sense, Okinawa's return to Japan was an opportunity for Japan's leisure-related industries to extend their business, which also met the local demand for investment. The plan for the investment in Okinawa as a new 'exotic South' was already underway prior to Okinawa's return in 1972. Encouraged by the great success of the Tokyo Olympics in 1964 and the World Expo Osaka in 1970, then Governor of the Ryūkyū Islands, Yara submitted the proposal of hosting the '75 World Expo in October 1971. The proposal was approved by the Japanese cabinet, followed by the International Bureau of Expositions in Paris. Reflecting on this move, the Foundation for the Okinawa Oceanic Expo (*Okinawa Kaiyō Hakurankai*) was established with Ōhama Nobumoto as the Chairperson. For Ōhama, a dedicated leader of the reversion campaign both in and out of the Satō administration, this became the last major service in his long career.

With participation from thirty-six countries from around the world, this largest international event that Okinawa had held in its modern history attracted public attention widely by highlighting Okinawa as a 'bridge' between Japan and its regional neighbours. That is to say, the recovery of this subtropical region was a key diplomatic opportunity for Japan to appeal its new international outlook to the international community, not only as a country in Asia but also as part of the Pacific, where the former colonial powers in Europe such as France, the UK, the Netherlands, as well as the countries belonging to the British Commonwealth, namely Australia and New Zealand, had maintained great political and economic influence. Some of the local communities in this vast oceanic region were becoming post-colonial independent nations during this period.

The Oceanic Expo '75 had a great socioeconomic impact in Okinawa, particularly around the host city, Motobu, and its adjacent communities in the northern part of Okinawa Island. The situation of this historically peripheral part of the Island remained underdeveloped even during the occupation period compared to the flourishing southern region. Yet, the Expo created a major economic demand for the construction and leisure industries. For this event, one of the world's largest aquariums and an offshore monument called the 'Aqua-polis' were built in an area off the coast of Motobu. Modern infrastructure was also rapidly established around the coastal communities of the Yanbaru region. The number of visitors from outside of the prefecture, which had already increased by 50 per cent each year since 1972, doubled up to one and a half million in 1975. If we judge the event by looking at those aspects, the Expo which was held over six months appeared to have ended in success in celebrating Japan's new era.

However, the popular perception was not necessarily the same as the governmental perspective. While the development certainly stimulated the local economy and helped improve the social infrastructure, the event became the subject of widespread controversy in the public. One criticism was due to the number of visitors being less than the original estimate. Yet, more imminent problems were attributed to the overdevelopment of the land which had caused run-off of red soil into the ocean. The coastline was coloured red as a result of deforestation of the mountains and soil had leached from the mountains when the region experienced heavy rainfall.

This leached red soil caused critical environmental damage to the native sea habitat such as the coral reef.[9]

Also, the sudden rise in investment caused an economic bubble creating a sharp rise in land prices in the region. *Ryūkyū Shimpō*, a local newspaper, reported that the price of land per square meter in Motobu Town, which was twelve yen in the early 1970s, had increased by almost a hundred times (approximately ten thousand yen) in a few years.[10] This drastic rise in land prices prompted the purchase of land primarily by mainland Japanese investors and significantly changed the local economy. In the end, however, upon the closure of the Expo boom, the bubble collapsed and added further confusion and distortion in the local communities.[11] This was later called 'the Oceanic Expo Shock' (or, '*kaiyōhaku shokku*').

Remaking the struggle

One of the major characteristics of the Okinawa struggle after 1972 is the emergence of rural residents, many of them not necessarily experienced activists, as the main actors of the movement. This grassroots activism led by local residents is often called residents' activism (or *jūmin undō*). In the postwar Japanese context, this type of social movement started slowly and sporadically from as late as the 1960s in different parts of the country. The term, *jūmin undō*, is often associated with civic activism against the ravaging of people's living environment such as water and air pollution. Perhaps, one of the most well-known cases in this context would be the series of political and legal actions taken by the residents of Minamata in Kumamoto.

In the early 1950s, local newspapers started reporting on the unattributable deaths of cats in the local community. While the cause of the deaths was unidentified, it was called 'the dancing cats disease' because those cats tended to thrash around restlessly as if they were dancing erratically before they died. As the disease gradually spread amongst humans, physicians began to study the cause of the unknown illness. There, they discovered that it was a neurological disease caused and developed by eating fish in the Yatsushiro Sea, which were contaminated by mercury released from the sewage of a major factory owned and operated by a chemical company, Chisso.

This mercury poisoning became known as one of the earliest cases of public environmental pollution in postwar Japan, which is also known as *kōgai*. The survivors, such as Ogata Matato, a local fisherman, filed cases to dispute at local, regional and ultimately the supreme courts against Chisso and its former president and municipal and national governments, and conducted directed actions in public.[12]

Minamata certainly has set a precedent of residents-oriented activism. Yet, it is also important to note that Minamata was one of the cases where individuals or a group of citizens stood up to organize protest campaigns against the destruction of their local environment at the time. Similar civic actions took place around the same period in other parts of Japan such as Yokkaichi and Toyama. While receiving support from other sectors of society such as lawyers and journalists, the residents-oriented activism established two significant meanings in the history of Japanese politics. First, it complicates the politics beyond the Cold War ideological rivalry between the Left and the Right by inserting a third perspective, who does not necessarily stand on either side of the political binary. This point can be developed further by adding that the residents-oriented activism was built upon a deep sense of place and resistance against the ravaging of not only living spaces but also the elements which sustain the community, such as personal or collective memory, convention and the (in)tangible relationships with other humans and nature. In this very sense, residents' activism can be conservative as well as progressive, and it is driven by spiritual reasons as well as materialistic purposes. Last but not least, as Simon Avenell astutely points out, civic activism was deemed as modern because 'citizens' (*shimin*) did not exist as a political concept in Japan before 1945.[13]

In the Okinawan context, too, residents-oriented activism took place and became a main driving force of local activism, including anti-base politics, in the post-reversion period. While the base issues continued to be a local concern, the hallmark of the Okinawan struggle since the 1970s was that activism sought ways to intervene in not only the base politics but also the political economy that constituted Okinawan and Japanese society.

In addition to the economic downturn and social confusion around the Oceanic Expo, the Japanese government implemented other economic stimulus policies in Okinawa in accordance with the First Promotion and Development Plan. This included establishing modern logistical infrastructure such as an airport, reclaiming land in the adjacent sea areas and creating other major and minor industrial facilities such as thermal power plants. However, these development plans were often implemented with little reflection on the concerns among the residents and the impact on the local ecological system. Therefore, the initiatives taken by both the municipal and the national governments caused anxiety among local communities and sometimes triggered protest campaigns. For example, on Ishigaki Island, a main island of the Yaeyama region, the local fishermen in Shiraho conducted a protest against the renovation of the local airport in 1979 because they were concerned with the impact on the natural environment around the coast. In the mid-1980s, residents in Awase in Okinawa City organized protests over the plan to reclaim the local intertidal flat to build a major commercial complex.

Although the scale of these movements was far from the mass protests in the pre-reversion era, civic activism that has emerged since the 1970s prepared a way to articulate local activism as the struggle for protecting the space of livelihood and against the imposed top-down transformation of the economy, environment and civic life. This had a critical impact on the ways of organizing anti-base activism. Activists began to mobilize various environmental issues. One notable example is the court case alleged by a civic group, *Kadena Bakuon Soshō-dan*, from the 1980s onwards, over excessive noise, which were constantly made by fighter jets and other aircraft at the Kadena Airbase. Others include the ongoing activism against the destruction of the sea and the forest due to the construction of offshore landing zones in Henoko and Takae since 1997 and the early 2000s, respectively. More recently, some civic groups such as Okinawa Biodiversity and the Informed-Public Project have been active on issues such as Agent Orange, which was discovered in rusty steel drums on the grounds of a former military campsite in Okinawa City, and the leakage of contaminated water with chemical compounds known as PFASs (per- and polyfluoroalkyl substances).[14]

In this context, the activism conducted by the residents of Kin Town is noteworthy as one of the earliest cases in post-reversion Okinawa during the 1970s and 1980s.[15] Located in the middle-eastern coastal area of Okinawa Island, Kin Town was designated as the site for the construction of a petroleum storage plant during the final years of the US occupation era by the Government of Ryukyu Islands in the late 1960s. At a time of rapid economic growth in mainland Japan, the demand for petroleum increased in the country, which urged the Japanese government to have a major storage facility (CTS, Central Terminal Station) and an oil refinery facility for safe resource supply. In 1967, then Chief Executive Matsuoka Seiho decided to attract foreign investors to build the CTS in Okinawa. After being refused by local residents in other places such as Yonagusuku, Matsuoka designated his hometown Kin Town as the site for this project.[16] Some major foreign energy firms such as Esso and Caltex showed their interest in bidding. Aiming to extend their business in the Asian region, these transnational petroleum firms saw Okinawa as an ideal place as the host of the major facility.[17] In this context, the Gulf Oil Corporation was selected.

Construction of the storage station beginning in 1970 attracted a further investment opportunity for establishing the roads and reclaiming land around Heianza Island, an adjacent island where the facilities were to be built. The construction of the storage affected the local fishermen in terms of the area in which to do their jobs. Yet, to make matters worse, shortly after the CTS started operation in 1972, the sea water around the coast of Kin Town became polluted due to leaked oil, bad odours from the petrol storage tanks and a change in the sea current caused by land reclamation, which caused critical damage to the neighbouring fishermen communities in this region.

Prior to the start of the CTS operation, concerned local residents and environmental activists founded the Society for the Protection of Kin Bay (SPKB, *Kin-wan wo Mamoru-kai*) in September 1973.[18] One of the leaders of SPKB was a former high school principal, Asato Seishin. Born in Okinawa, Asato returned from Korea after the Second World War, where he had taught as a local high school teacher during the Japanese colonial occupation. After his return, he was a senior regional organizer for the Okinawa Teachers and General Staff Association (OTGSA) in the central region of Okinawa Island while continuing his teaching career. The local residents of Kin Town, mostly fishermen, were also active members of this newly established protest community.

By inviting environmental experts and civic activists, they voluntarily organized a study group on damage related to CTS. Also, Asato and the local residents conducted protest campaigns by collaborating with other Okinawan civic groups from different regions. Their campaigns were successful in securing support from workers' unions such as the Prefectural Government Workers' Union and the OTGSA, which had a significant influence on progressive politics, including the newly elected Governor Yara. Reflecting on the surge of opposition to the oil facilities, Yara decided to withdraw the approval to start operating CTS in Kin Town in January 1974.

However, urged by Gulf Oil and other investing firms such as Mitsubishi and Mitsui, which participated in establishing a joint venture with Gulf Oil, the Japanese government tried to overturn Yara's decision, fearing the possibility of ruining a huge investment deal and its own face vis-à-vis the global US oil company.[19] It was a year after the oil shock in 1973. Against this backdrop, Nakasone Yasuhiro, then Minister for International Trade and Industry, stated that Japan had to increase the oil storage capacity by cooperating with the local residents and dismissed Yara's decision.[20] Other stakeholders such as Okinawa Mitsubishi Development also lobbied to overturn Yara's policy.[21] The same goes for the case of Okinawa Development Agency, hinting at the change of government development subsidies for the next term. At this point, there were no policy options Yara could choose except for rescinding his earlier decision. As such, the operation of the CTS was resumed in October 1975.

After its voice was dismissed, the SPKB filed a lawsuit in the Naha District Court against Yara and Okinawa Mitsubishi Development. This court case created a split between Yara and Asato, once Yara's close colleague. Yet, more importantly, this was the conflict over the meaning of 'peaceful' and 'independent' Okinawa, which Yara promised during his election campaign with his supporters. The SPKB expressed a strong critique against the operation of CTS, particularly its possibly hazardous consequences for Okinawa, which was against the 'peaceful industry' the Yara administration raised in their policy manifesto.

By raising issues such as sea contamination from leaked petrol and construction of the storage tanks, the activism by the residents was crucial in enhancing public awareness of the environmental problems and their impact on people's everyday lives. Moreover, the protest movement urged the public to reconsider the meanings of 'wealth', 'development' and 'rationalisation' promoted by the initiative of the Japanese government. In this context, Yara's political compromise was criticized as subservience to the Japanese government not only by the members of the SPKB but also by the wider public.[22]

The court battle between the SPKB and Okinawa Prefecture lasted for nearly a decade. In the end, the request for a provisional injunction to stop the operation of the CTS was dismissed with no further appeal from the SPKB in October 1982. However, the protestors' defeat in court did not discourage people from taking further action. On the contrary, as I mentioned above, the anti-CTS struggle became a key reference for other grassroots civic activists as a role model. In this sense, it opened up a new horizon in the history of the Okinawan struggle.

The archipelago of resistance

The SPKB was a group joined, through various channels, by participants from both in and out of Kin Town. Among them were young academics and journalists such as Arasaki Moriteru, who had moved to Okinawa from Tokyo just recently, and Arakawa Akira, an already renowned journalist, and a harsh critic of the reversion movement. With other friends and colleagues, including Okamoto Keitoku, Irei Takashi and an environmental expert, Yamakado Ken'ichi, who had also recently settled in Okinawa, these intellectuals in their thirties brought a fresh breath by starting a new and supportive society for the SPKB's activism.

This group, the Society for the Promotion of the Anti-CTS Struggle (*CTS Soshi Tōsō wo Hirogeru-kai* or *Hirogeru-kai* for short), was established in September 1974. Arasaki, who was still a junior academic at Okinawa University, became the coordinator of the group.[23] He and other founding members including Arakawa decided to organize the group in order to spread information about the anti-CTS struggle among people living in different areas of Okinawa Prefecture.[24] Although the Kin Bay struggle was initially started by a small group of local residents in an isolated environment, their activism drew attention from other communities in Okinawa, including other islands. In this context, the *Hirogeru-kai* played a vital role in creating the network. Based in Naha, the activities of this Society included regular updates of the SPKB's activism in the local newspapers, offering various kinds of assistance and organizing venues such as study groups for those who were not always able to participate in the protest movement in Kin Town.[25]

An equally important activity was to visit other islands in Okinawa Prefecture for research and networking purposes. In those places, too, the waves of investment and development were arriving, which prompted concerned people to take action, including protests. Their visits were not necessarily organized as the Society. Due to the nature of the Society, which was joined by individuals with various skills and professions, the reasons for trips were often dependent on individual members. So, as Yamakado documents, he had been to rural areas such as Ishigaki Island and Taketomi Island to interview and discuss with the locals issues such as constructing hotels and other leisure facilities to attract tourists.[26] What the members always cared about was how to create a residents-centred economy, which tended to be side-lined at the leadership level when major facilities were introduced.

Building upon those activities, the *Hirogeru-kai* was renamed the Activism by the Residents of the Ryūkyū Arc (ARC, *Ryūkyū-ko no Jūminundō*) in January 1976. As the name suggests, one of the major purposes of this group was to create a common platform for the activists and the concerned residents who were involved in protest movements on rampant development projects in respective locales of the Ryūkyū Islands from Amami region in Kagoshima Prefecture to Yaeyama, the nearest region to Taiwan. As in Kin, the construction of CTS was becoming an issue in other places. For example, a few years after the establishment of the SPKB, there was a plan to construct another major petroleum storage facility in Tarama Island, a further southwestern island from Okinawa Island. Similar stories were heard in Amami-Ōshima Island, Yonaguchi Island, Izena Island and other places in Okinawa and the southern islands region in Kagoshima Prefecture. In most cases, those targeted places had already been too exhausted to organize collective actions due to the decline in population, ageing and lack of infrastructure to sustain their communities. In this context, the ongoing struggle at the site and court that the SPKB conducted was an important source of reference for other communities. Likewise, for the activists from Okinawa Island, this was an opportunity to create a solidarity movement.

Here, the use of the 'Ryūkyū Arc' in the name of this new society represents the intention of their activism. Originally, it is a geological region referring to the chain of islands, which is also called *Nansei Shotō*, which means the 'southwestern islands', or *Okinawa Shotō*, which means 'Okinawa islands'.

However, the 'southwest' was not seen as appropriate as it indicates the gaze of the Japanese mainland, and the same goes for the latter one as it excludes Amami, which had been part of Kagoshima Prefecture. The ARC's aim was to create a region-wide collective action on the rampant intrusion of developmentalism and to reterritorialize their space of indigenous livelihood beyond the frame of 'Okinawa'.

Joined by over ten civic groups from different parts of the Ryūkyū archipelago, the establishment of the ARC heralded the beginning of a new chapter of residents-oriented activism. Coordinated by Arasaki and his colleagues, the ARC played a crucial role in consolidating different regional activisms through organizing the annual joint study camp, held in various locations from 1979.[27] Aside from the camp, the members saw each other at casual and formal events throughout the year, reporting on and exchanging updates of their activities. This camp continued for over ten years until 1989.

Additionally, the ARC had published a community journal under the same title as their society.[28] This journal was first published in 1977 as the medium to share the reports from different sites of protest movements in the Ryūkyū Islands and it was continuously published two to three times a year until the last issue in 1990. The journal covered local activism in other parts of Japan such as by the Ainu population in Hokkaido and environmental activism in Kumamoto and Kagoshima. Also, it occasionally featured international activists such as a Chamorro environmental activist, David Rosario, who visited Kin in 1980. As Uehara Kozue explains in detail, the island communities in Micronesia suffered similar experiences to the Ryūkyū islands such as the construction plans of the CTS at the time and Japan's radioactive nuclear waste.[29] In this sense, the journal was not exclusively about and for activists in the Ryūkyū Islands. Rather, it was more accurate to say that it was the social medium about various kinds of indigenous activism, while centred around the Ryūkyū Archipelago.

Okinawan activists learned about this way of articulating the Ryūkyū Archipelago as a communal concept through the works of Shimao Toshio, an author and essayist based in Amami-Ōshima from the 1950s until the early 1970s. Known as a master of surreal novels, Shimao was also an acclaimed critic of Japan's homogenous ethnocentrism and a zealous advocate for geo-cultural diversity. Particularly, his essays on *Japanesia* (pronounced as *yaponeshia*) breaks apart the Japanese archipelago to redefine the country as a compound of three major regional domains in the southwest, the middle and the northeast. It had a significant impact on his contemporaries. Among them were Arakawa Akira and Kawamitsu Shin'ichi, journalists at *Okinawa Times*, and Okamoto Keitoku, an early career academic, teaching Japanese and Okinawan literature at the University of Ryukyus. Those three, as well as others who were involved with a literary journal, *Shin Okinawa Bungaku* (*The New Okinawan Literature*), were keen readers of Shimao's works.

Particularly, Shimao's concept of *Ryūkyū-ko* or the Ryūkyū Arc, which regards the southwestern islands region as one of prime cultural foundations, upon which modern Japan has been built as a country and nation, fascinated the Okinawan intellectuals. Inspired by Shimao, some local intellectuals such as poet Takara Ben raised a concept called *Ryūkyūnesia* that essentially shares a common ground with Shimao's *Ryūkyū-ko*, which is nonetheless a more politically radicalized concept, evoking the Ryūkyū Islands region as a nation. Along this line, journalist Miki Takeshi proposed *Okinesia*. Arakawa Akira, who later became a good friend of Shimao, published a book *Shin Nantō Fudoki* (*The New Culture and Geography of the Southern Islands*) during his posting in Ishigaki Island, one of the southwestern borderlands of Japan, facing Taiwan and China. Arakawa recalls that he would not have published that book, which became a foundational text for his later thought of anti-reversionism, without encouragement by Shimao and his wife Miho.[30]

Arasaki also admits the critical value of the concept, which, he argues, lies in the 'rejection of uniformity of Japan as a nation and society'.[31] Yet, compared to Arakawa, Arasaki did not entirely agree with Shimao's articulation. While recognizing Shimao's insight, Arasaki diverts our attention not to be fully taken by Shimao's abstract concept. Arasaki claims that the idea of the Ryūkyū Arc is distinctively a literary concept, and he emphasized that their use of *Ryūkyū-ko* had to be built upon more practical and strategic reasons and objectives to create solidarity with various social movements in this region and to challenge the existing political establishment, including the major progressive parties. In other words, Arasaki was critical of Shimao's articulation of *Ryūkyū-ko* because he saw it as too abstract, which did not sufficiently reflect the differences, or what he calls 'insularity' (*kakuzetsu*), among local communities within the Ryūkyū Arc. While finding the concept useful overall, what Arasaki and his colleagues envisioned was regionalism, rooted in and derived from people's struggles.

This was the frustration that the activists felt more acutely as the solidarity movement grew. While the idea of solidarity was necessary, Arasaki and his colleagues from Okinawa Island had to overcome their centrality to create a sustainable solidarity movement. This issue intertwined in their activism gradually enabled Arasaki and his colleagues to be reflective of their positionality. This realization was crucial, as it would otherwise have been disregarded if their conceptualization of *Ryūkyū-ko* had remained only at the abstract level. That is to say, the ARC was able to re-articulate Shimao's cultural concept at the societal level precisely because of their collaboration with activists from different islands in practical terms. In other words, the insularity, locality and difference within *Ryūkyū-ko*, which could have been seen negatively, functioned powerfully by enabling the activists to articulate a mode of grassroots regionalism that is built upon multiple values and different forms of local contexts while sharing the common cultural ground.

Regionalizing the local space, community and life

One of the implications we can draw from this early mode of grassroots regionalism in Okinawa was that, through bringing forth the network among different island communities, the ARC complicated the meaning of Ryūkyū and of the Okinawan struggle beyond the insularity and monolithic representation entailed in the discourse of 'Okinawa'. As such, the members of the ARC articulated Shimao's idea of *Ryūkyū-ko* as a concept that represents a kind of social identity of those who were struggling against the disruption of their lives. In other words, *Ryūkyū-ko* was a centrepiece for considering the meaning and context of the Okinawa struggle and 'Okinawan identity' in post-reversion era.

Delving into this point further, the legacy of the ARC is that it raises a simple yet profound question on the conditions of thinking about 'identity'. This is still relevant and has been addressed continuously by those who are involved in the movement. One of the crucial points to note is that this continuous process of reflexivity about their identity disallows a cultural homogeneity or ethnic unity of Okinawans or Ryūkyūans. Instead, their use of *Ryūkyū-ko* denotes regionality as a multidimensional and multi-nodal space of social struggle. It means that 'Okinawan identity' is deemed to be a product of diverse social practices and networks of civic activism emerging from different locales within the Ryūkyū Islands and beyond. Put differently, the concept of regionality suggests to us a form of 'Okinawan identity' that is collective yet decentralized. By including local struggles in different parts of Okinawa, this new layer of 'Okinawan identity' opened an opportunity to seek an alternative foundation for communal integrity, which is less exclusive while maintaining a common ground to build a sense of community.

The search for alternative integrity was, of course, not an issue that can be resolved overnight. This was just the beginning of a new journey for the activists and activism in Okinawa. However, as Arasaki says, in the environment where traditional progressive politics during the reversion movement had become 'non-progressive' (*hi-kakushin-teki*) vis-à-vis civic struggles at the local community level, it was deemed unavoidable for activists to re-create common ground for the real progressive politics.[32] In 1993, the ARC was renamed as the New Okinawa Forum (NOF, *Shin Okinawa Fōramu*). Built on the experience of the ARC for more than fifteen years, the members of the ARC felt the need to refresh the Society. Focusing more on the importance of the publication and networking, one of the newly adopted objectives is to establish a public forum for sharing and discussing issues on *jichi* ('self-governance' or 'independence') of regional communities primarily of Okinawa and yet also other parts of Japan and beyond on such platform as a new quarterly journal, *Keishi Kaji*.[33]

The increasing momentum of grassroots regionalism also led to the establishment of the Institute of Regional Studies (IRS, *Chiiki Kenkyūjo*) in 1988 at Okinawa University, where Arasaki served as the President then. That was also the year marking Okinawa University's thirtieth anniversary as one of the first private tertiary education institutes in Okinawa, along with Okinawa International University. Based upon the university's motto: 'rooted in, learning from, and living with the region', the IRS was founded to be a centre for research and education on Okinawa Island and the other islands in the southern region. By using the word 'regional', however, IRS did not intend to limit its research to the narrowly defined Okinawa Prefecture. The first Director of the IRS, Ui Jun, a renowned scientist of the drainage system and well-known activist on environmental pollution since the 1960s, raised two different scopes of region: the Arc of the Ryukyus and the broader Asia and Pacific Region.[34] As such, today we can see the legacies of the SPKB, the ARC and other forms of individual and collective struggles in post-reversion Okinawa which have been materialized as the institutional culture and which have been placed as a cornerstone in the contemporary history of the Okinawan struggle.

Conclusion

In this chapter, I have examined the development of post-reversion Okinawan civic activism by focusing on the rise of environmental activism and regionalism. As I have discussed, the Okinawan struggle is not only about anti-base politics; and one of my intentions in this chapter was to highlight the diversification of the problems local activism addressed. Yet, this diversification was necessary for Okinawa's progressive politics in identifying the very cause of the structural discrimination imposed upon and endured by the people in the Ryūkyū Islands and for reconstructing progressivism. In other words, the activism in the post-reversion Okinawa revealed the forms of violence structured around the marginality of this borderland community, in which the old progressive political parties could bring little influence. In this environment, the reconstruction process took place at the grassroots level. While the resources to mobilize were limited, activists exerted all that they had to offer. Unionists split their organizations, such as the OTGSA, to participate in sit-ins, journalists issued relevant news, academics researched and taught at the universities and students also participated in protests before, after or by not attending school. However, the central actors of the struggles were the local residents who feared losing the means and sites of production rather than choosing 'compensation'. Their collaborative effort, as it was shown in the establishment of institutions such as the IRS, has prevailed in society and secured recognition instead of being kept silent.

Importantly, this period was also the era in which the grassroots anti-base movement developed, which I will discuss about later in this book. For example, in 1976, the local assembly and municipal government of Yomitan Village, where more than half of the territory was occupied by the US military facilities during that period, opposed further provision of the land for the construction of a communication facility in Sobe. Also, in 1982, local anti-base activists started a society called *Hitotsubo Hansen Jinushi-no-kai* (the *Hitotsubo* Anti-War Landowners Association). Inspired by a strategy used by the protest movement against the construction of the New Tokyo International Airport (Narita Airport) in the 1960s, this was a type of anti-base activism in which Okinawan activists bought a land right from the original owners in order to complicate the procedures regarding the land lease contract upon the time of renewal. Divided land into the size of *histotsubo* (which is equivalent to about three square meters), individual activists bought the ownership of the lands, which were under a lease contract with the Japan Defense Bureau, the government agency in charge of facility management for the US military in Japan, from the original owners. The activism of the *Hitotsubo* Society became more extensive with the increase of its members not only from Okinawa but also from Japan, and their tactics method was later adopted by the anti-base US activists in South Korea as well. Also, while it is not directly related to the anti-base movement, a society called the Society of One Feet (*Ichi-fito no Kai*) had started its campaign which was to buy one-foot long of the recording film of the Battle of Okinawa, archived at the National Library of America.

As such, the Okinawa struggle in the early post-reversion period was in fact the time when the foundation of the future struggle was created. Like the case of the Kin Bay protest, that activism took place largely due to the participation and contribution of individual citizens across Okinawa Prefecture and beyond. In this very sense, unlike how opponents tend to call, those actions cannot fit into the category of NIMBY (Not-In-My-Backyard). The movement needs to be construed at least as an Okinawa-wide movement. Furthermore, although people such as Ramseyer or Maher see the Okinawa's protest movement as conducted by a group of elites, that is clearly a distortion of the history when each movement had developed through the participation of concerned citizens of different age, gender and socioeconomic and cultural backgrounds. What those denialists of the Okinawan struggle misarticulate was *kyōdō no chikara* (the power of cooperation) among Okinawan activists, if I borrow Uehara Kozue's articulation.[35]

4

Shimao Toshio's cultural resistance

Ripples from the Pacific

The first phase of grassroots regionalism was an action led by a collective of activists such as Arasaki Moriteru, Okamoto Keitoku, Arakawa Akira and numerous others. Although they interpreted it in various ways among themselves, the idea of the Ryūkyū Arc, or *Ryūkyū-ko*, proposed by Shimao Toshio, was a common source of inspiration for re-contextualizing and defining their cultural and political identity. In this sense, exploring the quality and meaning of Shimao's discourse is an essential task to imagine and understand its impact on young Okinawan activist scholars. This chapter elucidates Shimao's cultural politics by examining the historical context around his much-underrepresented article 'Amami and *Japanesia*'. Unravelling the story will answer how the series of works by Shimao excited young Okinawans of those days and help us understand the thoughts behind their decolonization struggle.

In August 1965, Prime Minister Satō Eisaku visited Okinawa as the first postwar Japanese Prime Minister. In the same month, there was a short article published in *This Is Japan*, the flagship English-medium monthly journal issued by *Asahi Shinbun*. The author was Shimao Toshio, who is perhaps remembered as one of the most celebrated authors in the postwar Japanese literary scene today. Yet, this rather short two-page-long essay by the writer was not about his newly published literary work but it was about an island, Amami-Ōshima (hereafter Ōshima), the main island of the Amami region, where he had moved to settle with his wife and children a decade ago. This essay, titled 'Amami and *Japanesia*', was probably one of the very few, if not the only, English essays by Shimao, except for his posthumously translated works.

This large print journal with over four hundred pages, which was published annually from 1954 until the last volume in 1971, was intended to be a comprehensive catalogue of the country for foreign, primarily American and European, readers. Of all, the thirteenth volume is particularly important for two reasons: to see how Japan, after the first Summer Olympics in 1964, was trying to build its international image; and how it portrayed Okinawa and the rest of the southwestern islands to international audiences beyond the US military occupation. As I have discussed earlier in this book, the administrative return of Okinawa to Japan was on the agenda between Tokyo and Washington, DC, by early 1965. In January, the Prime Minister, Satō, visited the White House to meet US President Lyndon B. Johnson, during which Satō, for the first time as the Head of Japan, expressed his 'desire' for the administrative handover of Okinawa and Ogasawara islands from the United States to Japan. The joint statement by the two leaders was followed by Satō's visit to Okinawa in August. Shimao's article on Japan's southwestern region in *This Is Japan* needs to be read in this political context.

In the time when the course of Okinawa's future drew strong attention among observers, Shimao's essay follows two relatively long reports written by journalists, Rowland Gould and Sydney White, respectively, highlighting local culture and politics. While Gould reports his island hopping from Okinawa to Miyako, describing crafts and festivals in detail, White writes a political report on Okinawa. Yet, they both see the importance of this southwestern island region in its geographical location between Japan and the other Asian nations. In this context, however, Shimao starts his essay by rejecting this common geo-cultural assumption in the very first paragraph.

> Studied as part of the Pacific Ocean rather than as part of the Asian land mass, the islands of Japan assume a new perspective and significance, with geographical affinity to other island groups in the blue vastness known as Polynesia, Melanesia, Indonesia, and Micronesia. One wonders why Japan was not called Japanesia.[1]

This provocative remark, written by the author whose name was relatively unheard of beyond the Japanese literary circle at that time, must have been read with puzzlement, if not ignored, by many readers. Yet, tracing Shimao's preoccupation with the southern islands as a site to envisage an alternative cultural reference for Japan unfolds the author's much underrepresented resistance to ever-increasing political, economic and cultural centrality of modern Japan that was coerced aggressively in the peripheral communities.

This resistance was embodied as the concept of *Japanesia*, Shimao's original term that indicates an alternative vision of Japan with emphasis not on cultural homogeneity but on geo-cultural multiplicity, and its key constituent, *Ryūkyū-ko* (the Ryūkyū Arc), which also had a tremendous influence on Okinawan young progressive intellectuals and activists, such as Arakawa Akira and his contemporaries, in the 1960s and the following decades. What would be the criticality of placing Okinawa, and Japan, alongside those island regions in the Pacific, when many of them were still under the European and American administration? This chapter probes the core of Shimao's cultural intervention by closely reading his essays, opinion pieces and his transnational journey.

One day in October 1955, a white ship approached the port of Naze in Ōshima. The ship, *Hakuryūmaru*, which means 'white dragon', was one of the few cargo-passenger ships that sailed regularly between Tokyo and Naha in Okinawa where public access from outside of the territory was heavily restricted by the local US occupation authority. There were only five passengers. Among them were Shimao Toshio and his wife Miho. After living in Kobe and Tokyo for a decade, the couple decided to settle in Ōshima where Miho's relatives were living.

After the island's administration was handed over from the US military administration to Japan's Kagoshima Prefecture in December 1953, land development took off in Naze under the Japanese government's initiatives. This largest city in the Amami region, however, still remained rustic compared to its mainland counterparts, and so was the living standard of the islanders. Yet, despite his upbringing as a typical urban middle-class intellectual, Shimao was soon captivated by this island which he chose as his new home, particularly its sense of wilderness. Since then, Shimao had lived in Ōshima for two decades and it became the place where he spent the longest and most fruitful period of his career.

Amami's complex culture, rooted in its difficult past with Okinawa (the Ryūkyū Kingdom), the Shimazu clan (a feudal lord who governed today's Kagoshima), and the United States, as well as its own indigenous culture, eventually enabled him to conceive an alternative vision of Japan. This vision was later conceptualized as *Japanesia* in 1961, which became synonymous with Shimao's career as an essayist. It is an interpretive concept through which Japan's decentralized archipelagic nature is foregrounded wherein the country is divided into three separate geo-cultural spaces of south, middle and north, and regards these archipelagic groups as different localities or 'islands'; hence he uses *nesia*, a plural form of *nesos* ('island') in Greek.

With this archipelagic perspective, Shimao sought to conjure up the imagery of Japan, not as an ethnically solidified homogenous modern state but as a country conjoined by different islands, both physically and metaphorically. Central to this vision is his place of residence, Amami, or more broadly speaking, the southern islands, which Shimao calls the Ryūkyū Arc or *Ryūkyū-ko* along with his place of birth Tohoku in the north, not as Japan's peripheral regions vis-à-vis the old and new capitals Kyoto and Tokyo but as one of the major constituents of the country. Through this imaginative interpretation, as Philip Gabriel succinctly summarizes, Shimao's *Japanesia* challenges 'unspoken assumption of Japan as a natural entity, and of an underlying oneness of Japanese culture' and unfolds the 'plurality of cultures within the confines of the nation we call Japan.'[2]

However, the question of the south as one of Japan's key cultural sites was not Shimao's own invention. Ethnologists Yanagita Kunio and Oka Masao, for example, are perhaps some of the most renowned scholars in this regard. Shimao received particularly strong inspiration from Yanagita's late works, in which he examined the southwestern sea routes to understand human and material flows to the Japanese mainland.

These early ethnologists were driven by the desire to identify the uniqueness, as well as complexity, of Japan in cultural terms. What needs to be emphasized here is the fact that in many cases these research projects were developed in parallel with Japan's southward expansion in the first half of the twentieth century. Scientific texts, travelogues, essays and novels on *nantō* (the southern islands) and *nanyō* (the southern seas) reflected the human mobilities enabled by the southward-spreading influence of the Japanese Empire since the end of the First World War. Therefore, today, these intellectual traditions cannot bypass critical assessment of their complicities with Japan's imperial expansion.

The controversy over Yanagita's positionality as a government bureaucrat and over his works typically exemplifies this complicit triangle of knowledge, intellectuals and their sociopolitical context, and Shimao is no exception in this sense. Shimao's first overseas experience to the southern ocean was when he participated in the youth travel program to Taiwan, Shanghai and Luzon in 1939, which was coordinated by the Japanese government. Importantly, however, we need to remember that this trip took place in the middle of Japan's aggression on the Chinese continent.

Given his social position as a male, middle-class Japanese mainlander from a successful entrepreneurial family, Murai Osamu's accusation of Shimao is important to note. Calling Shimao Yanagita's 'defender', Murai argues that Shimao's *Japanesia* is a fantasy in which the southern island region is portrayed as a cultural unit that is only 'subtly different' from homogenous Japan.[3] Murai suggests that the fantasy about the southern islands was a Japanese version of Orientalism, referring to Edward Said's seminal text.

It is reasonable to say that Shimao's view of the southern islands is not free from the historical context around Japan. Also, contrary to his contemporaries such as Mishima Yukio, Yoshimoto Taka'aki or Takei Akio, Shimao did not directly engage in political activism nor make explicit comments regarding Japanese and international politics, especially in relation to the Japanese imperial past. Therefore, his attitude towards the history of and the current issues around Japanese politics is sometimes regarded as that of an uncritical intellectual.

Despite those criticisms, I argue that Murai's accusation about Shimao only partially makes sense, since he draws a genealogical linkage between Shimao and Yanagita by highlighting only limited works on *Japanesia* by the author. Thus, Murai's criticism fails to reflect on the development of Shimao's idea and its reception within Japanese society, especially among various progressive intellectuals. While admitting the ambiguity of Shimao's political position, I intend to develop the thesis that *Japanesia*, particularly the concept of the Ryūkyū Arc, has progressed the ways to critically address the discourses on the homogeneity of culture, centrality of social formation and 'linearity' of time in the modern Japanese state in terms of Japan's internal colonialism of the southern island communities.

Also, I contend that Murai's critique of Shimao does not pay enough attention to the social relations in which Shimao was enmeshed. For the last two decades, there has been an increase in historical research on Shimao and the period he lived in. For example, Terauchi Kunio, one of Shimao's disciples from Kobe University of Foreign Studies, has written a remarkable reference book, *Shimaoki* (*The Record of Shimao*), published in Japanese in 2007.[4] Two years prior to Terauchi's work, Kōsaka Kaoru and Nishio Nobuaki published an edited volume that compiles Shimao's biographical research essays as well as interpretive essays on Shimao's works.[5] Similarly, in 2010, Shimao's son, Shinzō, and Shimura Kunihiro published an edited volume that includes some biographical chapters.[6] More recently, Kudo Kunihiko's research gives us a useful account of Shimao's activities during his tenure as the Director of Kagoshima Prefectural Library's Amami Branch.[7] These existing studies offer ways to re-examine not only how to read Shimao's works but also where we can situate the author's life and views in a broader and more complex historical context.

In this sense, it is very important to highlight the influence of Shimao's *Japanesia* and the Ryūkyū Arc upon intellectuals and activists in Okinawa, which he considered to have been subjected to Japan's internal colonialism. Along with Arakawa Akira and radical anti-reversionists, Hokama Shuzen is also one of those who received profound inspiration from Shimao on the location of Okinawan culture. By referring to Shimao's works, the leading authority of the Ryūkyūan and Okinawan classics proposed the idea of the 'Pacific cultural space' (*Taiheiyō bunka-ken*) to reconsider Okinawa's cultural affinity in regional terms. He argues that it enables us to see the history and culture of Japan's southern islands not only as one of Japan's regions but also as a place shaped by the rich interactions in the maritime worlds constituted by the island communities in the Pacific and Southeast Asia.[8]

To advance Hokama's thesis, however, we need to discuss the issue that is not manifested in his concept of the Pacific cultural space. That is: Why the southern ocean and island communities are such an important reference for Shimao? In other words, what kind of cultural imagination did Shimao intend to bring in through discussing the Ryūkyū Arc and ultimately *Japanesia*? What I try to bring to the fore as a key term to consider those questions is *decolonisation* which was just beginning to be felt in the Pacific, including the maritime Southeast Asian nations.

His reference to Indonesia, which became an independent nation in 1945, might confuse readers due to the established image of that country as one of the key players in Southeast Asia. Yet, Shimao's reference to Indonesia as part of the *Pacific* does not mean that he was ignorant about the regional political demarcation. Rather, it derives from the common perception of the concept of the Pacific for his generation, in that the region was not as rigidly territorialized as it is today. For example, when the Research School of Pacific Studies, the world's first research centre dedicated to the studies of Pacific region, was established as part of the four research schools that constituted the Australian National University in 1948, the scope of their research extensively included much of what we today call Southeast Asia as well as the Melanesian and Polynesian regions.[9] The same goes for the Japanese term *nanyō*, which denotes the southern maritime region. In the institutional context, the term was used to specifically mean today's Micronesian islands after Japan's succession of former German island territories in the north of the equator. While the Japanese called this region 'the inner southern seas islands', there was 'the outer southern seas', region which was more extensive, including the south of the Chinese continent and Polynesia.

This vast oceanic region across the equator came to the fore of global attention as a site of political struggle after Japan's surrender in 1945. Along with the independence of Indonesia from the Japanese and the Dutch occupation in the 1940s, other former colonial territories also embarked on the journey of decolonization in the southern maritime and continental regions, such as the Philippines (1946), Burma and the Federation of Malaya (1948) and Cambodia (1953), and those ripples of post-colonial nation building reached Polynesian and Melanesian communities such as Samoa (1962), Fiji and Tonga (1970) throughout the 1960s and subsequently to Micronesian islands in the following decade. Indonesia, in this sense, sent an example and was seen as the regional hub of the decolonial project of the Pacific and one of the propelling forces of the global decolonization movement along with other key regional players such as India and the People's Republic of China and Egypt. Given this context, perhaps it is not unreasonable to infer that Shimao deliberately included Indonesia to indicate his alternative vision on Japan by relating Amami and the southern island communities with the Pacific. In other words, he considered the Pacific Ocean to be the cultural space that gives voice and meaning to Amami which was regarded as 'worthless' by both the local islanders and the mainland Japanese. So, in what way did Shimao conceive of Amami's significance and how did he relate this peripheral island territory with the Pacific?

Against absence of the historical past

Amami is the name of an archipelago that lies between Kagoshima in the south of Kyūshū Island and Okinawa Island. These days, this region may sometimes appear in Japanese popular dramas such as *Segodon* on NHK, featuring its 'exotic' and 'unorthodox' Japanese culture.

On this small island that sits at the margin of then Japan's borderline, Shimao and Miho arrived in the late autumn. As often said, the couple's relocation from Tokyo to Amami partly resulted from Miho's aggravated psychological state caused by Shimao's extramarital affair. This experience disrupted both his married life and also his career. They eventually decided to leave Tokyo to Ōshima, where Miho's relatives lived. In the interview with Okuno Takeo, Shimao said that in those days his psychological state only allowed him to live day by day, so he thought that the family had no choice but to leave Tokyo to live in Amami, a place that is close to Miho's hometown, Kakeroma Island.[10] The relocation was to restart their lives.

Shimao got a casual teaching job at local school shortly after his settlement on Ōshima, which he continued only for a short period of time. In March 1958, Shimao left his teaching job to assume the Directorship at the Amami Branch Office of the Kagoshima Prefectural Library. This appointment was a turning point in Shimao's career. Through this job, he was introduced to various local communities in and outside of Ōshima.

The appointment was made through the recommendation from the Director of Kagoshima Prefectural Library, Kubota Hikoho, also known as the children's book author, Muku Hatojū. Shimao first met Kubota through the introduction of their mutual acquaintance, Nakamura Chihei, who was once a friend and compared with his 'rival', Dazai Osamu. Nakamura was once the Director of Miyazaki Prefectural Library in the early postwar era. Yet, he had resigned from that position to succeed his father's business as the President of Miyazaki Sōgo Bank. Shimao had befriended Nakamura since Shimao was a student at Kyushu Imperial University.[11] Shortly after he moved to Ōshima, Shimao wrote a letter to Nakamura in which he asked for the introduction to Kubota.

Kubota and Nakamura were perhaps some of the most passionate advocates of community libraries in postwar Japan. They believed that libraries should be open, public and the centre for civic life. Later, people called them with respect *bunjin kanchō*, which means a writer or *literati* who is also the library director. They invested in creating new facilities such as a function hall for social events such as film screenings, music events and public lectures. Also, they adopted the new classification system called Nippon Decimal Classification for Japanese readers to ease their access to the library collections. For those who lived in rural areas, they started to offer an outreach service called *nōson bunko* (village library) and *rinkai bunko* (seaside library). So, when Shimao was appointed the Head of Amami Branch, Kubota gave him two major tasks: first, the improvement of the library collections, both academic and non-academic books, and loaning service in Amami region, including to remote islands; and, second, the preservation of regional culture and history. Also, since Shimao had no prior work experience as a librarian, he was sent to Kumamoto College of Commerce (today's Kumamoto Gakuen University) to receive proper training as a librarian.

Shimao put his tasks into action swiftly. Later that year, he organized an event *dokusho shūkan* (a reading week) for the first time in Ōshima. For this event to take off, he coordinated diverse local communities such as bookshops, the cultural division of the prefectural government and Catholic churches. Although the event itself was fruitful, it was only the first small step towards addressing the larger and deeper problems around the literary culture in the region. For example, the rural communities outside of Naze City were left out. The seven remote islands in the Amami archipelago needed particularly serious improvement of their library facilities, since in those days there were only a few old libraries in the entire region.

However, in this process, Shimao found out that one of the major problems which discouraged people from going to the libraries was the stereotypes attached to 'reading books' among the local islanders. In the regional newspaper column published in October 1958, Shimao raised this issue by arguing that there was a 'quite thick layer' of islanders who held the 'misconception' that 'reading distracts people' from working outside, and so disregarded it as an activity for 'lazy people'.[12] To change this view, he tried to create a modern library as the cultural centre, by purchasing books for everyday usage written in plain language, as well as expensive research texts and films and music. Also, he organized seminars for the islanders, teaching them about the usefulness of these modern cultural activities such as a story of farmers' wives who had learned about how to make a financial profit by reading books on agriculture and livestock.[13] Yet, earning the trust of the islanders was, quite understandably, not an easy job, let alone having them at the library.

The Islanders' attitude towards literary culture led Shimao to realize a deeper cause of the problem, which was a lack of general interest in lettered culture among the majority of society. It created a serious challenge to Shimao in order to fulfil not only promoting modern library culture but also finding written records of local culture and history. The scarcity of historical documents and old architecture such as religious institutions in Amami made Shimao anxious. At first, he even thought that there was no cultural artefacts which embodied the communal history in the region. For example, shortly after he moved to Ōshima, Shimao wrote that on the island, he discovered almost no 'scratches made by the people in the past' and said it sometimes makes him feel as if he came to 'a deserted island which has nothing but reeds.'[14] It is true that writing the history of Amami was seen as 'impossible' in those days, as recalled by Haraguchi Torao, a historian at the University of Kagoshima who later compiled the history of Naze.[15] For centuries, the communal past was kept as memory and descended through the generations orally rather than in written form. The written records only existed sporadically, and they were not sufficient for research purposes. Therefore, when a group of university historians, led by Haraguchi, started editing *The History of Naze City* in 1963, they had to refer to and compare with sources in other communities in Amami to write a communal history of Naze.

The absence of major Buddhist temples was critical in this context. Normally in other areas of the country, they were regarded as the institution for preserving the historical record. Nevertheless, Buddhism did not become ingrained in the soil in the Amami region as it had in mainland Japan. Instead, the local religion, mainly influenced by the Rūkyūan shamanism, survived as the dominant popular religion until the introduction of Shintoism. Shortly after Shintoism, some Buddhist schools such as the Tenri School became one of the popular religions, as well as Roman Catholicism. Yet, these religions were only recently introduced from outside of the island in the nineteenth century. Also, due to Amami's discriminated position as a penal colony and a sugarcane plantation throughout the Edo period, the Shimazu clan of Satsuma did not construct stonewalled castles on the islands after they incorporated the territory in 1609. In Shimao's view, who was a student of Chinese history during his undergraduate degree, the place at first appeared to be a historical desert.

Despite all the difficulties, however, this cultural desertedness became a source for Shimao's literary imagination. For example, in one of his essays presented in front of the local council members in Amami in June 1962, he said: 'In Amami, there is no equivalent to cultural heritage, and that was shocking. At the same time, however, it was very fascinating to me. There is nowhere that has nothing to this extent.'[16] This hyperbolic remark, which reflects Shimao's early impression of an absence of history in Amami, is also a deliberate simplification of the local island culture. While this simplification leaves his positionality as a mainland Japanese intellectual ambiguous in relation to the local islanders, his fascination with the 'absence' of major cultural artefacts also signifies the presence of things that are left in the absence. So, here the issue that needs to be considered should be what was that in the space of 'nothingness' that fascinated him.

In fact, Shimao was a committed local historian from his early days on the island. For example, he chaired a society of local historians called *Amami Kyōdo Kenkyū-kai* ('Amami Local Community Research Society'), a society dedicated to the discovery and documentation of local history. It was originally started as *Amami Shidan-kai* ('Amami History Discussion Group') by five members, including Shimao, in 1956, led by Kazari Eikichi, a former journalist and the Director of the Japan-US Culture Center Amami Branch Office, which was merged as part of Kagoshima Prefectural Library Amami Branch Office. Kazari was a renowned researcher who wrote the first monograph on local folklore in the Amami region in 1933. When Shimao was first introduced to Kazari, he was about to complete the cultural history of Amami. Kazari's approach to history involved analysing the language, old tales, poems, songs and other cultural heritage that had succeeded throughout generations in intangible formats, as well as historical documents. What this story tells us is that Shimao was already a committed member of the local history study circle. Shimao took over Kazari's position as the Director of the Japan-US Culture Center after his sudden death in 1957. Yet, it was not only the job and the society which Shimao succeeded, but also the history project Kazari founded and his folkloristic approach to history. With other members of the local history society, Shimao utilized all possible means of cultural inquiry to record local history in this 'history-less' place. Therefore, his remarks about Amami's history being a 'desert' need to be understood in that context.

So, what could be the possible reasons for Shimao to describe Amami as a 'historical desert'? One of the ways to interpret this concept is that by deliberately using the word 'desert', Shimao might have tried to describe a way in which the past exists in a condition that would otherwise be seen as an absence of communal history. If so, this metaphorical use of the words needs a careful consideration of its meaning and the contexts in which these words were employed. In fact, two years prior to the above statement, in 1960, he contributed a short essay to the New Year edition of *Nankai Nichi-nichi Shinbun*, a local Amami newspaper. In it, he says:

> The basic solitude of life in Amami is (although, of course, this is my literary exaggeration) that I feel there is no single ruin in this place. When I speak about the classical documents, too, I said that those things were not left in Amami. But we've come to see that there are many left, even though they are scattered around and often in a poor condition.[17]

As in the quote above, Shimao had recognized that his earlier assumption was not accurate by the time he wrote this piece, which was five years after his settlement in Ōshima. His confirmation about the plenitude of historical resources was reinforced three years later in his New Year column in the same newspaper, where he said:

> While living in Amami, it is impossible not to catch signals sent from daily life, trying to indicate to us the location of the historical truths which have been buried. But even if I tried to trace the shape of them, the documents which can be a clue to trace the shape of them seemed to have disappeared. Just like the island residents in Amami seem to refuse the creation of art

objects, they seemed to have deep reasons not to allow for any written records. That was a fault of my imagination. A careful investigation would enable us to find fragments of documents that are almost disappearing.[18]

Shimao's carefully chosen wording implies the difficulties, and his frustration, to find well-kept written records to use for research purposes. But this passage could be interpreted as his rejection of the discourses of the absence of history in Amami. Reading this urges us to raise a question as to why he referred to such metaphorical clichés as a 'desert' if he was a committed worker to recording the local history. In other words, why did he choose to use those metaphors in highlighting the plenitude of 'signals' of the past that can be translated as 'historical' yet remain uncaptured within the scope of conventional historical studies? So, how is it possible for us to argue that the 'desert' as a metaphor indicates the plenitude of the historical resources?

'Desert', according to the *Cambridge English Dictionary*, is explained as 'an area, often covered with sand or rocks, where there is very little rain and not many plants.'[19] Although Ōshima is far from a desert, we are reminded that the island is contoured by sands before entering the sea. Between the land and water, there is an extra layer of whiteness: the pieces of tarnished corals, oxidized and made into thousands of white blocks, and large and small shells of different sorts. If the desert is characterized as being full of sand and rocks, the shore is also a type of 'desert' with shells and dead coral as well as sand. Shimao's close observation of the shore enabled him to realize plenty of those natural resources from the 'desert' were used in a traditional graves, which is made of limestone rocks that contain sand, corals and shells. That was one of the common types of graves in many communities of Amami and elsewhere in the Ryūkyū Arc, including Okinawa Island. This must have inspired Shimao's historical imagination. In April 1964, he wrote a piece for *Nishi Nihon Shinbun* newspaper:

> These travellers would think that they have not encountered any manmade objects that block their visions. They would feel irritated by monotony and vulgarity around them, and they would witness the incurable poverty spreading out before their eyes. [...] My Amami started from that deadlock. After suffering the monotony and poverty, I cannot deny the abundance that was increasingly spreading in my mind, although I don't exactly know how

to put it. In the graves that are made of bone-like limestone corals under the dazzling sun, whispers of the people who lived and died on the island become a lively murmuring. They would arise by pushing aside the tombstone and walk towards me. The islanders' undocumented life histories, which are exposed to the sea breeze, are small yet deeply carved, and accumulate through generations like eternal children, serve to support the existence of our nation in the depths of history, although they received no recognition, no way to understand themselves, and are imagined to be a matter only for their small, limited islands without any relationship to other places.[20]

This is an important quote that shows how Shimao sought to make sense of the past of the community. It strongly expresses his frustration about the past of the community that has never been paid significant attention in Japan and how this negligence has forced the islanders throughout generations to feel they are 'worthless'. In a nutshell, this is his objection to the marginalization of Amami which has inflicted the 'history-less' situation on the local culture. To articulate this point, he compares ignorant travellers and himself, who had realized the abundance of the historical culture. The travellers, or perhaps the ordinary mainland Japanese, who feel 'irritated' by 'monotony', or 'poverty', are those who are blind or senseless to feel the 'signals' of the dead. Importantly, however, the image of the Japanese travellers in this quote reflects Shimao himself in the early days of his life in Amami. Therefore, this quote is the mirror of Shimao, showing his divided self and the dynamics of how the island changed his understanding of history.

By now, it should be clear that Shimao's commitment to researching and making the history of Amami was not a project limited to making the 'History' as defined in the academic sense. He approached the realm of the past more broadly as something rooted in the local geo-cultural landscape. Graves were one of the sources of his historical imagination, and the analogy of 'signals' implies it is up to individuals if they can be attentive or not. In this very sense, I would argue that Shimao's discovery was the *presence* of the past through which the recollection of the past becomes possible.[21] As Ewa Domanska discusses, it is this presence that makes us see 'the material aspects of traces of the past in a context other than semiotics, discourse theory, or representation theory, and to focus the analysis of those traces on an aspect that is marginalized or neglected by traditional notions of the source.'[22]

Enacting Japanesia

The research on Ōshima and travels to the regional remote islands for the first few years of his Directorship of the Amami Library helped broaden Shimao's literary and historical imagination in space as well as time. In other words, those intensive years between the late 1950s and the early 1960s were a formative period of his representative concept, *Japanesia*. As I discussed above, the metaphor of the 'desert' is not the same as the emptiness of history. Rather, it was to bring to the fore the 'presence' of the past. Yet, how is 'the Pacific' relevant in Shimao's resistance to accepting the absence of history? To consider this question, I will probe Shimao's transnational journey to various island communities in the second half of this chapter. But before going into the details of his travel, I wish to briefly explain a bibliographical aspect of this concept.

The concept of *Japanesia* was publicized for the first time in 1961 in the twenty-first volume of *Sekai Kyōyō Zenshū* (*The Complete Volumes of World Cultures*) as an appendix under the title 'Yaponeshia no Nekko' ('The Roots of *Japanesia*'). The importance of the concept was often understood to be its perspective that revisits the multipolarity of Japanese culture, which is built not only upon the political centres, or what Shimao calls the middle region of Japan, but also upon the marginalized south-western regions, centred around the Ryūkyū Arc, as well as the north-eastern part of the country. Through this critique, Shimao raised two major issues of modern Japanese culture that *Japanesia* critically engages with. The first issue is Japan's long-held cultural orientation towards and adherence to the continental worlds as the origins of the world's great civilizations. The second issue was this passivity, which, in turn, causes negligence of 'the other' significant cultural influence that was vital in the formation of Japanese history and culture. That was influence from the Pacific. In other words, Shimao's celebration of Japan as an archipelagic and a multipolar world was not only to criticize the cultural homogeneity within the country but to reveal the unconsciously biased thoughts and behaviours deeply ingrained in popular perception of the formation of modern Japanese society in civilizational terms by bringing the oceanic influence into the discussion.

Despite Shimao's already established fame as a writer and the novelty of the concept, however, it took almost ten years until *Japanesia* drew wide public attention. According to Okamoto Keitoku, an Okinawan literary scholar, one of the turning points was when an influential folklorist Tanigawa Ken'ichi published an essay titled 'What Is *Japanesia*' on the first page of the New Year's Day edition of *Tosho Shinbun* (*The Book Newspaper*), a weekly newspaper dedicated to promoting and reviewing recently published books, in 1970.[23] In his essay, Tanigawa argues that *Japanesia* allows us to address the problems of Japanese nationalism by not simply accepting internationalistic perspectives that are imported from outside of Japan but finding factors that implode the nationalistic representation of Japan.

Tanigawa further argues that *Japanesia* shows us 'polyphyletic' lines of time (*takeiteki jikan-jiku*) that enable us to see Japan as a 'cultural complex' (*bunka fukugoutai*) made of different historical spaces, multi-layered consciousnesses (*ishiki no jūsōsei*) and an abnormal development of capitalism. The core argument of *Japanesia* in Tanigawa's reading is to recapture the nation from difference within, and from this difference, he contends that we are able to have a 'coeval' (*kyōjiteki*) perspective on the progression of national history, which, in his view, counters 'chronological' (*tsūjiteki*) views.[24] Tanigawa's interpretation of *Japanesia* was foundational for the readers at the time as one of the first texts that reviewed the concept and as a work that translated Shimao's literary expressions into a solid theoretical discussion by contextualizing the concept in the Marxist-inspired tradition of Japanese folklore studies.

In his book *Yapoesia no Rinkaku* (*The Outline of Japanesia*), Okamoto says the increasing popularity of *Japanesia* can also be attributed to political and social situations in Japan, especially Okinawa around the turn of the 1960s, such as the handover of Okinawa from the US military administration to Japan.[25] As I have discussed in Chapter 2, Okinawa's return to Japan also reverberated strongly with Japanese and Okinawan civil societies by creating pro- and anti-reversion campaigns. In the time when some Okinawan activists were concerned about the future course of their territory after its re-incorporation into Japan, they read Shimao's critique with enthusiasm as it gave the meaning of their place to critically intervene with the centrality of national politics.

Furthermore, Okamoto referred to the appearance of progressive politicians as the heads of municipal governments in Japan in the late 1960s until the early 1970s as a reason that prompted the popularity of Shimao's works in Japan along with the mass students' movements in mainland Japan.[26] The emergence of progressive municipalities during those periods was a result of the rapid yet uneven industrial development and distribution of wealth in the country such as population drain in the rural areas, air pollution in urban areas and lack of appropriate social infrastructure. This was a period in which Japan's high centralization of political and economic powers was put in doubt.

Yet, at the same time, it is important to note that those two decades were the periods when Japan emerged into the international forum as the host of the Olympic Games in 1964 and the Expo in Osaka in 1970. Also, overseas travel became available for ordinary citizens.[27] To discuss trade agreements, the Japanese leaders such as Ikeda Hayato and Sato Eisaku visited Australia and New Zealand in the 1960s. What it suggests is that this period was a key milestone for Japan in the postwar era to show its new international outlook as a member of the liberal democratic countries in what was later called 'Asia and the Pacific'. The Japanese government's engagement in Okinawa's return needs to be contextualized in relation to its Cold War diplomacy in the region.

It was in this context that Shimao developed his idea of *Japanesia*, particularly the meaning of the Ryūkyū Arc, to turn it into a critical concept of modern Japan. The key moments were between 1963 and 1964, in which he took transpacific travels: to mainland United States, Hawai'i, Puerto Rico and occupied Okinawa, including its southwestern end. These journeys not only enriched his overseas experiences, but they were also crucial instances for him to reconsider the scope of his experience and the discourse on Amami to recontextualize them in an extensive region of the oceanic islands of the South.

With the support of the United States Information Agency (USIA), particularly the Fukuoka American Center, Shimao was invited to the United States as a guest. Shimao's interaction with the US diplomatic agency dates to the earlier period when he was appointed the Director of the Amami Branch of the Kagoshima Prefectural Library. Prior to Amami's return from the US military administration to Japan in December 1953, the office was one of the six Ryukyu-America Cultural Centers in the US-occupied territory in the southwestern part of Japan, including Okinawa and Amami. One of the roles of those Centers were to serve the local communities as a hub of social interactions, including library services, film screenings and other events, between the military administration and local islanders. Shimao's appointment as the Director of the Library took place in the middle of the handover period of the facility from the US government to Kagoshima

Prefecture, yet partial funding was still coming from the USIA. According to the memoir by Shimao's son, Shinzō, the officers of the USIA, especially the former Head of the Fukuoka American Center, Charles Medd, and his then wife Iola, often visited Shimao in Ōshima.[28]

Shimao's visit to the United States was arranged by the US Department of State under the People's Exchange Program scheme. Through this same channel, a number of academics and non-academic intellectuals have visited the United States, including Oe Kenzaburō and Nosaka Akiyuki, the author of the *Graves of Fireflies*. As his son, Shinzō, recalls, at first Shimao did not have a positive impression of this former enemy nation. Also, like many other writers in those days, he was a member of a progressive writers association, *Shin Nihon Bungaku-kai* (The New Japanese Literature Association), which was originally founded by Japanese pro-communist writers. Therefore, in light of the context of the Cold War, Shimao's political stance meant he was not necessarily an ideal guest to invite to the United States. In fact, the US embassy had been in frequent contact with conservative leaders until the turn of the 1950s.

However, the US public diplomacy policy changed around 1960 and the USIA began to contact and send progressive Japanese intellectuals as well as conservatives. This change resulted from the issue of a 'growing gap' between Japanese and American views on each other, as Edwin O. Reischauer warned in one of the seminal texts on *Foreign Affairs*, 'The Broken Dialogue with Japan'. This gap was explicitly felt around the time of the historic mass protest against the renewal of the security treaty between Japan and the United States in 1960, or the so-called 1960 Ampo protest. In this situation, cultural diplomacy, especially the exchange program of the cultural leaders, was believed to be one of the effective investments to construct mutual understanding between the two countries.[29] In this political environment, Medd approached Shimao to discuss issues around the handover of the Amami Library. It is not surprising that Medd later 'targeted' Shimao, the survivor of a suicide bomber unit during the Second World War who also insisted on the reduction of American collections from the library, as one of the next guests. Likewise, we can see that there were a number of academics and local intellectuals in the Kyūshū region who were sent to the United States through this invitation scheme, including Kubota Hihiko, in the mid-1950s.[30]

Although the invited guests usually travelled to the US mainland, Shimao was one of the few, if not the only, visitors who requested to visit Puerto Rico. He thought this small island might 'show poverty, and thus I might be able to feel more similarities to our lives.'[31] In Puerto Rico, he spent one week in San Juan and walked around the city and neighbouring communities, relaxed his tense body in the local tropical climate and saw the sugarcane plantations that cover the vast space of the island. Obviously, Shimao could not help but feel similarities to Amami. In Hawai'i, too, the sugarcane plantations drew his attention. For him, those plantations were reminiscent of his home village, and he also thought they were the symbol of the life of the southern islanders in the sense that the locals would have to produce sugar, not to consume, but to export. He wrote:

> The fact that this island could produce the sugarcanes was a reason that drew the island into its destiny. Perhaps, the islanders were forced to sacrifice other jobs to plant sugarcanes, the sugar that was produced would serve for people living overseas. (I cannot resist thinking of the islands of Amami because they have been stranded as the sugarcane plantation once by Satsuma, and today by mainland Japan.)[32]

While travelling to those 'sugarcane islands', Shimao also visited major cities in both the north and south of the US mainland, from Seattle to Washington, DC, from New York to New Orleans and from Phoenix to Los Angeles. In Seattle, he visited the University of Washington to meet its first professor of Japanese literature, Richard N. MacKinnon. Yet, other than that, much of his memoirs of the United States are about his trips to the remote islands. From this, we can see that visits to these islands were one of his main purposes during his American journey. While visiting the islands, both of which had complex histories of racial and ethnic relations with the United States, Shimao confirmed the similar fate of life on the small island communities in the shadow of the mainland.

Shortly after returning from the United States, Shimao travelled to Okinawa Island and further south such as to Miyako and Ishigaki Islands, all of which were still under US control, in 1964. This trip was an important moment, through which he learned a new view and language to discuss the occupied Okinawa by comparing them with the American island territories and Amami. Although his first reference to Okinawa dates to the late 1950s, he had never been to Okinawa prior to this trip because of the travel regulations imposed on both Japanese and Okinawan citizens. Under the US military administration, travel between the two places was strictly controlled by the US authority in Okinawa. For example, visitors to Okinawa from the rest of Japan had to submit travel application forms, including visa applications and their reasons and places to visit. They also had to obtain a Japanese passport. Although Okinawa was still considered part of the Japanese sovereign territory in theory, travelling to the whole region was as difficult as going overseas until Okinawa's return to Japan in 1972. Shimao stayed in Naha for the first five days, and then flew to Ishigaki Island where he met Arakawa Akira who was a journalist for *Okinawa Taimusu* (*Okinawa Times*). From Ishigaki, he flew to Miyako before going back to Naha.

During his two-week trip to Okinawa, Shimao projected images of Puerto Rico and Hawai'i onto Okinawa's landscape from time to time. For example, by looking at the fields filled with sugarcane in Miyako and Ishigaki from the plane, he remembered Hawai'i. The narrow runway surrounded by the tall canes was reminiscent of Lanai Island. The streets and cities of those southern islands, he felt, were evocative 'somewhat of *Espania* [which he calls "Isupania"]'.[33] The signs in English and the American soldiers and their jeeps only made the memory of his recent trip to the United States more vivid.

However, he also saw the lives of these islands from the perspective of an islander from Amami. The bulky stonewalls made of corals and rocks that surrounded old houses were the same as those in his hometown. Likewise, the traditional Ryūkyū dance performances he saw in Naha and Ishigaki were identical to those he sometimes went to see in Ōshima. These were reminders of the shared history of the Ryūkyū Arc. This trip to Okinawa introduced further complexity to the meaning of the southern islands to Shimao. The analogy of the American island territories and the cultural connections with the old Ryūkyūs suggested the translocal, or transnational, applicability of Shimao's experiences in Amami across the Pacific Ocean.

Shimao's transpacific journeys expanded his views on island lives in different parts of the world. He had been overseas in the past, including to the Philippines, Korea and Manchukuo in his youth, yet the impact of his pre-Second World War experiences was not comparable to his recent trips.

As I briefly discussed above, the mid-1960s was the time Japan was re-entering the global stage, although the country was still far from being in the club of the 'advanced' countries. The wounds of the war were still salient in international and domestic life. In this social reality, what Shimao saw was the affluence and pride of the United States as the world centre and the island communities as in the shadow of this global superpower. By drawing threads from these transpacific journeys, he was re-positioning Amami, not as part of postwar democratic Japan, but as one of these 'sugarcane plantation islands' ('*satōjima*') also in the shadow of its 'mainland'.

The Ryūkyū Arc, the Pacific and Shimao's anti-colonial politics

Shimao's little-read text, 'Amami and *Japanesia*', which I introduced at the beginning of this chapter, was written in this context. This two-page-long article is certainly not the one that represents his whole literary career. Yet, the value of the text is that it has the essence of his view on the Ryūkyū Arc and *Japanesia* after all the trips he made first to Ōshima and adjacent islands in Amami, then to the United States, Puerto Rico, Hawai'i and finally to the southern borderlands of the US-occupied Okinawa.

Shimao's discussion in the essay is twofold. First, he contextualizes the past of the southern islands as a tragedy, such as the subordination by the Shimazu clan and subsequently by modern Japan. Shimao emphasized that Shimazu's incorporation of the Amami archipelago in 1609 was the defining moment of socio-economic transformation of the region into sugarcane plantations, which coerced the islanders 'to dedicate all of their labour' to this industry.[34] By using the term 'plantation', it is reasonable to infer that Shimao tried to compare Satsuma's perpetual domination, which resulted in the impoverishment of the local productivity and community on the islands, with his recent visit to Puerto Rico and Hawai'i. In other words, he uses the word 'plantation' not to suggest an idyllic, local agricultural landscape, but to mean the involvement of superior power that incorporated the local society into Japan's proto-capitalist economy.[35] This discriminatory treatment of the Amami islands under Japanese rule, he further maintains, prepared the soil for an inferiority complex among the islanders that has made them 'falsify or conceal their background' as 'relatively worthless' vis-à-vis its colonial master.

At the same time, however, he also highlights the historical position of the Ryūkyū Arc as a hinge or a 'passage' that connects Japan and the southern islands in history. To elaborate on this point further, he argues that, as the place located on the northern borderline of the Ryūkyū world, Amami should be seen as the most relevant area in understanding the southern influences on Japanese history. In this spirit, Shimao argues that 'the mainlander's almost total ignorance of life on the islands' needs to be overcome by reconsidering the place of Amami as the point of connection between southern and northern cultures in Japanese history since the prehistoric age. For example, the use of *takakura*, a thatch-roofed storehouse, which is no longer visible in the mainland, is not only a historical artefact but needs to be interpreted as a critical source of historical imagination of where 'we Japanese' came from. Similarly, he thought that the local dialect, which researchers thought retains the language used in mainland Japan from the Heian period (794–1185), could be a significant opportunity to see an underrepresented part of the country. In this sense, he mentions the fact that modern researchers see the Amami islands as 'living fossils' or a 'treasure box' that can fill in the 'missing links' about the origins of Japan, as it still 'retains much more of ancient Japanese tradition than does modern life on the mainland.'[36] His interpretation of the local culture, such as *takakura* and the dialect, was an unorthodox translation of the history of those days. However, his local observations enabled him to see them as the medium that unfolds the past of the community not only of the islands but also of the modern nation.

Shimao's reference to the Pacific region, which he introduced at the beginning of the essay, needs to be remembered in this context. The vast maritime region is the key to opening up a regional space that gives an alternative voice and meaning to Amami and ultimately the roots of the Japanese, aside from the continental connection. Although it is true that his knowledge of the region was limited and he had never gone across the equator, his transhemispheric vision caught the tidal waves towards a postcolonial era, which was perceptible in the northern fringe of the ocean. Shimao's *Japanesia*, therefore, can be read as a reflection of his intervention in the cultural representation of Japan at the time when the country, once again, sought to enact its international outlook as an archipelagic maritime nation. Yet, the very criticality of his cultural politics was not to engage in the effort to re-centre postwar Japan as a nation that belonged to the club of modern liberal democratic countries. Rather, his project was to foreground the Pacific as the foundation upon which Japan's insignificant southern islands can not only reconstruct themselves but also offer a fresh meaning and identity for the rest of Japan as a more culturally archipelagic or decentralized country. In this sense, it is possible to interpret Shimao's enactment of the Ryūkyū Arc as well as Japanesia as a home-grown version of decolonial cultural politics.

5

From Okinawa to Asia

Entry denied

On the 5th of September 2012 at around 12.45 pm, three Japanese anti-base activists from Okinawa arrived at the Incheon International Airport in Seoul, South Korea. Those individuals, namely Takahashi Toshio, Tomiyama Masahiro and Tomita Eiji, were en route to Cheju Island to attend a conference organized by the International Union for Conservation of Nature (IUCN), which has been run annually since 1948. The purpose of the conference was to bring together national governments and non-government organizations (NGOs) for discussing the protection and promotion of natural heritage around the globe. With an official letter from a member of the South Korean National Assembly, the three Japanese individuals were invited guests of the conference.

Yet, as they disembarked at Incheon Airport, an immigration officer approached and told them to go to the administration office, where another immigration official required the three visitors to submit their passports and took their fingerprints. Handing in the letter of invitation, Takahashi, who was fluent in Korean, asked for an explanation for their treatment, but the official did not respond to his enquiry and just told them to wait until further notice. In the meantime, Takahashi called the Japanese Embassy in Seoul. He told the Japanese official that they had been detained at the airport. However, this Japanese official told him to contact the Japanese Embassy again if their entry was declined. At the immigration desk, they were taken to a different room at the corner and told to wait for further notice.

After two hours, two immigration officers told Takahashi and the others that their entry into South Korea had been denied, and they were to leave the country on the same day. A return ticket had already been prepared by Asiana Airlines. Takahashi argued that this order from the Korean authorities without any reasonable explanations would not be acceptable and he asked for the official letter by the Korean Ministry of Justice that explained the reason for declining their entry into the country, but all of his requests were dismissed by the officials. So, around 4.00 pm, Takahashi called the Japanese Embassy in Seoul again, and explained what had occurred. He asked a Japanese official to negotiate with the Korean Government, saying that this decision for the visitors to be deported without any clear reason was a violation of their human rights. However, the official at the Japanese Embassy said to Takahashi that the decision was made by the Korean Government, and therefore there was nothing that the Japanese Embassy could do to help. In the end, they had no option but to get on the plane and return to Fukuoka.

Upon their return to Naha, those three individuals held a press conference at which they reported the news, which was published in local newspapers in Okinawa the next day. Both the Japanese and South Korean governments remained silent on this issue. Later, it was revealed that the South Korean government declined the entry of other Okinawan visitors, as well as a number of Japanese and other environmental activists, to participate in the IUCN conference, and the Okinawan activists speculated that the Korean government was concerned about the escalation of the anti-base movement in Gangjeong Village on Cheju Island.[1] Six months earlier, the then President of South Korea, Lee Myung-bak, and his government had decided to destroy the rocky shoreline in preparation for the construction of a new naval base to be used jointly by the South Korean Navy and its US counterpart. The rocky shore, which was listed as a world heritage site harbouring rare local species, was designated as the central site of the base's construction.

While this incident might not have drawn wide and lasting media attention, the news also shed light on the increasing exchanges of civic activists across the national borders between Okinawa and South Korea over environmental conservation and the military base problems to the public. In this chapter and the next, I probe the roots of this transnational anti-base activism between Okinawan and South Korean citizens by examining the case of a local Okinawan activists' group called Okinawa-Korea People's Solidarity (OKPS) to which the above-mentioned activists belonged. By delving into some of the key events and a series of challenges and difficulties in the eyes of Okinawan activists, this chapter unravels what I call the 'second wave of grassroots regionalism' through which Okinawa became one of the key sites, along with South Korea, for transnational anti-base activism in Asia and the Pacific.

A street corner house

One early evening in late November, 2011, I was walking on Kokusai Dōri Street towards the western end of Naha City. Despite the off-peak season, this main street of the city was bustling with tourists just like in summer. Walking several blocks down, I could feel the sea breeze on my face. The wind came from Naha Port, where ferries, cruises and tankers take their passengers and cargo to and from different parts of Asia. My destination, Uruma Chapel, was located near the port called Tomari Takahashi. At first, the chapel was rather difficult to identify as the building was in the middle of a residential neighbourhood with no signs or religious symbols. Like other buildings on the street, it was only a grey two-story concrete building. The entrance had two sliding doors to which the schedule of bible study reading group information was attached. That was the only sign for me to understand what the place was meant to be.

I knocked on the door, and a tall elderly man appeared. He was Nishio Ichirō, who was a pastor of the United Church of Christ in Japan, a father with one daughter, the owner of a local kindergarten and also one of the founding members of OKPS. He told me to wait for his friends to arrive for the interview I had scheduled. Meanwhile, he gave me plates of cucumbers and carrots, which, he said, came from his vegetable garden. Soon after, a middle-aged man with long black hair flecked with grey arrived: this was Tomiyama Masahiro, who is also one of the founding members of this protest community. Although Tomiyama said he came directly from his office, he looked rather relaxed, as though he had just come back from a local beach. While Nishio wore a white shirt with a pair of trousers, Tomiyama was more casual in shorts, sandals and a t-shirt, even in the cool weather of late autumn. Shortly after Tomiyama's arrival, they were joined by Ōta Kunio, another member of the group. Ōta and Tomiyama are more or less of a similar generation, in their late fifties. In the relaxed atmosphere, with nibbles and drinks on the table, the three men started chatting about their recent news. This was my introduction to the OKPS, the 'protesters' who were banned from entering South Korea.

OKPS was founded in 1998 by five activists from Okinawa and mainland Japan – Nishio Ichirō, Tomiyama Masahiro, Takahashi Toshio, To Yusa and Arasaki Moriteru. Arasaki, once a young activist scholar, was the most senior member at that time, participating in the community as an advisor rather than being involved in it as an active member. Tomiyama Masahiro has been an active participant in the anti-base movement since his teenage years. He was born in Miyako Island, where the local people, he says, are known for a 'rough character' compared to the people in Okinawa Island, and he seemed proud of that roughness of 'Miyakonchu' (which denotes the Miyako islanders). He relocated to Okinawa Island with his mother who was a school teacher and an ardent activist. So, he thought it would be an obvious course of life to be involved in anti-base activism. Compared to Arasaki who was a devoted activist through pens and papers and who was once Tomiyama's teacher during his undergraduate period, he calls himself a 'field player' by which he means someone who stands in the frontline of protest sites. He told me numerous episodes about his past involvement in physical confrontations. His opponents ranged from police officers, including the riot squad, and *karate* athletes who were hired by right-wing activists. 'Although people call Okinawans peace-loving and anti-base activism is non-violent, that's not always the case' was a phrase he would sometimes tell me in our meetings since then.

While Arasaki and Tomiyama have their ancestral roots from different parts of Okinawa Prefecture, Nishio and Takahashi Toshio came originally from the mainland in the 1970s and 1980s, respectively. Although there are differences in generation, both of them were involved with student activism prior to their relocation to Okinawa. After they moved to Okinawa, Nishio started his missionary activity as a pastor while running a local kindergarten. On the other hand, Takahashi continued to work as a student activist for a while even after he moved to Okinawa. Yet, later, he started working as a social worker after he withdrew from his previous career. To Yusa, too, became involved with OKPS from outside Okinawa. As an Osaka-based Korean activist, To has been involved with political activism including helping anti-war American GIs to desert during the Vietnam War and supported the democratization movement in South Korea from Japan.[2] The members of OKPS, though they came from different walks of life, became friends while being involved in local anti-base activism such as *Hitotsubo* Anti-war Landowners Association (see Chapter 3). These individuals gathered to establish OKPS with the aim of internationalizing Okinawa's anti-base struggle, particularly by establishing links with South Korean anti-base activism.

Today, over thirty people are registered as members of this community, but they are widely dispersed. Many of them are residing on Okinawa Island, and some of them are living in mainland Japan and South Korea. In a strict sense, members are expected to pay 500 yen as a monthly membership fee to cover the costs of group activities. But because of the nature of the membership, it is difficult to collect money from all of the members. Thus, in a practical sense, this rule is applied loosely and irregularly. Also, as another principle, the members are expected to attend a monthly meeting to discuss activities, policy and other administrative matters. However, this has never been made mandatory because it is hardly ever possible to bring all the members together because of their dispersed locations. Likewise, although OKPS has an annual assembly where all the members are supposed to gather, in fact, it is usually organized as one of the regular monthly meetings. However, these loose aspects of the membership and organizational structure do not mean that the group is inactive. There are members who regularly attend the meetings every month from cities, towns and villages including Naha, Urazoe, Futenma and Yomitan. These people serve as core members in implementing various group activities, corresponding with a widely dispersed network of individuals outside of Okinawa.

Remembering the other war-dead

Although OKPS was founded in June 1998, its origins go back to the late 1980s. One of the earliest occasions was when five South Koreans visited Okinawa in November 1986. They were survivors of a group of labourers who were brought to various places around Okinawa from colonial Korea after the Pacific War started. According to a historical study, about three-hundred fifty Koreans, including the five men who visited Okinawa, were brought to work in different places in the Kerama Islands, located forty kilometres away from the mainland of Okinawa in June 1944.[3] They were part of a total of the whole group of Korean labourers, which was estimated no less than three thousand, who served in various places in Okinawa towards the end of the War.[4]

Most of the Koreans in Kerama Islands came from North Gyeongsang Province. Arriving in Kerama, they were put to work building the secret shelters used to house small boats. These boats were to be used for suicide attacks against the Allied Powers under the orders of the Japanese Imperial Army. This mission was called *marure*. During the Battle of Okinawa, about eighty Korean labourers in Kerama were believed to have died from malnutrition, and some of them were executed by the Japanese soldiers. Struggling with hunger, they stole potatoes from local farmland, but were found by the local villagers and reported to the Japanese military officers. In the end, two-hundred and fifty-seven people survived and they were captured by the American soldiers and repatriated to their homeland.

After they returned to Korea, these survivors had been longing to take back the remains of their fellow Korean conscripted workers to their homeland. So, they established an organization called the Pacific Fellows Association (*Taiheiyō Dōshikai*) together with other former Korean conscripted workers engaged in different parts of formerly Japanese-occupied territories during wartime.[5] This is how the five Koreans came to visit Kerama Islands, particularly Aka Island and Zamami Island, in order to commemorate the spirits of those who could never return to their country.

The visit of the five Korean survivors inspired not only Okinawans but also some ethnic Koreans in Japan. Among them was an independent documentary maker, Park Sunam. She filmed the Korean survivors' journey to Kerama and made a film titled 'Ariran no uta: Okinawa kara no shōgen' (*The Song of Arirang: Testimony from Okinawa*), which was released in 1991. Born in Mie Prefecture as a second-generation ethnic Korean resident in Japan, Park started her career as a journalist and activist for her fellow Koreans in Japan in the early 1960s, most famously known for her book about the killing of two young females in the so-called Komatsugawa Incident.[6] Park produced a number of films related to Koreans during wartime, including Koreans who became victims of the atomic bombs in Hiroshima and Nagasaki in 1945. With the help of her Okinawan friends such as senior activist Fukuchi Hiroaki and photographer Ishikawa Mao, Park embarked on her journey in the Kerama Islands at the time of the visit of the five Korean former conscripted workers.

The visit of the Korean survivors unveiled some crucial aspects of Okinawa's wartime history. Although local historians such as Miyazato Kiyogorō, the founder of the Kerama Oceanic Culture Museum, were collecting and telling the stories of Korean conscripted workers in Kerama Islands, they were otherwise hardly remembered in Okinawa. Especially, memories of the execution of Koreans were kept by only a limited number of local residents. In this sense, unravelling the history of Koreans in Okinawa during wartime introduced a new perspective on the history of the war in Okinawa. But for some locals, the forgotten history of the Korean conscripted labourers posed difficult questions for Okinawa's historical narratives. In particular, the presence of Korean workers complicated the view of the Okinawan 'victimhood' narrative during the Battle of Okinawa and its historical position in modern East Asia. While the exact number of Korean labourers, which includes young Korean females who were conscripted workers to serve as so-called comfort women, is not known, the memory of Koreans in wartime Okinawa made it necessary to see local history from the perspective of 'another victim' of the war.

In other words, the five Koreans' visit raised the question of Okinawa's historical position in relation to East Asian communities. Like other cultural minority groups from the territories outside of the Japanese mainland, Okinawans, too, were often discriminated against by the Japanese and had to endure colonial cultural relations vis-à-vis Japan. However, despite all the discriminatory treatment, Okinawans were not the same as Koreans and Taiwanese. While people in these places, which had more recently been incorporated into the Japanese Empire, were categorized as people of 'the external territories' (*gaichi*), Okinawans were regarded as people from the internal region of Japan proper (*naichi*). This was related to the political administration used to govern the empire. While Koreans and Taiwanese were administered by the Governor Generals who represented the authority of the Japanese government, Okinawa was one of the Japanese prefectures. From this perspective, we can understand the complexity of Okinawa's modern experience, in that it was not a colony but was treated in a discriminatory manner by some of those from mainland Japan.

The re-appearance of Korean labourers in Okinawa's history confronted Okinawans with ambiguous problems of self-recognition as (on the one hand) the domestically colonized subject under Japan's imperial expansion who were incorporated into modern nation-state and located in a peripheral position, and (on the other) as people who were not the same as other colonized, regional neighbours such as Korea. However, this was a crucial moment in the history of OKPS, gradually enabling Okinawans, such as Arasaki who helped Koreans to visit Kerama, to conceive of their position in relation to and in the context of the East Asian region.

From Okinawa to Asia

The Okinawan activists' encounter with former Korean conscripted labourers was a crucial moment. It was the first experience for many of them to hear their memories directly. Also, the significance of this period lies in the fact that this trip became the earliest occasion on which some key members of OKPS met to work together on the issue related to Korea. By joining the commemorative trip to Kerama, the founders of OKPS came to recognize another colonial history in Okinawa, which also influenced local activists to consider Okinawa's historical present in relation to other Asian neighbours. But this encounter with former Korean labourers was not the direct trigger to start the international anti-base solidarity movement with South Koreans.

Okinawa's international anti-base solidarity campaign started in the early 1990s. One of the leading groups consisted of local feminists, led by Takazato Suzuyo, an activist who was also a member of the Naha City Assembly. Along with the feminists, Tomiyama Masahiro and other activists who later became the founders of OKPS were also considering the chance to extend their activist network overseas. After two decades since Okinawa's return to Japan, they were concerned about how long their activism would have to continue, and more importantly, whether it was possible to achieve a base-free society only by the effort of the Okinawan people. Knowing that there were other places where people organized their anti-base struggle, these concerned Okinawans began to feel the necessity to create an international solidarity campaign.

There was another reason that encouraged them to further develop their activism. In November 1990, a renowned progressive academic, Ota Masahide, won the gubernatorial election and became the fourth publicly elected leader of Okinawa Prefecture. This victory by the former professor of the University of Ryukyus, who was widely recognized as the representative voice of Okinawa's progressivism, against his opponent and the incumbent governor, Nishime Junji, who had been in the leadership position for twelve years, was seen as the arrival of a new era for the local anti-base politics.

One of the first countries the activists approached was the Philippines. Okinawans felt hope for the new era by witnessing the Philippines' democratization movement, especially with its success in ending the authoritarian regime under President Ferdinando Marcos in 1986 (the so-called People Power Revolution). Also, Tomiyama had a friend, Arakaki Tokiko, who founded the Society for Friendship of Okinawa and Philippines, which was an organization for cultural exchange between these two historically and geographically close places. So, through her introduction, Tomiyama first visited Manila in the late 1980s.

Following Tomiyama's first visit, he and his fellow activists made trips to the Philippines almost every year until the mid-1990s. Their main contact was a progressive nationalist organization called Bayan (Bagong Alyasang Makabayan or the New Nationalist Alliance). As an umbrella organization made up of many different leftists and nationalists, Bayan was founded in 1985 and conducted general strikes as a means of protest against Marcos' dictatorial regime. Together with communist and other progressive communities in provincial areas, Bayan was a core force behind the People Power Revolution in 1986.[7]

The drastic change in the Philippine political landscape in the late 1980s was of strong interest to Okinawan activists. Yet what attracted Okinawans most in that period was the 1991 agreement for the transfer of the Clark Airbase from the US Air Force to the Philippine government, which was put into effect in the following year. Like Futenma and Kadena Airbases in Okinawa, the Clark Airbase had also played a crucial role for the US military during the Vietnam War. Therefore, the closure of this US airbase, which was one of the largest of this kind in the region, was seen as a historic event not only by the Philippine citizens but also by Okinawan activists. As such, when they heard the news, some Okinawans thought that they should learn from this neighbouring country, and they started organizing trips to the Philippines.

To strengthen Okinawa-Philippine solidarity, Tomiyama, Arasaki, Nishio and other like-minded activists organized a group to study the history and current political and economic situation of the Philippines. The main aim of this study group was to have a better understanding of how the Philippines had been able to close the Clark Airbase. They also studied the relations between the Philippines and Japan, including the history of the Japanese wartime occupation of the Philippines, and contemporary issues such as the local impact of Japanese trade and investment.[8] In the meantime, Tomiyama visited the Philippines several times. After Tomiyama's visits over several years, the Okinawan side decided to organize a symposium to learn about the Philippine experience of anti-base movement activism. In this context, Nishio, Tomiyama, Takahashi, Arasaki and their friend To Yusa started a group called the Action Committee for Solidarity with Asia (ACSA or *Ajia to Rentaisuru Shūkai Jikkō Īnkai*) in 1994.

However, the correspondence between Okinawa and the Philippines was not consistent and did not last long after 1994. Like many grassroots activist movements, ACSA faced problems such as insufficient membership, lack of language skills to communicate with the Philippine activists and funding to support its activities. Yet, even though the members of ACSA had some problems with communication, language was not the real problem. Nishio retrospectively said that the Philippine and Okinawan activists were able to communicate adequately with each other because the situations in those two places were very similar.[9] But one of the major reasons why this early period of Okinawa's solidarity ended in failure was (ironically) because of the very fact of the closure of the US bases in the Philippines. After withdrawal of the US military from the Clark Airbase, American military bases were no longer the major issue among the Philippine activists. Besides, the anti-base movement had not been the main reason for the establishment of Bayan. The umbrella organization was created to tackle broad social and economic inequality and to realize more just and democratic politics in the country. American imperialistic involvement in Philippine politics and society, including its support for the

Marcos regime, was an important issue during the democratization period. Insofar as the American presence continued, the US bases were a symbol that represented its influence in the Philippines. But after 1992, this symbol was not a major issue any more for the local citizens.

From ACSA to OKPS

The turning point for the activity of ACSA came rather coincidentally in late 1996 when an activist named Kim Yong-han visited from South Korea. Kim was one of the young activists who were involved in anti-US base activism in South Korea, which was increasingly becoming a significant issue in the country. One of the key moments in this regard was in October 1992 when a young local woman was murdered after being raped by a US military personnel in Dongducheon, called the Yun Kuem-Yi case. The Yun Kuem-Yi case was a brutal murder case that triggered a nationwide protest campaign, seeking a fair criminal judgement against the US military and the revision of the Status of Forces Agreement between the United States and South Korean governments. A year after the case, in 1993, the local activists founded a group called the Headquarters of the National Campaign for the Eradication of Crimes by US Troops (*Juhan Migun Beomjoe Geunjeor Undong Bonbu*, or *Jumibun* in Korean), which has been playing the leading role in the anti-US military base movement in South Korea.

One of the purposes for Kim to visit Okinawa was to meet activists and hear the story of the 1995 island-wide protest which was triggered by the sexual assault of a local woman committed by three US military personnel. The news was also reported in the South Korean newspapers, which impressed Kim not only as a story of mass protest, but also because this mass protest upset Japanese and US leaders and unsettled the security alliance system between the two countries. In the wake of the rape case, the Japanese Prime Minister Hashimoto Ryūtarou and his cabinet responded swiftly with their US counterparts to the rising tension over the bases in Okinawa by establishing the Special Action Committee on Okinawa (SACO). The SACO was established to discuss the future of the US bases, including the reduction of the US military facilities, and the Status Forces Agreement between the two countries. Looking at the political events triggered by Okinawa's mass protest campaign, Korean activists considered that there might be some hints in the Okinawan activist community that they could learn from for the development of their own anti-US base movement. In such an intense political environment, Kim arrived in Naha with the help of his fellow Korean activists in August 1996.

This first encounter with Kim Yong-han was also a great opportunity for Okinawan activists. As Arasaki recalls, although Okinawans had known about the end of military government and the political democratization of South Korea since 1988, the knowledge that Okinawan activists had about Korean social activism was limited to media coverage, and thus the domestic situation of South Korean society was hardly visible to Okinawan activists.[10] In this sense, Kim's visit to Okinawa was one of the earliest opportunities for Okinawan activists to learn about the South Korean anti-US base struggles, including the unequal status of the security treaty with the United States which guaranteed the extraterritoriality of the local US soldiers and personnel.

This first encounter prompted the creation of a new channel of communication between activists from the two countries. Seven months later, in February 1997, Kim came back to Okinawa with over forty-two South Koreans. One of the main reasons for the Koreans to visit Okinawa was to observe the public hearing at Naha Regional Court of a case between *Hitotsubo* Anti-war Landowners Association and the Japanese government about the issue of forced leases of privately owned land to the US military. This was the crucial moment that enhanced mutual awareness between South Korea and Okinawa.

After this second meeting, the interaction between Korea and Okinawa became increasingly active. Even though both Koreans and Okinawans were not well-informed about each other, what bound Okinawan and South Korean activists together was all sorts of common social and political problems which derived from the presence of the US bases. While there had been a number of sporadic solidarity movements with overseas activists, it was unprecedented in the history of the Okinawan anti-base movements that local activists engaged with a transnational coalition to this scale and frequency. Through collaboration between Okinawa and Korea, activists in the two countries sought to reframe the anti-US base struggle as a Northeast Asian regional problem. According to Tomiyama and Nishio, activists in Okinawa felt that their struggle was not isolated any more when they came to learn about South Korean activism.[11] After hosting a meeting with the forty-three Korean activists, which was attended by over two-hundred Okinawans, the founding members of ACSA decided to dissolve and rename the group. This is the start of *Okinawa-Korea People's Solidarity* (the formal name of the group is: *the Association that Aims to Create People's Solidarity through Anti-US Military Base Movement in Okinawa and South Korea,* or *Okikan* or OKPS for short) in June 1998.

Like ACSA, OKPS was based in Nishio's Uruma Chapel. However, what the members thought that they urgently needed was a basic knowledge of Korean social movements. While some members such as To, Takahashi and Nishio had been individually involved in the Korean democratization movement in the past, their basic knowledge of South Korean society was limited. With the help of renowned scholars such as Suh Sung, who had been detained in South Korea for nineteen years due to his political involvement in the anti-authoritarian regime campaign, the OKPS members held social and cultural events from late 1997 until early 2002 to study the base problems in South Korea and, more generally, the politics of the country. While studying about Korea at home, Okinawans travelled to the country to do 'on-site learning'. During this period, some OKPS members visited Korea a few times a year. The reasons for the trips were diverse. Sometimes they organized an informal study seminar or more formal public symposia, and sometimes they travelled to participate in direct actions taking place in various places. Koreans also frequently visited Okinawa for the same reasons. In the end, the number of people's exchanges during this period became twenty-five times. Through the exchanges, both Okinawans and Koreans became acquainted with each other.

From 1998, the members such as Takahashi and Tomiyama started studying Korean with the help of a Korean student studying at the University of the Ryukyus. They were working during the daytime, and at night they attended the class to study the language. In the classroom, they also met those who were interested in the activities of the OKPS. These new members, such as students and housewives, were not necessarily knowledgeable or familiar with anti-base activism. But they still joined the OKPS through their interests in the society and culture of Korea. So, Tomiyama once told me that 'OKPS's popularity was owed to K-pop'. Yet, as the visits from South Korea to Okinawa grew in number and the purposes of visits diversified, including school excursions, the range of activities of the OKPS also became more extensive. Those new demands made the membership of the community more flexible and open as they desperately needed people who could help with their activities.

Mutual preconceptions

The visit of the Korean activists to Okinawa in 1997 was indeed the beginning of a more substantial and sustainable bilateral relationship between the two places. However, this does not mean that their solidarity campaigns were all successful. Rather, this early period was the time when Okinawans, as well as Koreans, had to grapple hard with ambivalence and scepticism towards each other. In other words, we might be able to say that the active exchanges of people between the two places reflected the anxieties and concerns that both Okinawans and Koreans had for their counterparts.

For Korean activists, their ambivalent feeling and scepticism were primarily attributed to the history of Japanese colonial occupation in Korea. In the mid-1990s, there were still a large number of Korean anti-US base activists who thought that the presence of US military bases in Japan prevented Japan from rearming. They saw the US forces as a 'jar lid', containing any possible resurgence of Japanese militarism.[12] From this perspective, many Korean activists were sceptical about the aims and philosophy of the Okinawan anti-US military base movement. Furthermore, there was a widespread perception in Korean society that US military bases helped South Koreans protect their country from the North Korean threat. So, in those days, Takahashi recalls from his memory, South Korean journalists who approached the OKPS were interested in knowing why Okinawan activists were opposing the US military bases.[13]

At the same time, Okinawans were also worried about developing a solidarity movement with South Korean activists for different reasons. Although military dictatorship had formally come to an end when President Roh Tae-Woo, a former General of the South Korean Army, declared the democratization of South Korea in 1987, Okinawan activists were still concerned about surviving elements from the former military regime, best represented by the issue of the National Security Act. As a second-generation ethnic Korean in Japan, also known as *Zainichi* Koreans, who also had a long-term involvement with the democratization movement of South Korea in Japan during the 1970s and 1980s, To Yusa knew only too well that many of his fellow ethnic Korean activists from Japan were imprisoned in South Korea under the National Security Act.[14] Tomiyama says that he and other Okinawan activists in the 1970s and 1980s had a preconception that there was no freedom of speech and no social activism in South Korea under dictatorship.[15]

Hesitation to deepen the solidarity movement with Koreans was not only attributed to the image of the South Korean military regime shared by the members but also to personal experiences. Some members had visited South Korea before 1987, where they had witnessed South Korean everyday life which was quite different from ways of life in Japan at that time. Some of them were deeply shocked by their experiences in Korea and stopped their involvement with activism related to Korea until the late 1990s. Among them was Nishio Ichirō. Nishio, who was studying at a theological school in Okayama called Nōson Dendō Shingakkō (the Okayama Theological Seminary for Rural Mission), flew to South Korea with his Korean friend in early August 1974. Although this visit was part of their religious training at a rural chapel in Seoul, he was also involved in left-wing student activism at his previous theological college, Tokyo Union Theological Seminary (Tokyo Shingaku Daigaku). Because of this political background, Nishio was anxious about his first visit to South Korea. On his arrival, he was greeted by the sight of Korean soldiers with machine guns at Seoul's Gimpo International Airport. His anxiety reached its peak when he was about to leave South Korea in mid August. At the immigration desk of Gimpo Airport, the officers confiscated his passport. Knowing little about his situation or the local language, Nishio was in a panic and only recalled what he was told by his friend: 'Never lose your passport.' Later he found out that this was because of the assassination of Yuk Young-Soo, the wife of President Park Chung-hee, by a young Korean resident in Japan, Moon Se-gwang. When this so-called Moon Se-gwang Incident occurred, South Korean police suspected that the perpetrator was Japanese. Therefore, all Japanese people who planned to leave the country around this period were blocked from departing.[16]

Face-to-face relationship

In the course of building trust with South Korean activists, the members of OKPS have kept one principle as the motto of their activity. That is to create and prioritize 'face-to-face relationships' (*kao no mieru kankei*) with South Korean counterparts. The former representative of OKPS, Nishio, said that, when he and his friends started the OKPS, they decided to build up a close relationship with South Koreans to the point at which they would be able to see their Korean counterparts as 'friends'.[17] First of all, they thought that an actual exchange of people between the two areas was crucial in gaining the trust of and getting to know Koreans. As we have seen, the relationship between the two different groups started with suspicion and unfamiliarity towards each other. With such a beginning, the best way in which the members of OKPS could break the ice with South Korean activists was to establish a regular cycle of movement of people. During the first few years, the members of OKPS frequently flew to Korea and also invited Korean anti-US base activists to visit Okinawa. Through the members' participation in events such as study groups, symposia, academic conferences, study tours and direct action, Okinawans increasingly learnt about South Korean anti-base struggles from first-hand experience.

Second, the principle of face-to-face relationships reflects a type of solidarity the OKPS intended to build, which was based on interpersonal relationships rather than organizational connections. This approach enabled Okinawan activists to create flexible and wide-ranging individual relationships with many different kinds of anti-US base activist groups in South Korea. Although this group's first encounter with the Korean anti-base movement was through Kim Yong-han, the members of OKPS were involved with anti-US base campaigns in other places including Maehyang-ri, where local villagers and supporting activists demanded the closure of a military base used as a target practice site including depleted uranium shells, and also with a protest campaign against the extension of the military training facility in Pyeongtaek. In recent years, some members of OKPS began to be involved with the anti-naval base construction movement in places like Gangjeon and Jeju Island.

Learning from Okinawa/Korea

Despite their initial unfamiliarity with each other, the OKPS and their Korean counterparts have created mutual trust. This was achieved in part through frequent communication that ensured Okinawans understood people's lived experiences and knowledge born out of the social contexts in South Korea. Through meetings at conference venues, being exposed to freezing water from the water canon of riot police in Pyeongtaek's cold winter at protest sites, and at downtown bars where they drink together, the OKPS has become one of the first Japanese anti-base groups which could successfully build a solidarity movement with Koreans over the issue of the US military bases. Inspired by OKPS, civic groups in other areas of Japan with US bases, such as Yokosuka in Kanagawa Prefecture, began to follow the OKPS model in creating collaborative projects with Koreans.

Meanwhile, the Korean activists also found Okinawa to be an important 'reference point' for the anti-base movement. Here, the notion of 'reference point' means that the Koreans not only refer to their Okinawan counterparts but also introduce ideas and strategies from Okinawa's anti-base movement into their local activism. The anti-base struggle is indeed a translocal movement in which Okinawan and Korean participants are connected through people and ideas across different local contexts. In this sense, the forty-three Koreans' visit to Okinawa in 1997 was profoundly important in that it was one of the earliest moments in which Korean activists learned Okinawan ways of conducting anti-base campaigns. Through this event, Korean activists learnt the strategy developed by the *Hitotsubo* Anti-War Landowners Association. This strategy was introduced into the struggle in Korea. By purchasing a portion of privately owned land collectively, Korean citizens in Maehyang-ri started to initiate their local version of anti-war landowners from the late 1990s. Bringing a court case against the Korean government over the noise from the US bases is also another strategy that was introduced from Okinawa. Following examples from places such as Kadena and Futenma, where local citizens organize groups to take legal action against noise pollution, Korean activists in places such as Pyeongtaek sued their government over similar problems.

However, it needs to be noted that 'learning from the other' is not a one-sided approach. The OKPS was started to create a bilateral relationship through which mutual learning between Okinawans and their counterparts overseas could be developed. In this sense, while Korean activists say that they should learn from Okinawa, Okinawans have also learned from Korean experiences. On this point, Arasaki's comment on Korean activism is helpful. Looking at the surge of nationwide Korean protest against the US military over an accident in which two local schoolgirls were killed by an American tank in 2002, Arasaki said:

> When I was studying South Korean base problems, I saw a pamphlet which says 'let's learn from Okinawa' but I thought this was an overestimation. The point (of the pamphlet) was 'Okinawa made the US apologize, but the US have never apologized to us (South Korea)' ... Although they (South Koreans) are saying that they should learn from Okinawa, I am doubtful about the current situation of the Okinawan anti-base movement. I rather think that Okinawans are encouraged by Koreans .... I keenly feel the importance of considering how we can learn from them.[18]

In particular, Arasaki thinks that the active participation of young people in the anti-base movement is a characteristic that Okinawa needs to learn from South Korea. From a different perspective, Tomiyama says that he is always amazed by the number of people which South Korean activism mobilizes and by their creative strategy for the anti-base campaigns in Seoul. He said:

> South Korean activism is always sensational and exciting. When I was marching with other fellow activists in front of Seoul Mayoral Building, people suddenly spread a big American flag. It was a massive flag. You know what happened? A few young guys ran in the middle of the crowd to cut the flag into two. I was thrilled. I wished we could also do that performance in Okinawa.[19]

Perhaps one of the most crucial things that Okinawa learned through interaction with the Korean anti-base movement was the significance of Okinawa's geopolitical location in the region. Kadena Airbase in Okinawa was one of the main sites from which American B-29 bombers were sent to the Korean Peninsula during the Korean War. After half a century, while the US military command has changed globally since 2001, reflecting 9/11 and the subsequent attack on Afghanistan, Okinawa is still regarded as a crucial place for America's regional strategy in the Asia-Pacific, especially in relation to Northeast Asian affairs. Although this fact has been widely known among local activists in Okinawa, the actual strategic connection between Okinawa and Korea was not known until the OKPS learned about this through their Korean counterparts. As To Yusa says, since the Korean War, the Headquarters of US Forces Korea, located in Yongsan near Seoul, has been a centre for US military operations in the Northeast Asian region including Okinawa. He also says that when the Commander of the US Eighth Army is changed, it has been conventional that the newly appointed officer is always taken on an inspection tour of the bases in not only Korea but also Japan, including places such as Futenma and Kadena in Okinawa and Atsugi, Yokosuka, Hokkaido and Yamaguchi.[20]

This intra-regional connectivity within Asia also raises ethical questions for the Okinawan anti-base movement. Tomiyama recalled that when Okinawan activists protested the use of depleted uranium bombs at the target practice site in Torishima, which was revealed in 1997, they did not even imagine the possibility of those bombs being moved to a base in South Korea. He said that he had not considered the potential negative impact of their activism on the neighbouring overseas communities, whether it be successful or not.[21] Learning about this sort of new inputs was possible through the interaction with Korean activists, which helped Okinawans reconsider the meanings of their activism in relation to other places in the region.

Five years of frequent exchanges with South Korean activists from 1998 until 2002 have brought slight changes to the Okinawan anti-base movement. Compared to the early days, visits of Korean activists to Okinawa are no longer unusual, and have instead become important annual events for Okinawans. Even though the OKPS still remains little known as a group even within Okinawa, the interest in the Korean base problems amongst Okinawan activists grew and so did the number of Korean visitors, which indicates various activities organized by this group for the last two decades at least created some impact on the culture of the Okinawan activist community. Furthermore, the variety of collaborative projects between the two places became more extensive beyond base politics or history by including other issues and types of activist communities, notably the environmental movement. Citizens from Okinawa and Korea started undertaking a collaborative survey of land contamination on the sites of former US military camps and adjacent areas from the mid-2000s. In this sense, it should be reasonable to say that the OKPS has added new layers to the history of the Okinawan struggle.

The Okikan style: '5.15' and the emergence of the younger generations

May 15 is an important day in the history of modern Okinawa. As discussed earlier, this was the day when Okinawa's administrative handover to the Japanese government was realized in 1972. So, to commemorate this day, every year, there have been prefecture-wide commemorative ceremonies and events that take place. One of the main ceremonies is usually organized by the Okinawa Prefectural Government, where the governor of Okinawa and high-profile political figures from mainland Japan come to give speeches. However, anti-base activists and like-minded citizens also organize events with different motivations to counter the ceremonious atmosphere filled with official events. Organizing public fora such as symposia, panel discussions and lectures, their critical exploration of the meaning of 'reversion' continues until today. Also, during the week, there has been a tradition of making a human chain that surrounds the US Futenma Airbase.

In 2012, this historic day was to have its fortieth anniversary. For this memorable year, both the prefectural government and civic groups had been working to organize events on a greater scale than in previous years. There were numerous posters and flyers displayed on corners of streets and on billboards. In this environment, the members of the OKPS had also been working on their events that they had been conducting since 2003. Together with the public talks with guests from diverse Korean activist organizations, the members of the OKPS become tour guides and take Korean visitors to Henoko and Takae to show them the ongoing protest campaigns.

The preparation for '*go ichi go*' (15 May in Japanese) usually starts half a year prior or so. Yet, for the one in 2012, the OKPS started planning their activities from late September 2011. The agenda items for the monthly regular meeting, which are not so numerous at other times of the year, gradually increase as the anniversary approaches. With senior figures such as Takahashi and Nishio as coordinators, the members discuss issues related to this week-long event. The agenda is extensive. Jobs that the OKPS is responsible for ranges from booking accommodation to arranging pick-up services for Korean guests from the airport, interpretation at formal and informal venues to set the stages for Korean performers and preparation of lunches. With an extremely tight budget and a limited number of active members who also have different private and professional commitments, eight months would not be as luxurious an amount of time as it sounds. Rather, the period would be just enough to barely cover all the preparations.

The highlight of the OKPS for this eventful week was to coordinate a stage performance by a Korean music company. Since 2009, OKPS has invited cultural performance groups such as *Deoneum* and *Kkottaji*. Deoneum is a group known for the traditional farmers' music called *pungmur nori*. Playing the drums and dancing in a circle, the performers not only showcase classic folk culture but also express protests against the political establishment. Based in Incheon, one of the industrial centres of the country, they have been collaborating closely with the local workers. Another group, Kkottaji, is also a renowned group who uses music performance as a means of social protest. While Deoneum plays traditional music, Kkottaji plays contemporary pop music.

In Okinawa, as well as in Korea, music is a central piece in the culture of the local protest movement, and the anti-base movement is no exception. Indie artists such as rappers Kakumakushaka and Chibana Tatsumi are among the singers whose works have been popular in Okinawa, particularly among youths. OKPS approached several local musicians and was able to book an Okinawan traditional music singer, Ayumu Yonaha, for the coming event of that year.

For this event to happen, young OKPS members, who are in their thirties and forties, played a crucial role by introducing emerging musicians such as Yonaha. Among them was Ishikawa Takashi, who proposed the idea of inviting Kkottachi. Originally from Chiba Prefecture, Ishikawa used to work in Tokyo as a medical doctor prior to relocation to Okinawa in the early 2000s at the invitation of a senior pulmonologist in Naha. His career as an activist started when he was a university student. When he was a medical student at Chiba University, Ishikawa started becoming involved with social activism to support workers affected by industrial accidents, particularly those suffering from respiratory disease. During that period, he met concerned medical students in South Korea who also worked with manual labourers. It was then that Ishikawa was introduced to Kkottaji, and the OKPS was able to invite the group through Ishikawa's connections at that time. As such, the involvement of the younger generations is not only helpful for the seniors, but also playing a vital role in introducing new kinds of activities to the OKPS. The young participants do not necessarily share the contexts and experiences of their elders. But the OKPS has gradually become better known among local activists through cultural events such as music concerts. In this sense, the spirit of the OKPS is developed inter-generationally by creating new collaborations in forms and styles between the two places.

Beyond anti-base

What I have discussed in this chapter was a micro-historical process, which created a trans-border space of dialogue and collaboration on the anti-base activism between Okinawa and South Korea by examining experiences and history entailed in the OKPS. I called this momentum the second wave of grassroots regionalism. In this sense, this chapter would perhaps be contributing to the discussion on the internationalization or transnationalization of Okinawa's anti-base activism, which is certainly drawing more scholarly interest in recent years.

However, as shown in earlier chapters with different cases, the range of issues that this chapter addresses goes beyond the narrow definition of the 'anti-base movement'. The project of building a transnational network was initiated by five local activists who felt a common imperative to seek new ways to develop Okinawan anti-base activism. But the founders of the OKPS were not just concerned about the base politics. By reflecting upon the historical relationships between Okinawa and South Korea, they learned ways to critically articulate the historical narratives of war, US hegemony in Northeast Asia and their own position as 'Japanese' as well as 'Okinawan' in the regional matrix.

Put in another way, what they have learned through direct engagement with Korean civil society was the significance of historical consciousness regarding Okinawa's postwar condition vis-à-vis Korea's postcolonial condition, and it is through this reflective and critical awareness towards the selfhood that the OKPS could succeed in building and reinforcing trust with its Korean counterparts beyond the preconceptions and misconceptions that they held towards each other in the early period. For this very reason, it is not unreasonable to say that what made Okinawa's anti-base struggle so successful beyond material, financial and technical constraints was not only the imminency to address the base-related problems, but also through the gradual realization and sharing process of the historical present that they live in.

6

Translocal lives in anti-base activism

In the previous chapter, I discussed at length the general history of the Okinawa Korea People's Solidarity (OKPS) to examine its formation and development, and also its achievement and challenges in creating transnational anti-base activism. One of the reasons for their relative success in gaining the trust of their Korean counterparts was perhaps attributed to the flexible and ad hoc nature of this community, which relied upon individual capacity in realizing their mission. Put differently, what it means is that, with its extremely limited resources to mobilize by exerting their activities, the OKPS, as it is the case for many other activist communities in Okinawa and elsewhere in Japan, is shaped by the interests and contexts of individual members as well as the national, regional and global political structure. Here, the key to the success in building this solidarity network with Koreans was the individualist nature of the community, and I argue their individually orientated forms of community are one of the core concepts that propelled their mission and activism.

With this spirit in mind, in this chapter, I elaborate on the integrity of the OKPS that is built upon the individual capacity in light of the personal contexts of some of the key members of the community. What I argue in this chapter through probing the life history of three members is the power of 'the invisible threads', which played a crucial role in weaving Okinawa's activism into the web of the regional, political and social context in Northeast Asia.[1] Different strands of the life history of three members (Arasaki Moriteru, Takahashi Toshio and Yu Yeongja) will be introduced here to unfold what constitutes the OKPS and its activism. Also, their stories show us the complexity entailed in the very notion of 'locality' of Okinawan activism. As such, the stories of committed members whose networks also branch out extensively in and out of Okinawa ultimately unravel not only the journeys of their lives but how the bottom-up regionalization of this activism, which would otherwise be framed as distinctively 'local', was made possible.

The life history of Arasaki, who was born as the second generation of Okinawan migrants in Tokyo in the 1930s, helps us to understand various socio-historical contexts that shape the thought and career of this historian who is remembered as one of the most prominent Okinawan scholars and activists. It brings to the fore the historical process by which this local anti-base activist gradually came to incorporate a regional perspective based on his interaction with South Korean citizens. Takahashi's story tells us about the involvement of former new left activists in the recent history of Okinawa's anti-base activism. While we tend to think of the notion of Okinawan people under the rubric of ethnicity or cultural identity, Takahashi's life history complicates this assumption and gives us a glimpse into the role of the Japanese new left activists and their engagement with South Korean politics in the 1970s. Finally, Yu's story shows the involvement of ethnic Koreans living in Japan, which provides us with yet another perspective on making Okinawa's grassroots regionalism. The story of Yu, as a non-Japanese and non-Okinawan, is important as it allows us to critically engage in the politics of local activism beyond identity politics, which is often built upon the simplistic dichotomy between 'local Okinawan' and 'the mainland Japanese'. From these three perspectives, this chapter examines how this multifaceted regionalism of the OKPS was formed in Okinawa.

Arasaki Moriteru

A scholar, educator, university president, public intellectual and activist, Arasaki Moriteru had been at the forefront of not only anti-base activism but numerous other political and cultural scenes related to Okinawa. Or, perhaps I should say that his wide-ranging professional careers show how every aspect of social life in Okinawa is related to base politics. As a professor of contemporary Okinawa history, Arasaki's works, including his seminal books on the subject such as *Okinawa Sengo-shi* (*The Postwar History of Okinawa*) and *Okinawa Gendai-shi* (*The Contemporary History of Okinawa*), are among the most well-read texts for understanding the development of the anti-base movement and Okinawa's political environment after the end of the Second World War. In recent years, Arasaki's texts have been published in other languages such as Korean and Mandarin. Regarding his relation to the OKPS, as I have discussed in the previous chapter, Arasaki was one of the founding members of the group, and has been an important Okinawan counterpart for Korean visitors since the time when the war survivors made a trip to Kerama in the late 1980s. Nevertheless, Arasaki's life history is little known beyond his family and close friends in spite of his works, which are internationally recognized. How was this high-profile critic and activist on contemporary Okinawan history created? What was the motivation for him to engage with Korea? I will probe Okinawa's grassroots regionalism in the eyes of one of the most iconic figures of Okinawan activism.

Arasaki Moriteru was born in Suginami, a western district of Tokyo in 1936. Living far from Okinawa, Arasaki spent most of his formative period in various districts of Tokyo. He was the eldest son of his father, Arasaki Seichū. He was originally from a noble clan, residing near the Shuri Castle. Arasaki's mother, Tawo, was also from an educated family in the Amami region.[2] Both of his parents migrated from Okinawa Island to Tokyo before Arasaki was born, and it was not uncommon for Okinawans, especially those who were not raised as the successor of the family, to migrate to major cities in mainland Japan, if not overseas, in those days.

Although his parents were not members of the social elite or wealthy, both of them were well educated. Tawo was a poet, writing and reading traditional Ryūkyūan poems, *ryūka*. Born in Tokunoshima Island, which currently belongs to Kagoshima Prefecture, Tawo finished her education at one of the most prestigious women's high schools on Okinawa Island. She had worked as a school teacher for several years, and she married Seichū, who also worked at a local public school in Okinawa. As I mentioned above, Seichū's family, the Arasaki clan, had been part of the former aristocracy before Ryūkyū was annexed by Japan. However, when Seichū grew up, his family no longer held any prestigious title. Rather, the family was struggling financially. Despite that, educational investment was seen as important in his family. So, for example, one of Seichū's elder siblings, Arasaki Seibin, proceeded to attend Tokyo Imperial University, where he majored in natural science, and later he became the first Okinawan-born Professor of Agricultural Science, studying algae.³ Like his siblings, Seichū also had a good educational background. He graduated from the local teachers' college and became an English teacher. However, he was not given any chance to study further at university. Priority in education was given according to seniority for financial reasons.

Nevertheless, Seichū did not give up on his plan to receive tertiary education. He decided to leave his home and job in Okinawa and go to Tokyo with his wife. Working during the day time as a national government bureaucrat, Seichū enrolled in a private university to continue his study as a night-class student. Unlike his scientist brother, Seichū's passion was in English literature, George Bernard Shaw, in particular, was one of his favourite authors. During my interview with Arasaki, he said that his father perhaps projected his own life onto the life of this Irish playwright.⁴ Although he had to abort his study due to other commitments, the intellectual curiosity that Seichū and Tawo had prepared a rich educational environment for their children.

While Arasaki was brought up by such caring parents, his early childhood was not easy because of poor health conditions such as tuberculosis and a heart problem. He had to take one year's leave from school to undergo medical treatment. Even after he returned from hospital, Arasaki's vulnerable health prevented him from participating in hard physical activities. Also, the air raids on Tokyo by the Allied Forces towards the end of the Second World War made his life difficult. Although Arasaki and his family were not directly affected by the bombing, Seichū and Tawo decided to flee to Kumamoto Prefecture in the south-western part of Kyūshū Island, where there was a large Okinawan community, including their relations.⁵ The family spent much of wartime in Kumamoto, away from Tokyo and their homeland, Okinawa.

Patriotic boy

One of the key terms to understanding Arasaki's early postwar experiences was 'patriotism' (*aikokushin*). As happened to most of the 'wartime generation' (or *senchū-ha*), which denotes those who were born around the 1930s, Arasaki grew up with a strong spirit of Japanese patriotism. Such children were later called 'patriotic boys' (*aikoku shōnen*). Despite his health condition, his dream was to become a soldier and fight the Americans on the battlefield.⁶

However, after the end of the Second World War, like many patriotic boys, Arasaki also had to face drastic changes in the social environment, which tremendously confused him. For Arasaki in his early teenage years, the most symbolic representation of this social change was his school teachers. He simply despised the sudden change in his teachers who had once supported the advancement of the Japanese Imperial Army and then suddenly started to denounce the previous regime and became advocates of American-style democracy. Therefore, the experience of the early postwar democracy education system remained in his mind as deep scepticism towards Japan's new era.[7]

The young Arasaki's suspicion towards postwar Japanese democracy became explicit by the time he was a high school student. When the San Francisco Peace Treaty came into force on 28 April 1952, the school principal of Tokyo Koyamadai High School, where Arasaki had recently enrolled, called all the students to the school grounds. There, the principal celebrated Japan's restoration of independence from the allied occupation with shouts of *banzai*.[8] Hearing the school principal's words, many students of this elite school criticized their principal. For the left-leaning students, the restoration of Japan's independence was in fact nothing more than incorporation into the American capitalist order. The conservative nationalist students, including Arasaki, criticized the school principal because they considered that independence had only been achieved through the strong support of the United States, which had been Japan's biggest enemy during the Pacific War.[9]

Although many politically concerned students of his high school belonged to left-leaning student clubs such as the Social Science Club, Arasaki was not a member of any of these groups. Instead, he chose to join the Debating Club because of its 'neutral political views'.[10] There he trained his oratory skills and became one of the most outstanding debaters in his school. During his first year, Arasaki became a finalist in the school-wide debating competition. The title that he chose was: *The True Way to Japan's Independence*. There, Arasaki insisted that the recovery of lost territories, including Okinawa, was necessary for restoration of Japan's territorial sovereignty in its true sense.

Although Arasaki had been a patriotic boy, it did not take long for him to realize the presence of a 'borderline between Okinawa and Japan, and between *yamatonchū* (Japanese people) and *uchinanchū* (Okinawan people)'.[11] The turning point came in 1952, during his first summer holiday after becoming a Koyamadai high school student. While reading a newspaper, Arasaki found Douglas MacArthur's comment on Okinawans, whom he described 'submissive' and 'ethnically different' from Japanese.[12] Arasaki was stunned by MacArthur's statement. For the first time, the young Arasaki heard someone describe Okinawans as 'ethnically' different people from the Japanese. Subsequently, Arasaki read another newspaper article written by an American journalist which increased his unease. It reported how the locals in Okinawa had happily welcomed the US occupation. Until that moment, Arasaki had strongly believed in the ethnic and cultural unity of Japanese people regardless of subtle differences in language and other cultural aspects. It was all about this assumption of 'sameness' that underpinned Arasaki's Japanese patriotism, which had co-existed with his Okinawan identity. However, his belief was critically unsettled after he read those newspaper articles. What if Okinawa was not part of Japan, but had been occupied by Japan, just as Americans had occupied Japan? What if Okinawan people were different from Japanese people? Were the local Okinawans really pleased to have Americans on their soil? These concerns emerged in his first year of high school and slowly made his intellectual interests shift from Japan to Okinawa and its local history.

In the same year, there was another crucial experience that shaped Arasaki's thought. During the summer holidays in August, one of his friends gave him the latest issue of *Asahi Gurafu*, one of the earliest Japanese photo journals. As Arasaki read the journal, some of its photos attracted his attention. They were images of the victims of the atomic bombing of Hiroshima. During the occupation, the Press Code for Japan strictly prohibited the publication of information which could 'directly or indirectly, disturb the public tranquility', and or which contained 'destructive criticism of the Allied Powers and anything which might invite mistrust or resentment of those troops'.[13] Photos showing the effects of the atomic bombings were also heavily censored, and therefore, it had not been possible to show the catastrophic images of the victims during the occupation period. Arasaki was shocked not only by the visual images of the victims but also by the enormity of civilian lives that were lost during the war, which compelled his naivety about warfare being fought primarily by soldiers. Not long after, Arasaki had a chance to read a novel about the Battle of Okinawa. The book was about the tragedy of the Himeyuri Nursing Unit at the end of the war. Many of this group of female students who were mobilized as a nursing unit during the Battle of Okinawa committed suicide towards the end of the war. Reading about these experiences made a significant impact on the young Arasaki, who was compelled to reflect on his ignorance about war and Okinawa.

Becoming an 'expert on the Okinawa problem'

After graduating from high school, Arasaki enrolled at the University of Tokyo in 1956. At the time, he was intending to have a professional career in journalism. Therefore, he chose sociology for his major, which was a common path for those who wanted to enter the industry. With his mentors, all renowned sociologists such as Fukutake Tadashi, Odaka Kunio and Hidaka Rokurō, he was introduced to the classics: Max Weber, Karl Marx and Emile Durkheim. Also, with Fukutake who specialized in rural communities, Arasaki joined field trips, which allowed him to be equipped with fieldwork methodology.

But it was Hidaka with whom Arasaki worked on his undergraduate thesis with. By this time, Hidaka had already established himself not only as an academic but also as one of the most influential advocates of the postwar Japanese peace movement. Under his mentorship, Arasaki began to conduct his first piece of academic research on Okinawa. The topic he chose to study was the early US occupation period in Okinawa. In particular, he was strongly intrigued by the first whole-island struggle that occurred when Arasaki started his undergraduate study. For Arasaki, this first mass uprising of Okinawan people against the US occupation was nothing but a historic event that should draw the public's attention along with the Hungarian Uprising against the occupation by Soviet Russia or the Second Arab-Israeli War, which occurred in the same year as the Okinawan protest. He regarded the people's uprising as an expression of Okinawa's dynamic political culture, which contrasted starkly with media reports about Okinawans as a 'submissive' people. Based on the principle of self-determination, Arasaki saw this as a strong demand by fellow Okinawans for the reunification of Japan. Although his choice of research was not appealing to some senior sociologists in the faculty such as Odaka Kunio, Hidaka Rokurō was supportive of Arasaki's project. This is how

Arasaki's first research paper on the Okinawan problem, which was entitled 'An Inquiry into the Reversion Movement to Japan: Notes on Understanding Okinawa Problems' (Nihon Fukki Undō no Kenkyū: Okinawa Mondai Rikai no Tameno Oboegaki) was written.[14]

When Arasaki was approaching the end of his student life, he was introduced to one of Hidaka's colleagues, Nakano Yoshio, who resigned recently from the position of Professor of English Literature at the University of Tokyo. Nakano had been actively participating in the campaign for Okinawa's return to Japan ever since he read the collection of essays written by Okinawan students in Tokyo, *Okinawa without the Homeland* (*Sokoku Naki Okinawa*).[15]

When Nakano met Arasaki for the first time in 1958, he was planning to establish a research centre on Okinawa in Tokyo. Nakano's project, which later materialized as the Okinawa Resource Centre, attracted attention from his friends and colleagues such as Yoshino Genzaburō, the chief editor of a current affairs journal *Sekai* at Iwanami Shoten who was also the organizer of the Council of Peace Studies; Kato Ichirō, a Professor of Law who would later become the President of the University of Tokyo; Uehara Senroku, a Professor of European History at Hitotsubashi University; and Umino Shinkichi, a lawyer who was the President of the Japan Federation of Bar Associations. Nakano offered Arasaki a job at this newly established civic think-tank. His office was a small room in Umino's office. Arasaki started his career as a part-time researcher at this institute, while also working as a public servant for the Tokyo Metropolitan Government. Also, it was during this period when Arasaki published one of his first books on Okinawa, *The 20 Years of the Okinawan Problem* (*Okinawa Mondai Nijū-nen*), with Nakano Yoshio in 1965, which was based on his undergraduate thesis.

In 1974, two years after Okinawa's administration transfer, Arasaki and his family relocated to Naha, Okinawa. He was offered a teaching job on modern Japanese and Okinawan history at Okinawa University. Established in 1961, Okinawa University was one of the first private universities in the prefecture. However, after Okinawa's return to Japan, the university was facing closure because the Japanese government planned to implement a 'one national and one private university' policy in Okinawa. The Japanese Ministry of Education planned to integrate Okinawa University with the International University, another major private tertiary education institution. Reflecting on this proposal from the national government, the university staff asked for help from concerned colleagues in mainland Japan as well as in Okinawa.[16] In such circumstances, Arasaki was one of those who responded to the voices from Okinawa by joining the campaign to maintain the university. He not only joined the campaign but also accepted the invitation to become a lecturer at the university, which was suffering severely from a lack of teaching staff. Although he had already established his career as an expert on Okinawa in mainland Japan, Arasaki was hoping to live in Okinawa, and felt that this was an opportunity to fulfil his plan.

Shortly after he moved, Arasaki began to be involved with not only the university continuation campaign but also the various activities related to the local anti-base movement. Together with his friends, Arasaki founded a support network for the environmental protection movement against the construction of an oil storage terminal in Kin Bay. Also, in 1982 Arasaki organized another movement called the *Hitotsubo* Anti-war Landowners Association (see Chapter 3). After he became involved in these new projects, his vigorous attitude gradually made him known within Okinawa's local activist community.

Thinking Okinawa as 'region'

Relocation to Okinawa enabled him to reflect on his earlier works on the Okinawan struggle and to take a different approach to the issue. Prior to his movement, his main targeted audience had been mainland Japanese who would otherwise have remained ignorant about the social situation in its southern island prefecture. Yet, after 1974, Arasaki began to take a more radical approach to the issue by learning from and working with critics and activists in Okinawa and he began to write pieces that were relevant to fellow Okinawans as well as Japanese. Some of his works written during this period, including *Okinawa That Became Japan* (*Nihon ni Natta Okinawa*) published in 1987 and *Okinawa: The Backlight of the Imperial System* (*Okinawa: Tennōsei e no Gyakkō*) published in 1988, reflect his changes in thought after he moved to Okinawa. A key aspect of his writing during the 1980s was that he tended to highlight the historical differences between Okinawa and the rest of Japan.

Yet, even after he became more critical of Okinawa-Japan relations, Arasaki's stance was considered to be idiosyncratic compared to some of the renowned local critics such as Arakawa Akira and Kawamitsu Shin'ichi who had been involved with the activism. While some of them started arguing in favour of the possibility of the independence (*dokuritsu*) of Okinawa (or the Ryūkyūs) from Japan, Arasaki was reluctant to follow that argument. Instead, what he adopted as his central motif was the concept of high autonomous status or self-reliance (*jiritsu*) of Okinawa based on its distinctive 'regional' characteristics in Japan. He argues:

> I think self-reliance is the state in which people's voices are reflected to the fullest extent to decide political, economic, social and cultural activities in one regional society. Therefore, this could ultimately mean independence as a state. At any rate, I think that the basis of self-reliance is [an autonomous] self-governance (jichi), and it means all levels from the limited sense of self-governance to independence ... The reason why self-reliance became a key issue in Okinawa today is because it is obstructed. It is obstructed by the centralized state power which rejects the regional characteristics (*chīki-teki dokujisei*), those who indulge themselves by enjoying benefits from the state, and those who accept [the status quo] without criticism.[17]

Here, we see his insistence and persistence in using *jiritsu* or *jichi* instead of *dokuritsu* to describe the form of 'autonomous' or 'self-reliant' politics. What we can see in his argument is not merely a cautious approach to the independence of Okinawa. He considered the pursuit of 'self-reliant' regional political institutions would allow Okinawans to be more realistically tactful and to have more analytical perspectives to understand the development of their social struggles. In this spirit, he even provoked controversy by arguing that the independence of Okinawa is a kind of topic people rant about at a bar, which upset many of his colleagues.

In developing this perspective, Arasaki sought to critically reassess the discourses of Japanese homogeneity, and it was in this context where Shimao Toshio's idea of the Ryūkyū Arc drew his strong attention, which he considered to be the foundation upon which Okinawa's distinctive geo-cultural characteristics need to be taken into consideration.

Yet, to understand the importance of Arasaki's intellectual journey and activism in the 1970s and the 1980s, we also need to consider another figure who also profoundly influenced Arasaki's concept of region: Tamanoi Yoshirou. Tamanoi was an economist who had recently retired from his tenure at the University of Tokyo. After his retirement in 1978, he came to teach at Okinawa International University, where his research interests shifted from classical economic theories to research on region, regionalism and ecology. As was the case in Shimao's works, Tamanoi too regarded the Ryūkyū Arc as an idiosyncratic region with its own culture, which cannot be subsumed into Japan. Yet, Tamanoi's concept of region emphasizes Okinawa's geographical significance and transnationality embedded in its local historical experiences of connections, especially with other Asian countries.[18]

One distinctive aspect of Tamanoi's concept of region is its emphasis on the need to incorporate ecology into economy, which he considered as a profound basis to constitute the local culture and society. He also thought that the local economy should be directed by local residents who inhabit in their environment that is attached to the economy and argued that economists have long neglected the importance of ecology as a quintessential part of economic system and how it serves as the basis for growth.[19] Humans are also part of this ecological system, and therefore he argued that we had to reconsider what we mean when speaking of growth.[20]

From this perspective, Tamanoi considers Okinawa, with its distinctive location, ecology and society, a model for recreating sustainable social and economic development. As Arasaki notes, Tamanoi's notion of region contributed to developing the Okinawan struggle in both theory and practice. In particular, his ideas inspired a number of local struggles in terms of ecology movements, including the Kin Bay Struggle.[21] Therefore, Arasaki says that Tamanoi 'showed a direction for the movement, encouraged the participants, and enhanced public awareness.'[22]

Furthermore, Tamanoi's regionalism did not only draw attention to the importance of restoring local autonomy but it also showed the possibility of considering local issues within a wider Asian region. Based at the Institute of Southern Islands at Okinawa International University, he sought to rediscover Okinawa's indigenous connectivity with overseas countries. By adopting the concept of reciprocity from economic anthropology, especially from the writings of Marcel Mauss and Karl Polanyi, Tamanoi sought to reinterpret the maritime networks between the Ryūkyū state and other Asian neighbours in the pre-modern period as having dynamic relations which were different from that of commercial trade in the modern period.²³ By doing so, he tried to lay out an extensive view of Okinawa's ecological world which goes beyond local and national domains. Tamanoi's concept of region was thus crucial and enlightening for Okinawan readers, including activists, in that it provides their local struggle with new historical and spatial meanings.

Finding colonial Korea in Okinawa, feeling Okinawa's 'pain' in Korea

Nevertheless, 'Asia' was not yet felt so close for Arasaki in relation to Okinawa's activism at that period. As I have discussed in the last chapter, a turning point arrived in the mid-1980s; when Arasaki was the President of Okinawa University, one of his colleagues, Shirato Shin'ichi, then Professor of Commerce at the university, asked if he was interested in inviting delegates of the Pacific Fellows Association, a civic group of surviving former Korean conscripted workers, to Okinawa. Shirato told Arasaki that these delegates were particularly interested in visiting Okinawa in commemorating the spirits of fellow Koreans who died at the end of the Second World War on some of the remote islands in Okinawa. However, travel between South Korea and Japan was still not easy for ordinary citizens in that period. This was a few years before the declaration of South Korea's democratization in 1987, and visas were not issued easily to South Korean citizens by the Japanese government. Hearing this story, Arasaki took swift action towards arranging the visit of the five Korean survivors and put forward a plan to invite these war survivors as special guest speakers for one of his classes. Arasaki contacted the Japanese Ministry of Foreign Affairs and managed to obtain visas for the guests.²⁴

This was one of his early interactions with Korean survivors which inspired Arasaki, and other fellow Okinawans, to take into account the history of Koreans during the Battle of Okinawa and its relation to Okinawa. Although there were several books on Koreans in wartime Okinawa which had been already published such as *The House of the Red Tiles* (*Akara no Ie*), which is about the lives of Korean women who were forced to serve Japanese soldiers at military brothels, there were no works that provided an overall picture on this issue.²⁵ Arasaki believed that the Koreans' visit and their memories of the Second World War would shed light on a crucial aspect of history which had been little known to Okinawans, let alone Japanese people.

Nevertheless, it was not for the first time for Arasaki to 'find Korea' in Okinawa's modern experiences and he had already been aware of the relevance of Korea's modern experiences to Okinawa. For instance, from very early on, Arasaki's writings mention the significant impact of the Korean War on the formation of base towns in Okinawa. In particular, his critical perspective on Japan's relations with Okinawa and Korea became explicit in the lecture he gave at an event called 'the Christian Youth Peace Seminar' organized by Takahashi Saburō, a minister and peace activist, in 1969. There, Arasaki argues that Japan's postwar economic prosperity was made possible precisely because of 'the blood that was shed in the Korean Peninsula' during the Korean War in which Okinawa was involved as an airbase.²⁶ While the economic boost due to 'special procurements' (*tokuju*) by the American occupation forces for Korean War purposes was commonly seen as 'a gift from heaven' (*tenkei*) in Japan in those days, Arasaki saw it as the other side of the war in Korea. Namely, he saw this event as one of the earliest occasions which defined the future course of Okinawa under the US military regime and separation from Japan.²⁷

In 1987, a year after the five Koreans visited Okinawa, the members of the Pacific Fellows Association invited Arasaki and another six Japanese citizens to participate in the commemoration ceremony including the unveiling event of a monument to the spirits of former forced labourers in Gyeongsang Province. Although Arasaki had visited the People's Republic of China in the late 1970s, Taiwan and the Democratic People's Republic of Korea in the early 1980s, he had never had a chance to visit South Korea until then. During the trip, he was taken to museums and historical sites which were related to Japan and the Japanese colonization of Korea. Arasaki, who had also visited the Revolutionary Museum in North Korea, witnessed unresolved divisions in the memories of North and South Koreans. He said that some of his companies from mainland Japan could not stand images of Japanese torturing Koreans in these museums, and expressed concern about the negative implications that those grotesque images conveyed for Japan-South Korea relations in the future. However, hearing this criticism, Arasaki riposted that '… after all, a man who steps on other people's feet does not feel their pain.'²⁸

This early interaction between Arasaki and the Pacific Fellows Association did not last long. This was mainly because the project to commemorate their fellow Koreans finished when the members of the Pacific Fellows Association completed the monument in their local region, but it was also related to the fact that Arasaki and Okinawan activists later found out that this Korean civic group was closely linked to the South Korean government which was still headed by the then President and former military general Roh Tae-woo. However, this early encounter left a strong impression among Okinawans by bringing 'Asia' into their vision. As I have elaborated in Chapter 5, this encounter with Koreans eventually led to the creation of an international anti-US base solidarity movement in Korea after a decade.

Born into an Okinawan migrant family and educated around the transition period of Japan from wartime imperialism to a post-Second World War liberal democratic country, Arasaki underwent a series of struggles to define himself as an 'Okinawan in Japan'. While Okinawa was still separated even after Japan's independence, Arasaki tried to overcome this identity dilemma by becoming a kind of nationalist both as a Japanese and Okinawan. Yet, his later career at the Okinawa Resource Center in Tokyo and subsequently at Okinawa University allowed him to conceive of an alternative space of subjectivity created by the Okinawa struggle beyond identity politics. Defining Okinawa's cultural and historical contexts as a social space, he conceptualized the region as a space of inhabitants, rather than that of the nation. This concept of region as social space later extended to include East Asia. Finding common ground and connection with Korea as a formerly occupied territory by the Japanese Empire, Arasaki incorporated Korean history within the local historical narrative. Arasaki provides an example of a notable Okinawan activist whose involvement with the anti-base movement led him to create another meaning of 'the local', which is considered in combination with not only 'the national' but also the alternative and more open-ended concept of 'region'.

Takahashi Toshio

A tall, grey-haired gentleman who is always quiet with a warm smile on his face, my early impression of Takahashi was that he seemed to be such a calm, middle-aged man. Yet, later, I was informed that he used to be a leader of one of the most militant and violent revolutionary sects in his youth. Although Takahashi Toshio originates from mainland Japan, he has become a highly regarded activist in the Okinawa struggle. He is one of the five founding members of OKPS and has also been acting as the main coordinator of the group. Whenever people receive notices of the next meeting and minutes of the previous meeting, it is always Takahashi who sends those emails. Takahashi is also one of the organizers of a protest community called 'the Citizens against the Noise from Futenma Airbase (*Futenma Bakuon Soshoudan*)'. Based in a main office in Futenma in Ginowan City, Takahashi and other members are working to bring a lawsuit against the local US military and Japanese government over the loud noise from the airbase in Futenma Town by collecting signatures from the local residents of the town.

Takahashi was born in Nangoku City, Kōchi Prefecture, in 1953.[29] As in many other parts of Japan, there was a large Korean community in Nangoku City. He said that the community was built in the early 1940s by Korean workers, who had been mobilized by Japan during the war to build local infrastructure, such as dams and airports. Takahashi's house was located near this local Korean community. He lived in Kōchi until he graduated from high school. In 1971, Takahashi became a university student of Tōhoku University in Sendai, the north-eastern part of the Japanese mainland. He chose to major in mechanical engineering. When he was a first-year student, Takahashi began to be involved with a progressive student activist group. For Japanese university and high school students, it was not unusual to participate in the progressive movement in those periods. Organizing student groups and workers' unions, young Japanese citizens in those periods were actively involved with social activism inside and outside their schools and workplaces. In particular, the university students who were concerned with issues related to social justice such as war, discrimination against cultural minorities, poverty and hard labour conditions became the main actors in the movement. In this context, Takahashi joined one of the student activist groups which played the leading role among many student groups at Tōhoku University in the 1970s.

While his friends gradually quit their involvement with activism, Takahashi's involvement became so serious that he could not continue his mechanical engineering studies. Takahashi left Tōhoku University without graduating in the early 1980s and moved to Kanagawa Prefecture with his wife. One of the reasons for this move was because his wife was appointed to a teaching position at a local primary school in Kanagawa. The other reason was that there was a base of his group, called the Revolutionary Workers Association, at Kanagawa University in Yokohama City during that period. There, Takahashi spent a short period as the leader of this group.

Takahashi joined the student movement in the early 1970s, a decade after the height of the movement in the history of Japanese new left student activism. The peak of Japan's new left student movement was from 1959 until 1960 when the Bund (*Bunto* in Japanese), an umbrella organization, gathered in the centre of Tokyo with other much larger progressive groups such as the nationwide workers' union, *Souhyō*, trying to prevent then Japanese Prime Minister Kishi Nobusuke from renewing the Japan-US Security Treaty. Over three hundred thousand people joined the public demonstration in front of the National Diet building in June 1960. Although the security treaty was renewed, Kishi and his cabinet had to resign. After the mass protest campaign, the Bund was dissolved, and a non-partisan progressive movement was continued by former members of the Bund and Trotskyists who did not belong to the Japan Communist Party or Japan Socialist Party. After the dissolution of the Bund, the student movement gradually lost its momentum and became radicalized, using violence to attack members of other groups. In this context, Takahashi was also involved with this violent struggle as one of the group leaders. Also, in order to increase the support for his group, and to avoid arrest, Takahashi sometimes changed his name and kept moving from one place to another. After he lived in Kanagawa for a while, Takahashi moved to Okinawa in the mid-1980s to create a local branch of his group and to construct hegemony over the local anti-base movement.

Walking on broken glass and becoming a 'local'

Initially, his stay in Okinawa went as he wished. Takahashi joined some of the local anti-base activist groups and developed his personal connections with fellow Okinawan activists. However, it did not take long for Okinawan anti-base activists to realize Takahashi's hidden intentions. After his identity was revealed, some local activists began a campaign to attack Takahashi as an infiltrator who disguised his career and name in order to use Okinawans and the Okinawan struggle for his own sake. Under the principle of non-partisan civic activism, Okinawan anti-base activists often had a strong distrust for mainland Japanese radical sects. Okinawans thought that these student activists were detrimental for them because they knew from experience that these Japanese activists intended to divide the local anti-base movement for their own purposes.

In this environment, Takahashi could not remain engaged in local Okinawan activism. Yet, returning to the mainland was not an easy option because his family, including two sons, had already settled in Okinawa. Also, his group, which was targeted by the police as one of the subversive 'extreme left violent groups', was no longer able to support Takahashi's lifestyle because their financial resources had been exhausted, and his former colleagues were gradually leaving political activism. Here, Takahashi's life as an activist had reached a dead end.

In such a critical situation, Takahashi turned to several people for help, including Nishio. He offered Takahashi his house to use as a temporary safe place, and this senior activist tried to persuade other Okinawans to pardon Takahashi's past and let him stay on the island. Through Nishio's and friends' efforts, Takahashi could remain in Okinawa with one condition: to leave his previous career and live as 'an Okinawan'. He did not have any other option but to convert his political beliefs. Takahashi described this period as though he were 'walking on broken glass with bare feet'.

After he left student activism, Takahashi started a new career as a social worker. Also, he gradually started studying the Korean language. Prior to this, Takahashi, who later became a Korean expert in Okinawa, had been to South Korea when he was a university student in May 1974. Takahashi was involved in a petition campaign to release his friend who had been jailed in South Korea. When this friend was visiting Seoul National University, he was arrested due to suspicion of involvement with anti-South Korean government activism. In those days, the political situation in South Korea was extremely tense. After the coup d'état in May 1961, the then President of South Korea, Park Chung-hee, had been strictly policing pro-Communists, socialists and student activists. Park's regime also targeted educated ethnic Koreans from Japan who came to visit South Korea, particularly those who were suspected of having relations with the General Association of Korean Residents in Japan (GAKR), which has a close tie with North Korea. After the execution of Cho Young-soo, an executive member of the Korean Residents Union in Japan (KPUJ), because of his active role in establishing the newspaper *The People's Times* (*Minzoku Jihō*) in December 1961, a number of *Zainichi* Koreans were arrested under Park's government.[30]

Park's regime became even more oppressive towards dissidents after he won the presidential election over Kim Dae-jung, an influential opposition leader and a long-term pro-democratization activist, who later became the fifteenth president of South Korea. After this narrow victory over his rival, Park declared martial law. To protest against the new system which reinforced governmental control, South Korean university students such as those from the Democratic Youth Student Association (DYSA) started taking political action, and nearly two hundred students were arrested, including Takahashi's friend. The purpose of Takahashi's visit was to submit a petition to the Japanese Embassy in Seoul on behalf of his fellow activists who were working on the release of this Korean student. Takahashi was chosen to visit Seoul as a delegate of his group because many senior activists had arrest records due to their involvement with activism, while Takahashi was one of the few with no record of being arrested.

After he arrived in Seoul, Takahshi was upset over witnessing the unpopularity of his government in South Korea with his own eyes. Stains and shells from the eggs thrown at the wall of the Japanese Embassy caused great embarrassment and shock to this young and responsible student. This was his first exposure to life under martial law, with restrictions such as nighttime curfew, which made Takahashi extremely anxious and exacerbated his sense of unease. He was perhaps one of the most well-informed about the harsh political oppression under Park's dictatorial regime and the anti-Japanese sentiment among South Korean nationals in Japan in those days. However, his trip to early 1970s Seoul remained a deeply disturbing and haunting experience. After this first visit to South Korea, he avoided being directly involved with the Korean political movement until he joined the OKPS.

A turning point came about ten years later when Takahashi had a chance to re-engage with Korea. He and future OKPS founders were introduced to Park Sunam, a *Zainichi* Korean film director who was interviewing Okinawan local islanders about the memories of Korean forced labourers and 'comfort women' in Okinawa. This trip to Kerama was a key moment that invited Takahashi and others to consider the entangled historical relationship between Okinawa and Korea. Together with other friends who helped Park's filmmaking, Takahashi participated in starting the project Action Committee for Solidarity with Asia (ACSA), which became Okinawa Korea People's Solidarity in 1997. Feeling the necessity of learning the Korean language, Takahashi and other OKPS members started going to Korean language lessons. While many other learners gave up, Takahashi was one of the few students who became fluent in both writing and speaking Korean to the extent that he could translate simultaneously from Korean into Japanese. Ever since, Takahashi has been playing a crucial role in the Okinawan activist community as a leader of the OKPS, a trusted friend to many of his Korean and Okinawan colleagues, and a public speaker on his own experience as a coordinator of trans-border civic engagement in Japan and Korea.

Yu Yeongja

Buddhist nun, mother and a second-generation ethnic Korean, Yu Yeongja's personal journey to OKPS reveals a highly complex set of boundaries that she had to negotiate. She is one of the very few participants in OKPS who has familial and cultural connections with Korea. Also, she is one of the few who have been instrumental in the group as a language expert since the mid-2000s. These aspects make her essential for the group, especially when Okinawans host Korean delegates or when they travel to Korea. But one of the equally important aspects is her presence neither as Japanese, Okinawan nor mainland Korean but as what she describes as 'a bridge' (*kakehashi*) among these places.[31]

Although she joined the group relatively recently, her likeable character, witty jokes and open mind towards others made her even more important in the group, respected and trusted by other members. Her presence also sheds light on the gendered world of OKPS, and more generally, the Okinawan activist community. Other OKPS members, who are either middle-aged or older males who have been involved with civic activism for decades, call her affectionately *nuna*, which means 'elder sister', a Korean word to address older women by younger men, or *haha*, which means 'mother' in Japanese. While they call her as such with respect, these nicknames also indicate metaphorically the roles that she is expected to act in her community. This personality is not her innate character. Rather, as the story shows later, it has been formed through various challenges she walked through.

Yu was born in Hiroshima in 1951. She was the youngest child of nine siblings. Her parents moved from Korea's Jeolla Province to mainland Japan during Korea's colonial period.[32] The family moved to Kobe when Yu was little. Kobe was one of the world's busiest industrial port cities. For this reason, Kobe was also known for its large international population, most typically people from Korea and also other parts of Asia. As a result, the ethnic Korean community in Kobe was active in the civil rights movement even under American occupation after 1945.

One of the earliest and the most well-known examples is perhaps the Hanshin Education Struggle in the late 1940s. The Korean League (*Chōsen-jin Renmei*) in Kobe and Osaka took direct action to protest against the local Japanese police and American Occupation Forces over the right to conduct ethnic education, and this eventually resulted in physical clashes with police and occupation forces. In Kobe, Yu went to the local ethnic Korean school run by the General Association of Korean Residents in Japan until high school. Although her family originated from the southern part of Korea, which was by then the Republic of Korea, Yu's parents, like many other households in this period, sent their daughter to a school closely affiliated with the Democratic People's Republic of Korea (DPRK or North Korea). However, political ideology was not such a major issue for her parents. Rather, they wanted Yu to be educated in a way that would maintain her Korean identity. Also, since neither of her parents was literate, they wanted their children to be educated as people in the new era.

At school, she learnt the Korean language and became 'ethnic Korean in Japan' or what she calls '*Chōsen-jin*'. Also, it was there she met her future husband who was a leader in student activism. Although Yu was never involved in student activism, she was still interested in politics around her community. So, she said, instead of becoming a social activist, she had a dream to become 'a wife of a famous Korean activist'. They married after graduating from high school. Yu's husband later became an art teacher at a local Japanese high school, and Yu began to run a Korean-style barbeque restaurant in Kobe while raising three children.

Nonetheless, she was gradually introduced to the world of the Korean civil rights movement. The first key occasion was the protest campaign against the compulsory fingerprinting of foreign residents in Japan.[33] Ethnic Koreans, who are categorized as 'special permanent residents', were the most affected, and targeted, people by the introduction of this system. In 1980, an anti-fingerprinting movement was started by a Tokyo-based male ethnic Korean, Han Jong-suk. Although he was risking a penalty, either one year in prison or paying a fine, Han chose to refuse to be fingerprinted, insisting that this system was against the International Covenant on Civil and Political Rights, to which Japan became a signatory in 1978.

When Yu saw fellow Koreans who participated in the campaign, particularly people from a similar generation to her, she could not help but join her friends. What inspired Yu most was the fact that this protest campaign was not started by the major ethnic activist groups such as the GAKR, the KPUJ or other political organizations or parties but by average fellow ethnic Koreans and concerned Japanese citizens who joined the campaign as individuals. However, when she decided to join the campaign, Yu's husband, who was once an activist leader, was not supportive of his wife's decision. Despite his ardent commitment to activism, he had already lost his interest in politics. Instead, he told Yu that this was a problem of Japanese society, which needed to be corrected by Japanese people, not 'us'. Her other family members also gave similar advice to Yu. Yet, the opposition from her family could not stop her, even after her husband finally said that he would divorce her if she still insisted on this issue. Remembering those days, Yu said that her answer was 'yes' to divorce. She even told him 'let's divorce and I won't bother your life.' She was confident with herself at that time and thought she would be able to live freely without him finally. In the end, she and her husband did not divorce. Instead, he and other family members decided to support her. Together with her Korean and Japanese friends, her first job was to publish a community journal called *Pīsu Pīpuru (Peaceful People)*. As a principal organizer, she wrote many articles, sitting at the table of her barbeque restaurant after business hours.

The next life-turning moment came soon after she started participating in the anti-fingerprinting campaign in the late 1980s. One of her friends introduced her to a local study group on the Second World War and Japan's colonialism in Himeji, a city not far from Kobe. The event was organized by a local Buddhist group from the Jōdo Shinshū School. At first, Yu was not interested in the event, because she was a strong atheist. But she was interested in hearing a talk by a guest speaker, Kinjō Minoru, a prominent Okinawan sculptor, writer and activist. This event was part of a whole series on the thought of the Japanese Buddhist monk Shinran (1173–1263) – the founder of Jōdo Shinshū. Participants not only read Shinran's texts but also learnt his way of thought to interpret the historical and contemporary problems of Japanese society.

The event was enlightening for Yu because of not only Kinjō, but also the thought of this school. Until that moment, she had considered that religion dealt with morals based on strict rules in order to have a good life after death. Also, Yu's impression of the Jōdo Shinshū School had been negatively affected by the events of history. While known as one of the largest Buddhist Schools, Jōdo Shinshū was also deeply involved in Japanese colonialism. Promoting a mixture of syncretic Buddhism with the national Shintoism, this school had played a crucial role in establishing Japanese Buddhism around Korea. In this context, many local Korean temples were either transformed into Japanese style or abolished.

However, what Yu learnt from one of the monks at the venue changed her views. Yu's scepticism towards Buddhism was shaken particularly when she learnt about the School's idea of the past, present and future. In Shinran's text, the monk told her, Buddha does not give any answer to the question of whether there is life after death. Instead, the monk continued, Shinran's Buddhism respects the present moment, which can be found when one realizes the calls from both past and future. Based on this view and on remorse about their politico-religious activities during the colonial period, the monks and believers participating in the study group were not complacent or tolerant, but unanimously critical of Japan's colonial history. This is how Yu became increasingly fascinated by Jōdo Shinshū and its thought.

This experience turned her into one of the regular participants of the class. Yet, it did not satisfy her intellectual interests. In order to know more about Shinran's thought, she decided to study at Ōtani University, one of the Buddhist universities founded by Jōdo Shinshū, where she was granted a qualification to become a nun at the age of fifty-two.

During her spiritual and intellectual training at Ōtani University, Yu met an ethnic Korean professor, Jeong Cho-myo (also known as Jeong Sanae), who was teaching ancient Korean history. It was Jeong who introduced the joy of studying the South Korean world to Yu. Like many of her fellow ethnic Koreans of her generation who were educated strictly to become 'a local delegate of the General Kim Il-Sun' at the ethnic Korean school, Yu did not really have a positive impression of South Korea. Despite the fact that South Korea was her parents' homeland, Yu knew almost nothing about that place. Jeong understood Yu's suspicion so she took Yu to South Korea in 1999. Born in Japan as a member of an ethnic minority, Yu found that her visit to South Korea was a moment where she could finally feel her ancestral roots, which filled in the space that had long been a blank space in her Korean identity.

Yu and her daughter moved to Okinawa in the early 2000s. Forty years after she had married, Yu decided to leave her home in Kobe. The reason for moving to Okinawa was due to Kinjō Minoru, who became a friend of hers by then, asked Yu to open a local study group on Shinran and Jōdo Shinshū. However, there was another reason that she decided to move. As she aged closer to sixty years, Yu desired to have some new challenges in her life. There was no better chance for her than the invitation from her friends in Okinawa. This time, her husband also supported his wife's decision to live separately for some time each year. Yu thus started living in Yomitan Village for part of the year and in Kobe the rest of the year.

She started organizing a study group shortly after she arrived in the village. The venue was in a corner of Kinjō's studio. Due to her likeable character and welcoming manner regardless of religious background, the class soon became popular among the locals. As she experienced in her first class in Himeji, Yu not only read and discussed the texts with people but she tried to associate those works with Japanese historical contexts. In doing so, however, she created her own manner of critical religious practice using her Korean background. This is demonstrated by the clothes she would wear for the class. When preaching in front of her students, she usually wears a black Buddhist gown called *kesa*. But occasionally she also comes to the class wearing *chima jeogori*, the traditional Korean women's dress. It was around this period when she started participating in the public gathering on Okinawa's base problems, where she was introduced to the founding members of the OKPS.

Although Yu's active involvement with the Okinawan anti-base movement was usually welcomed by many fellow activists, this was not always the case. One unforgettable event took place in 2010, when she attended a public gathering in front of the Okinawa Prefectural Government. Prior to this gathering, she was told by her friends that the next protest demonstration would aim to pressure Okinawa Prefecture by representing 'the voices of all Okinawan residents' who disagreed with the new base construction plan in Henoko. Therefore, Yu thought that she should attend the event in her favourite Korean dress. However, during the protest, she was surrounded by a group of local female activists. One of them asked her why she came with 'such a strange dress'. Yu replied that it was her dress which represented her cultural origin and also said that it is a formal dress to wear at a public event. Yet the woman told her that it was 'inappropriate' to wear that sort of dress because the protest should be a gathering for and by 'Okinawans'. After this event, she seriously started considering returning to Kobe.

However, many of her close Okinawan friends tried to persuade her to remain in Okinawa. They were frustrated that such a divisive view was prevalent within certain groups of fellow Okinawan activists. Of those friends, there was Miyagi Setsuko, one of the most highly respected senior activists who said 'Okinawans needed a person like you'. Furthermore, her strong supporter Kinjō Minoru, who is a community leader in Yomitan Village, also said that Okinawans should work together with ethnic Koreans in Japan as they both share unresolved historical wounds caused by the Japanese. Hearing this encouragement, Yu was reassured that her decision to move to Okinawa was not the wrong choice. Yu's life in Okinawa was not always easy. Above-mentioned cases or similar ones still occur 'occasionally', she said. But after living in Okinawa for nearly fifteen years, Yu also found many reasons to stay. In Yomitan Village, Henoko and elsewhere, she has good communities. Inspired by Yu's life and religious views, some of her friends including influential local politician and activist, Chibana Shōichi, started studying Jōdo Shinshū, and Chibana later became a qualified Buddhist monk.

Complex boundaries

The life histories of Arasaki, Takahashi and Yu, respectively, take us to the memory of social struggles that these individuals experienced and the OKPS, and more generally, the transnationalization of Okinawan anti-base struggle can be a site to see the interaction of those individual threads. The three respective stories show the moments, events and human relations that are involved in and navigate their lives. Furthermore, these highly personalized accounts touch upon the aspects of the social struggles that Japan experienced after 1945. The involvement of Okinawans in student radical activism in the Japanese mainland and the Korean civil rights movements are some of the cases among many stories which have rarely been told in the context of Okinawan activism. Also, Arasaki, Takahashi and Yu's respective journeys showcase how seemingly different political domains in modern Japan – Okinawa and mainland Japan – are in fact related to one another. While these areas tend to be considered in separation, their stories always bring us back to the point where we see the two places in one context of postwar Japanese social activism. Moreover, the translocal lives of these individuals show detailed accounts of how place-based activism such as the Okinawan anti-base movement became a civic movement that fosters a social imagination beyond local and national boundaries. In this sense, therefore, translocal lives are the essential empirical reference for imagining new representations of the social collective that overarch multi-levelled spatial scales.

7

Invisible threads of regionalism

So, what does the history of Okinawan activism tell us when it is seen through the lens of translocality? Before we wrap up this book, I want to return to this question, to clarify the overall theme of this book, to revisit the significance of thinking about and acting upon transborder journeys undertaken by the Okinawan activists, and to think through the present from this particular mode of historical perspective. I will undertake this task in the form of a personal reflection as a person who has crossed paths with numerous colleagues, friends and other like-minded people in different places and as a scholar, who is not only contextualizing but also contextualized in the myriad threads of individual, social and intellectual endeavours undertaken in and around the history of Okinawan translocal activism. In this short concluding essay, I wish to discuss how the tradition of grassroots regionalism is practised today by younger generations of people who have inherited the spirit from their predecessors. Understanding contemporary practices helps us imagine what Tessa Morris-Suzuki calls 'invisible regionalisation', which is a historical process which makes and re-makes a distinct public sphere and a sense of community that are autonomous from top-down strategic regional architecture such as 'the Indo-Pacific'.[1]

As I have discussed throughout this book, Okinawa's grassroots regionalism as an idea or as a movement has rarely been organized as a solid and consistent social movement. Rather, it emerged sporadically and spontaneously in response to certain historical moments. As we have seen in Chapters 3–6, the efforts to create extended linkages with activists in other locales beyond Okinawa Island were led by individuals who were concerned about the isolation of their activism in both the 1970s and 1990s, which I have called the first and the second waves of grassroots regionalism. Those were the historical periods when international political and economic environment experienced great change. The United States' withdrawal from Vietnam and the Sino-US Rapprochement are some of the notable examples, along with the 1973 Oil Crisis, which also had a crucial influence on Okinawa's geopolitical position in the region in the 1970s and the following decade (see Chapters 3 and 4). The late 1980s and the early 1990s were transformative periods, given the end of the Cold War in the North-Atlantic world and the Gulf War, as well as the democratization of South Korea, Taiwan and the Philippines (see Chapters 5 and 6). The Kin Bay struggle and the 1995 mass protest rally, from which derived the first and second grassroots regionalism movements, took place in those key historical moments as a local response to the changing international political environment.

It is perhaps true that the importance of people's transborder linkage-building activities have been seen as *less* important compared to the 'main' activism, such as protest rallies and direct actions. But one of the historical lessons we have learned from Okinawa's grassroots regionalism movements is that the activists were not only focusing on local politics, but they were also aware of broader political issues and relations. This includes some historical events I have not mentioned in detail in this book, such as Okinawans' involvement in the Third World Movement and transnational anti-racism campaign in the 1950s and the 1960s, and indigenous and environmental activism with other communities overseas in more recent years. It is this broader political consciousness that I wanted to bring to the fore in this book. Without their regional awareness, no grassroots regionalism or internationalization of the Okinawan struggle would have taken place.

While examining the origin and development of some activism in-depth, there is one question that remains unexplored. That is, how did Okinawan activists feel an affinity with unfamiliar places such as South Korea or the Philippines or even other remote islands of the Ryūkyū archipelago? This emotional aspect is essential in the making of grassroots regionalism. What are activists thinking, and feeling, when they arrive at these foreign lands and meet the locals? In the rest of this chapter, I intend to consider this question through my personal reflection on some occasions I experienced. Although the following story is about my personal experiences on my trips to Darwin and Okinawa in the early 2010s, it is still worth documenting since it gives some ways to trace, imagine and reconstruct the feelings that some other trans-border activists might have had when they went across the borders.

On feeling at home in an unfamiliar place

In early January 2012, I was in my hometown, spending the holidays with my parents. One day, a friend of mine from Wollongong rang me, saying that he wanted to introduce me to two friends who were visiting Japan from Darwin, in the Northern Territory of Australia. I went out to meet them in Yokohama, where a major anti-nuclear protest rally was being held.

A year had passed since the triple disaster that happened in March 2011. The trauma of the nuclear power plant explosion still haunted many people's minds, including overseas. Therefore, the rally attracted activists' attention from around the world, including the two guests from Darwin – Justin and Cat. They told me that they were planning to visit Okinawa next. The reason for their visit to Okinawa was to see the sites of anti-base activism in Henoko and Takae, and they asked me if I would be able to come along with them. Coincidentally, one of my friends in Okinawa contacted me around the same time to see if I would be interested in joining a tour with two Australians as an interpreter. Of course, the Australians were Justin and Cat. This type of coincidence happens often in the world of social activists, which is small and dispersed, yet closely interwoven.

Coming to Tokyo from Darwin was already exhausting as there is no direct flight between the two places. So, Justin and Cat had to take multiple domestic and international flights. The difference in seasons between mid-winter Tokyo and mid-summer Darwin made the trip even more tiring. On top of that, Tokyo's urban landscape, full of cement and grey concrete skyscrapers, was draining psychologically. Wearing winter coats was not enough for these visitors from the mid-summer of the Top End to cope with the different environment. It also required patience.

When I met them again in Naha, Justin and Cat somehow looked different. Cat grinned and said how grateful she was to come to Okinawa because of the warmth and moisture in the air, which made her feel as if she was in her home in Darwin. It was not only the climate that reminded them of home. From time to time, looking at the massive military bases in Futenma, Kadena and Henoko, both of them made similar comments. Even though they had travelled far from the place they lived, they felt something akin to their home by feeling the air on their skin, seeing the landscape through their eyes and hearing the roar of the fighter jets. With little knowledge of Darwin, not to mention its climate, I was hardly able to understand what she meant at that time.

As I briefly mentioned in Chapter 1, Australia's active involvement was crucial to the reinforcement of a new US regional military strategy in the region, the so-called Re-balance to Asia. In recent years, the Australian government has announced a plan to establish a new security dialogue with the United States, Japan and India (the so-called QUAD) along with a trilateral security pact (AUKUS). The 'Re-balance' policy was a precursor that was announced about a decade earlier. On 17 November 2011, then US President Barack Obama stood side by side with Julia Gillard at the Australian National Parliament in Canberra, where he announced the new plan for basing US troops in Asia and the Pacific. The presence of the PRC was increasingly seen as a major and imminent concern for the White House. In this new international political environment, the Obama administration had decided to shift its security focus from the Middle East to Asia and the Pacific. One of the key highlights around the early 2010s was the rotational deployment of the US Marines in three different locations in the western Pacific to deter China's advance in the region. Darwin, which was already a major military port city, had been chosen to host the US Marines, together with Guam and Okinawa.

Australia has long been a US ally in the South Pacific ever since the Second World War. About a week prior to Japan's signing of the San Francisco Peace Treaty on 8 September 1951, the delegates from Australia and New Zealand signed a military alliance treaty with the United States, called the ANZAS Treaty (Australia, New Zealand and the United States Security Treaty). Although New Zealand's collaboration has been limited due to the dispute over the introduction of nuclear arms since 1984, the alliance between Australia and the United States still continues to develop to this day, including the joint operation of military facilities such as Pine Gap, a major satellite tracking station near Alice Springs. The Royal Australian Airforce Base in

Darwin and the Darwin Port are no exception. They have been used jointly by the Australian military and its US partner for a long time. However, what was unprecedented, at least to the majority of the public, was that both governments agreed to host more than two thousand US military personnel on Australian soil for an indefinite period. Given this official announcement, Justin, Cat and other concerned citizens decided to start a group called the Base Watch to monitor the progress of the situation, while learning about the social and environmental impact of US military bases from overseas, including from Okinawa and South Korea.

After a year since the Australians' visit to Okinawa, in early February 2013, I flew from Sydney to Darwin with three friends from Okinawa, Abe Kosuzu, a renowned academic and activist, and her two postgraduate students. Kosuzu was invited as a keynote speaker at a conference in Canberra. After a few days of seminars and discussions, we travelled to Darwin to meet Justin and Cat and to see their activism.

None of us, including myself, had ever been to Darwin, nor had we much knowledge about the local region, including the mid-summer weather. Justin said that there were only two seasons in Darwin: the 'dry' season and the 'wet' season. Compared to the dry season, which is between June and August, the wet season, which starts from January to March, is 'not the best season to visit', he warned us more than once. The level of humidity in Darwin was a whole new experience for me, coming from Canberra's dry, sizzling summer. Apparently, most households in Darwin have a capacious refrigerator to keep not only fresh food but even peanut butter and other staples that would usually be kept in the pantry. Cyclones and squalls are also common from early to late summer. The most notorious one was Cyclone Tracey, which had hit Darwin on Christmas Day in 1974, and it caused catastrophic damage, destroying about 80 per cent of the entire city. The memory of this tragic historical event is still remembered keenly, often with a strong sense of trauma, by the local inhabitants, as demonstrated by exhibitions at the local galleries and museums.

From the very first day, Darwin left a strong impression on me. The land I came to was surely Australia, yet of a different kind. The city compelled me to feel the limits of my language and senses to understand the place, partly because of my ignorance about the rest of Australia, although I had lived in Canberra for an extensive period by then. Or it could have been that my understanding of Australia was confined so narrowly and rigidly to the industrial and political centres below the Tropic of Capricorn that made me feel that I was in a 'different world'.

In the next moment, however, I realized that I was the only person who had been lost in translation. Darwin's climate seemed to relax my friends' tense bodies and souls, so they became more chatty and livelier. Like me, they saw another Australia in Darwin. But the way they perceived it was different to me. One of them said it felt as if she was back home in Okinawa. Spending an intense period in Canberra, her first overseas trip must have been nothing but exhausting. Her plight was reflected in her face. It was not only the climate that absorbed her energy, but the broader city environment distressed her. One day, when we were walking on Australian National University's (ANU) campus, she took off her socks and shoes and started walking with bare feet, saying that feeling the texture of green grass made her calm down. Until we got to Darwin, she did not have even a pocket of time and space to be herself. So, the humidity and storms of Darwin felt like nothing but a blessing to her mind.

When I heard her saying that she felt she was back home, I recalled Cat's comments when in Okinawa about a year before. Coming straight to Tokyo's winter from Darwin's humid summer, and attending a week-long rally, Justin and Cat perceived Okinawa's lukewarm clear weather not as 'the southern tropical winter' but it reminded them of the 'dry season' of their homeland, which Justin described succinctly as 'perfect weather'.

Those remarks I heard in Okinawa and Darwin still linger in my head, and I sometimes reflect on the meaning of 'feeling at home' in an unfamiliar place and environment. Even though the group of us were all foreigners in Darwin, I could not even conceive of the same feeling as my friend because I was just captivated by the sharp contrast, instead of the similarity, between Canberra and Darwin. I am not trying to bring up such accounts as environmental determinism that grants the natural climate the decisive factor in our mode of thought. Rather, the key focus I raise is a kind of consciousness that makes us 'feel at home', however momentary or unorganized the feeling may be.

This 'sense of (un)familiarity' is conceived and developed through recognizing relevance in material terms, including the local climate. There are two points I am trying to raise here. The first is emotional sensation, which reminds us of home; not always because we have rich global experiences but precisely because of our innate deep knowledge about the political, cultural, natural and material landscape of home. In fact, my Okinawan friend had never before been anywhere overseas except for the Japanese mainland. The local climate was only one of the examples through which the deep-seated bodily experience of Okinawans was recalled. While walking around different sites of Darwin and its adjacent areas, such as a road next to the long fence of the Airforce Base and a mangrove forest, our Okinawan friends mused about how similar the landscape was. Therefore, it was the experiences of their homeland that were mobilized in locating themselves in an unfamiliar world.

However, it is nothing special that we use our past experiences in understanding our whereabouts when we are in an unfamiliar place, and locating ourselves in this way does not always give us the right answer. It sometimes causes various misunderstandings of the other place and community, which can provoke conflicts. However, this does not diminish the importance of the act of mobilizing the bodily experience of home in locating oneself. On the contrary, it leads us to wonder why we keep mobilizing this experience towards identifying our location. My thought is that the very reason we tend to locate ourselves through bodily experience is that it is one of the intrinsic ways of establishing our communication and negotiation with others. As implied in its very notion of 'locating', it is an action for arranging, establishing and fixing oneself in a certain geographical and social and cultural environment and context through which we will tell ourselves about how to relate to others. Therefore, 'locating oneself' in this way inevitably requires reflexivity of oneself to some extent, trying to come to terms with one's position outside of one's actual home. In other words, it is the very first step towards finding and arranging affinity and linkages with others.

The second is that this deeply grounded sense of 'home' which enabled Okinawans to find themselves in Darwin enables us to imagine how the activists and thinkers we have discussed in this book might have seen others when they travelled overseas and how they conceived of, articulated and created grassroots regionalism with other communities. For example, in Chapter 4, Shimao Toshio saw geo-cultural similarity between Amami, Puerto Rico, Hawai'i and Okinawa by observing their similar histories and landscapes as a southern island community, and used the ocean, beaches and sugarcanes as symbolism in his writings to discuss the destitution and impoverishment of islanders' lives in these otherwise distant places. For the people of the OKPS, such as Tomiyama Masahiro, South Korea felt like home not because of its local climate, which is radically different from Okinawa, but because of Korea's civic political culture that developed in parallel with the Okinawan struggle.

This practice of making and finding one's position and affinity in a foreign land can be regarded as the elementary stage for the establishment of grassroots regionalism or trans-border community. As it is elementary, the quality of the connection is still fragile, and it can be disrupted by various structural, technical, logistical and personal problems. Yet, it is true that any form of trans-border society at the grassroots level would not have taken place without this elementary stage. Often grappling with the constraints of financial and other resources compared to major international non-governmental organizations, emotional affinity is crucial to initiating and developing grassroots cooperation. In this very sense, when we try to understand the motivations of translocal activism we need to take into account personal and emotional reasons as well as the ideological.

This is the reason why I call grassroots regionalism 'invisible', as it starts spontaneously, carried out by individuals who are motivated by personal causes. We need to be attentive to small stories that are hardly ever kept in the public records to see this invisible movement. But we also need to remind ourselves that invisibility is not same as absence. Shimao's imaginative endeavour to discover and reconstruct the history of Amami shows that recognizing invisibility invites us to seek the deeper layer beyond the visible surface to find fragmented pieces or traces of past endeavours for building linkages across the boundaries. As demonstrated in this book, Okinawa's grassroots regionalization has steadily progressed over time despite numerous challenges, and we must acknowledge their journeys, which are crucial to making and remaking the world of Okinawan activism.

Notes

Chapter 1

1. See, for example, *The Targeted Village* (2012) [Film] Dir. Chie Mikami, Japan: Ryukyu Asahi Broadcasting.
2. The region includes the entire Okinawa prefecture and Amami region, although the latter was returned in December 1953. The process of Amami's return is detailed in Robert D. Eldridge, *The Return of the Amami Islands: The Reversion Movement and U.S.-Japan Relations* (Lanham: Lexington Books, 2003).
3. The United States Military Government of the Ryukyu Islands was responsible for the early period of Okinawa's occupation until the establishment of the US Civil Administration of the Ryukyus in 1950.
4. Tadao Yanaihara, *Shuchō to Zuisō: Sekai to Nihon to Okinawa ni tsuite* (Tokyo: Tokyo Daigashu Shuppankai, 1957), 191–2, 214–16.
5. Moriteru Arasaki, *Arasaki Moriteru ga Toku Kōzōteki Okinawa Sabetsu* (Tokyo: Tōbunken, 2012).
6. Naoki Uemura, 'The Colonial Annexation of Okinawa and the Logic of International Law: The Formation of an "Indigenous People" in East Asia', *Japanese Studies* 45, no. 2 (June 2003): 213–22.
7. Akiko Fujita, 'U.S. Diplomat Replaced After Calling Okinawans "Lazy" and "Master of Extortion"', ABC News, 10 March 2011, https://abcnews.go.com/International/us-diplomat-kevin-maher-replaced-outrage-surrounding-okinawa/story?id=13100614.
8. Mark Ramseyer, 'A Monitoring Theory of the Underclass: With Examples from Outcastes, Koreans, and Okinawans in Japan', (24 January 2020): 1–61. https://extranet.sioe.org/uploads/sioe2020/ramseyer.pdf.
9. Shinnosuke Takahashi, 'Mobilizing Places: Beyond the Politics of Essentialism in Okinawa Anti-Base Struggle', in *Cultural and Social Division in Contemporary Japan: Rethinking Discourses of Inclusion and Exclusion*, ed. Yoshikazu Shiobara, Kohei Kawabata and Joel Matthews (Singapore: Routledge, 2017), 103–17.
10. Michel Foucault, *Security, Territory, Population*, trans. Graham Burchell (New York: Palgrave Macmillan, 2007), 104–5.

11 Tessa Morris-Suzuki, 'Beyond Consumasia: The Neglected Challenges', in *The Social Sciences in the Asian Century*, ed. Carol Johnson, Vera Mackie and Tessa Morris-Suzuki (Canberra: ANU Press, 2015), 120.
12 The term itself was first coined in the late nineteenth century at the time of Okinawa's annexation by the Japanese empire. See also, Ichirō Tomiyama, *Ruchaku no Shiso: 'Okinawa Mondai' no Keifugaku* (Tokyo: Inpakuto Shuppankai, 2013).
13 Annmaria Shimabuku, 'Petitioning Subjects: Miscegenation in Okinawa from 1945–1952 and the Crisis of Sovereignty', *Inter-Asia Cultural Studies* 11, no. 3 (August 2010): 355–74.
14 See also, Shinnosuke Takahashi, 'Katarisuto toshite no "Okinawa Sengo-shi"', *PRIME* 42 (March 2019): 74.
15 Moriteru Arasaki, 'Okinawa kara Nani ga Mieruka', in *Chiiki no Jiritsu Shima no Chikara*, Vol. 2, ed. Moriteru Arasaki (Tokyo: Komonzu, 2006), 72–3; 'Ajia no Kuniguni to Kyōtsū Suru Shiten wo', in *Okinawa Dōjidaishi 1988–1990: Yawarakai Shakai wo Motomete* (Tokyo: Gaifusha, 2004), 71–2.
16 Ikuo Shinjō, *Okinawa no Kizu toiu Kairo* (Tokyo: Iwanami Shoten, 2014).
17 Yasuhiro Tanaka, *Fūkei no Sakeme: Okinawa Senryō no Ima* (Tokyo: Serika Shobō).
18 Ewa Domanska, 'The Material Presence of the Past', *History and Theory* 45, no. 3 (October 2006): 337.
19 Tessa Morris-Suzuki, *Hihanteki Sōzōryoku no tame ni: Gurōbaruka Jidai no Nihon* (Tokyo: Heibonsha, 2013), 65–6.
20 On the concept of place-based politics, see also, Arif Dirlik, 'Globalization, Indigenism, Social Movements, and the Politics of Place', *Localities* 1 (2011): 80–4.
21 Keisuke Mori, 'Okinawa Shakaiundou wo 'Kiku'koto ni yoru Tagenteki Nashonarizumu-hihan ni mukete: Okinawa-ken Higashi-son Takae no Beigun Heripaddo Kensetu ni Hantaisuru Suwarikomi wo Jirei ni', *Okinawa Bunka Kenkyū* 39 (March 2013): 159–208; Kosuzu Abe, 'Repetition and Change: Direct Action in Okinawa', *Seisakukagaku Kokusaikankei Ronshū* 13 (March 2011): 61–90.
22 Kosuzu Abe, 'Radikaru na Okinawano "Toujisha"', *Okinawa Bunka Kenkyū* 38 (March 2012): 294–6, 309–12.
23 Fujimoto Yukihisa's documentary film *Marines Go Home: Henoko, Maehyang-ri, Yausubetsu* (2008) is an important source of reference to see the formation of protest community in Henoko.

24 Julia Yonetani, 'Appropriation and Resistance in a "Globalised" Village: Reconfiguring the Local/Global Dynamic from Okinawa', *Asian Studies Review* 28, no. 4 (August 2004): 391–406; Kelly Dietz, 'Transnationalism and Transition in the Ryūkyūs', *Transnational Japan as History: Empire, Migration, and Social Movements*, ed. Pedro Iacobelli, Danton Leary and Shinnosuke Takahashi (New York: Palgrave Macmillan, 2015), 211–42.

25 Yuichiro Onishi, *Transpacific Antiracism: Afro-Asian Solidarity in 20th Century Black America, Okinawa, and Japan* (New York: New York University Press, 2013).

26 Kosuzu Abe, 'Re-thinking the Resistance and the Constellation of Minorities in Okinawan Politics', *Seisakukagaku Kokusaikankei Ronshū* 10 (March 2008): 33–47.

27 Tessa Morris-Suzuki, 'Liquid Area Studies: Northeast Asia in Motion as Viewed from Mount Geumgang', *Positions: Asia Critique* 27, no. 1 (February 2019): 217.

28 Ibid., 218.

29 Moriteru Arasaki, *Okinawa Sengo-shi* (Tokyo: Iwanami Shoten, 1976), 1–7.

30 Upon his visit to Okinawa in August 1965, then Japanese Prime Minister Sato Eisaku manifested that 'there will be no end of "postwar" unless Okinawa's reversion to homeland is achieved'.

31 Kosuzu Abe, '"Sengo" ga Mitsukaranai', *Shunjū* 521 (August 2010): 12–14.

32 Heonik Kwon, 'Remembering the Cold War', *Situations* 10, no. 1 (2017): 94–5.

33 On the concept of the post-colonial Cold War, see, for example, Heonik Kwon, *The Other Cold War* (New York: Columbia University Press, 2010).

34 Satoshi Gabe, '"Kokumin Bungaku" no Hensei to Teikō: "Ryūdai Bungaku" ni okeru Kokumin Bungakuron', *Gengo Jouhou Kagaku* 7 (2009): 212.

35 Ge Sun, 'Minshū no Shiten to Minshū no Rentai', *Changbi* 151 (Spring, 2011), https://magazine.changbi.com/jp/archives/89058?cat=2481.

36 Kuan Hsing Chen, 'Editorial', *Inter-Asia Cultural Studies* 15, no. 1 (March 2014): 1.

37 Moriteru Arasaki, 'Can Okinawa Be a Catalyst for Peace in East Asia?', *Inter-Asia Cultural Studies* 15, no. 1 (March 2014): 43–62.

38 See also, Laura Hein and Mark Selden, eds., *Islands of Discontent: Okinawan Responses to Japanese and American Power* (Lanham: Rowman and Littlefield, 2003); Glenn D. Hook and Richard Siddle, eds., *Okinawa and Japan: Structure and Subjectivity* (Abington: Routledge, 2003); Gavan McCormack and Satoko Oka Norimatsu, *Resistant Islands: Okinawa Confronts Japan and the United States* (Lanham: Rowman and Littlefield, 2012).

Chapter 2

1. Therefore, in this thesis, I use the term 'the US military government' to describe USCAR as well as the US Military Government of the Ryukyu Islands.
2. The civil administration under military control was possible for two reasons. First, Okinawa was considered to be a key area for America's defence line of the western Pacific. However, there was no legal basis to claim Okinawa be a part of the United States. Therefore, as the long-term control was determined, the US Military Government transformed itself to the civil administration which not only aimed to possess Okinawa for the strategic purpose but also to establish a democratic political system in Okinawa under the supervision of the United States. USCAR was the local authority delegated by the Far East Command until 1957, and by the US Department of Defence until 1972.
3. Historian Ōta Masahide investigates the difference between the Deputy Governor and the High Commissioner and discusses the superiority of the High Commissioner to the Deputy Governor in terms of the power they were given. As one example, he mentioned that while the Deputy Governor was the local delegate of SCAP in Tokyo, the High Commissioner was placed directly under the US Department of Army. He states that the High Commissioner was wearing 'the four hats', which represent the Heads of (1) the US Ryukyu Commands; (2) the Coordinator of the US Army, Navy, Air Force and Marines in Okinawa as the representative of the Command of the US Pacific Command; (3) the Commander of the Nine Division of the US troops and (4) the US High Commissioner of USCAR. For more detail, see, for example, Masahide Ōta, *Okinawa no Teiō Kotobenmukan* (Tokyo: Kume Shobō, 1984).
4. Prasenjit Duara, 'The New Imperialism and the Post-Colonial Developmental State: Manchukuo in Comparative Perspective', *Japan Focus* (30 January 2006), http://www.japanfocus.org/-Prasenjit-Duara/1715/article.html.
5. The administration system that was implemented in US-occupied Okinawa was perhaps comparable with the local experiences in Saipan and other island communities in Micronesia, which were incorporated into US administration as the Trust Territory of the Pacific Islands.
6. The American Presidency Project, *Dwight D. Eisenhower, Executive Order 10713 – Providing for the Administration of the Ryukyu Islands*, 5 June 1957. https://www.presidency.ucsb.edu/documents/executive-order-10713-providing-for-the-administration-the-ryukyu-islands#:~:text=Criminal%20jurisdiction%20may%20be%20withdrawn,is%20so%20designated%20by%20him (accessed 14 May 2023).

7   Ōta, *Okinawa No Teiō: Kōtōbenmukan*.
8   The United States Central Intelligence Agency, *The Ryukyu Islands and Their Significance*, 6 August 1948. https://www.cia.gov/readingroom/docs/CIA-RDP78-01617A003200010001-4.pdf (accessed 26 February 2024).
9   Ibid.
10 See, for example, Pedro Iacobelli, 'The Limits of Sovereignty and Post-War Okinawan Migrants in Bolivia', *Japan Focus* (August 2013), http://japanfocus.org/-Pedro-Iacobelli/3989/article.html.
11 According to the survey, the population per camp in the northern region was as follows: 10,000 for the camp in Ogimi Village, 57,000 for Haneji and Taira, 30,000 for Nakagawa and Kanwa, 30,000 for Kushi and Henoko, and Sedake 30,000. See, for example, Masa'aki Aniya, 'The Pacific War', in *Yomitan-son Shi*, Vol. 5 (Okinawa: Yomitanson-shi Henshū-īnkai, 2002).
12 Ibid.
13 Ibid.
14 Chiyo Wakabayashi, 'Jīpu to Sajin: Senryō Shoki Okinawa Shakai No "Henyō" to "Hen'I"', *Okinawa Bunka Kenkyū* (March 2003): 2423.
15 Atsushi Toriyama, *Okinawa: Kichi-shakai no Kigen to Sōkoku 1945–1956* (Tokyo: Keisō Shobō, 2013), 106.
16 The number of the former local residents who could not return to their homelands in 1949 is as follows: over 30,000 people for Naha City, 7450 for Yomitan, 7700 for Chatan and 4980 for Kadena. (Toriyama. *Okinawa: Kichi-shakai no Kigen to Sōkoku 1945–1956*), 106.
17 Wakabayashi, 'Jīpu to Sajin: Senryō Shoki Okinawa Shakai No Henyō to Hen'i': 252.
18 Particularly, some districts of the south and middle lost large portions of the private land including farmland due to high concentration of the US military bases and facilities by the beginning of the 1950s. In the case of Chatan Village, the loss of the farmland was 96 per cent.
19 Toriyama, *Okinawa: Kichi-shakai no Kigen to Sōkoku 1945–1956*, 42.
20 Shōkō Ahagon, *Beigun to Nōmin: Okinawaken Iejima* (Tokyo: Iwanami Shoten, 1973), 127.
21 Ibid., 132.
22 According to Arasaki, the US military government began land inspection in order to identify owners from the late 1940s. They completed compiling the cadastre by 1951. Based on this record of private landownership, USCAR issued

certificates of landownership to the owners. See, Yoshio Nakano and Moriteru Arasaki, *Okinawa Mondai Nijyūnen* (Tokyo: Iwanami Shoten, 1965), 71.
23 United States Civil Administration of the Ryukyu Islands, Office of the Deputy Governor, *LAND ACQUISITION PROCEDURE*, APO 719, CA ORDINANCE NUMBER 109, 3 April 1953. http://ryukyu-okinawa.net/pages/archive/caord109.html (accessed 3 September 2013).
24 Ibid.
25 Ahagon, *Beigun to Nōmin: Okinawaken Iejima*, 90–2.
26 According to Proclamation, there were some exceptional ways to appropriate farm land without the actual consent of the landlords; for example, the fifth clause of Article 2, which says 'Should it be deemed of urgent necessity by the CG, RYCOM, that the use and possession of land or other real property be taken by the United States after the publication of a Notice of Intent, but prior to the acquisition of the estate or interest required, the Deputy Governor shall issue an order directing the vacating of the premises.' (UNITED STATES CIVIL ADMINISTRATION OF THE RYUKYU ISLANDS, Office of the Deputy Governor, *LAND ACQUISITION PROCEDURE*, APO 719, CA ORDINANCE NUMBER 109, 3 April 1953).
27 Toriyama, *Okinawa: Kichi-shakai no Kigen to Sōkoku 1945–1956*, 107.
28 Makoto Sakurazawa, *Okinawa no Fukki Undō to Hokaku Tairitsu* (Tokyo: Yūshisha, 2012), 75–6.
29 Ibid.
30 The civilian police system was originally established in the camps during wartime in order to maintain public order in the community. Some civilians in the camps were appointed to perform communal services including acting as civilian police in the camp.
31 Sakurazawa, *Okinawa no Fukki Undō to Hokaku Tairitsu*, 76–8.
32 'Fukki-mae no Okinawa, Beihanzai Yaku Issen-ken', *Shinbun Akahata*, 27 November 2010, http://www.jcp.or.jp/akahata/aik10/2010-11-27/2010112702_04_1.html.
33 Moriteru Arasaki, *Okinawa Gendai-shi e no Shōgen* (Naha: Okinawa Taimususha, 1982), 75–7.
34 Toriyama, *Okinawa: Kichi-shakai no Kigen to Sōkoku 1945–1956*, 75.
35 Ibid., 75–6.
36 Mikio Higa, *Okinawa: Seitō to Seiji* (Tokyo: Chūkō Shinsho, 1965), 109.
37 UNITED STATES CIVIL ADMINISTRATION OF THE RYUKYU ISLANDS, Office of the Deputy Governor, *ESTABLISHMENT OF THE GOVERNMENT*

OF THE RYŪKYŪ ISLANDS, APO 719, CA ORDINANCE NUMBER 13, 29 February 1952. http://ryukyu-okinawa.net/pages/archive/caproc13.html (accessed 4 September 2013).

38 See, for example, Higa, *Okinawa: Seitō to Seiji*, 104, 191. Also, see Ōta, *Okinawa No Teiō: Kōtōbenmukan*, 121–5.
39 Special Subcommittee of the Armed Service Committee, House of Representatives, *Report of a Special Subcommittee of the Armed Service Committee, House of Representatives Following the Inspection Tour, October 14–23 November 1955*, June 1956. http://ryukyu-okinawa.net/pages/archive/price.html (accessed 3 August 2013).
40 Ibid.
41 Ibid.
42 Toriyama, *Okinawa: Kichi-shakai no Kigen to Sōkoku 1945–1956*, 245.
43 Miyume Tanji, *Myth, Struggle and Protest in Okinawa* (Abingdon: Routledge, 2006), 70–1.
44 Yoshio Nakano and Moriteru Arasaki, *Okinawa Sengo-Shi* (Tokyo: Iwanami Shoten, 1976), 84–5.
45 Ibid., 107.
46 Yoshio Nakano and Moriteru Arasaki, *Okinawa Mondai 20 Nen* (Tokyo: Iwanami Shoten, 1965), 133–4.
47 Chōbyō Yara, *Yara Chōbyō Kaikoroku* (Tokyo: Asahi Shuppan, 1977), 38–9.
48 UNITED STATES CIVIL ADMINISTRATION OF THE RYUKYU ISLANDS, Office of the Deputy Governor. *ESTABLISHMENT OF THE GOVERNMENT OF THE RYŪKYŪ ISLANDS*, APO 719, CA ORDINANCE NUMBER 13, 29 February 1952.
49 *Fukki-kyō* (復帰協) is the acronym for *Okinawa-ken Sokoku Fukki Kyōgi-kai* (沖縄県祖国復帰協議会).
50 Eiji Oguma, *"Minshu" to "Aikoku": Sengo Nihon No Nashonarizumu to Kōkyōsei* (Tokyo: Shinyōsha, 2002), 604. Journalist Jon Mitchel argues that the US bases in Okinawa including Camp Schwab were the main airbases not only for the air-raid mission but also aerial application of Agent Orange. See, for example, Jon Mitchell, 'Agent Orange on Okinawa – The Smoking Gun: U.S. Army Report, Photographs Show 25,000 Barrels on Island in Early '70s', *Japan Focus* (30 September 2012), http://www.japanfocus.org/-Jon-Mitchell/3838/article.html.
51 However, a CIA document declassified under the Freedom of Information Act reveals that the US Central Intelligence Agency, in collaboration with a senior politician of the Liberal Democratic Party Kaya Okinori, was planning

to conduct a covert operation directed at influencing the result of the election. (The United States Central Intelligence Agency, *Central Intelligence Agency Japanese Imperial Government Name Files, Kaya Okinori*, document 75, FJTA 55122, 25 September 1968, http://www.foia.cia.gov/search/site/Kaya%20Okinori (accessed 2 September 2015).)

52 Nakano and Arasaki, *Okinawa Sengo-shi*, 172–4.
53 With this issue, the Japanese Prime Minister Satou Eisaku expressed reluctance to allow the US troops to bring in the nuclear weapons on to the ground of Okinawa. However, the type of nuclear weapons that the Japanese government refused to contain was the dated long-distance rocket such as MGM/CGM-13 or so-called Mace B on which it was possible to attach a nuclear warhead. Moriteru Arasaki, *Okinawa 70 Nen Zengo*, 163.
54 'B52 Kadena ni Tsuiraku', *Ryūkyū Shimpō*, 19 November 1968, http://ryukyushimpo.jp/news/storyid-170304-storytopic-9.html.
55 Kōichirō Yoshiwara, ed., *Okinawa: Hondo Fukki no Gensō* (Tokyo: San'ichi Shoten, 1968), 28.

Chapter 3

1 The Japanese government justified the need for Okinawa's rapid economic growth, which, they argued, was disrupted by ravages of the hard-fought battles (*karetsu na senka*) with the United States during the war and its long-term separation from Japan (*naganen ni wataru hondo to no kakuzetsu*). The official document of the plan reports that the Japanese government must make efforts to provide basic infrastructure to support the independent development (*jiritsu-teki hatten*) of Okinawa. However, Arasaki harshly criticized this policy since he saw it as the forcible integration of less developed areas of Okinawa into the Japanese market. See, for example, *The Cabinet Office of Japan, Dai Ichiji Okinawa Shinkō Kaihatsu Keikaku* (Tokyo: The Cabinet Office of Japan, 1972), 1; Moriteru Arasaki, *Okinawa Gendai-shi* (Tokyo: Iwanami Shoten, 2005), 51.
2 Takayoshi Egami, 'Fukki-go no Okinawa Shinkō Kaihatsu Keikaku', *Opinion* 47 (August 2003). http://www.waseda.jp/jp/opinion/2003/opinion47.html (accessed 18 November 2014).
3 Japanese Ministry of Land, Infrastructure, Transport and Tourism, *Zōho Shin Zenkoku Sōgō Kaihatsu Keikaku*, 1969: 9–10.
4 Ibid., 80.

5   Ibid.
6   Ibid.
7   Ibid., 81.
8   Shoichirō Miyazaki, 'Kankō Seisaku Kenkyū: Miyazaki-ken no Rizōto Kaihatsu wo Jirei ni', in *Sasutenaburu Shakai to Kōkyō Seisaku*, ed. Kansai Daigaku Keizai Seiji Kenkyū-jo (Osaka: Kansai University, 2007), 149–87. https://www.kansai-u.ac.jp/Keiseiken/publication/report/asset/sousho143/143_04.pdf.
9   Arasaki, *Okinawa Gendai-shi*, 53.
10 'Tochi Kaishime, Chika Kōtō', (*Ryukyu Shimpō*, 2 December 1972), http://ryukyushimpo.jp/news/storyid-150894-storytopic-9.html.
11 Osamu Tada, *Okinawa Imēji no Tanjō: Aoi umi no karuchuraru sutadīzu* (Tokyo: Tōyōkeizai Shinpō-sha, 2004).
12 See, for example, Robert Stolz, *Bad Water: Nature, Pollution, and Politics in Japan 1870–1950* (Durham: Duke University Press, 2014).
13 Simon Avenell, 'Making Japanese Citizens: Civil Society and the Mythology of the "Shimin"', in *Postwar Japan* (Oakland: University of California Press, 2010); also see, for example, Avenell, 'Regional Egoism as the Public Good: Residents' Movements in Japan during the 1960s and 1970s', *Japan Forum* 18 (2006): 93; also, as an introduction to the study of the Japanese residents' movement, see: Kamon Nikarai and Jiro Matsubara, *Jūmin Undō no Ronri: Undō no tenkai katei, kadai to tenbō* (Tokyo: Gakuyō Shobō, 1976).
14 In terms of the US military bases, in 1982 around nine hundred local residents in Kadena Town brought a lawsuit against the Japanese and US governments due to the noise pollution from the jets from Kadena Airbase. Inspired by the citizens in Kadena, in 2002, concerned residents in Futenma Town also started taking legal action against the US military in relation to the loud noise from Futenma Airbase. On the issues of agent orange and other environmental damage caused by the US military bases, see, for example, John Mitchel, *Poisoning the Pacific: The US Military's Secret Dumping of Plutonium, Chemical Weapons, and Agent Orange* (Lanham: Rowman and Littlefield, 2020).
15 The local pronunciation of Kin puts strength on 'n' sound. Therefore, in Okinawa, the English name is written as 'Kinn' instead of 'Kin'. However, for the sake of convenience, this book uses 'Kin'.
16 Arasaki, *Okinawa Gendai-shi*, 54.
17 Moriteru Arasaki, *Okinawa Sengo-shi*, (Tokyo: Iwanami Shoten, 1976), 205–6.
18 Among recent studies, Uehara Kozue is a leading researcher who has written an introductory essay on anti-CTS struggle. (Kozue Uehara, 'Minshū no "Seizon"

Shisō kara "Kenri" wo Tou: Shiseiken Henkan-go no Kinn Wan, Han CTS Tōsō Saiban wo Megutte', *Okinawa Bunka Kenkyū* 39 (2013): 128.)

19 The Okinawa Development Agency (or Okinawa Kaihatsu-chō) was established in May 1972 with the aim of overseeing economic promotion in Okinawa. As its mission, this government agency was responsible for creating Okinawa's economic development plan and the supervision of Okinawa Development Finance Corporation (Okinawa Shinyō Kaihatsu Kinyū Kinkō).

20 Uehara, 'Minshū no "Seizon" Shisō kara "Kenri" wo Tou: Shiseiken Henkan-go no Kinn Wan, Han CTS Tōsō Saiban wo Megutte', 29–30.

21 Ibid., 29.

22 Moriteru Arasaki, *Okinawa Dōjidai-shi 1973–1977: Yogawari no uzu no nakade, Jiritsu e no shikōsakugo* (Tokyo: Gaifūsha, 2004), 37.

23 For Arasaki's biographical information, see Chapter 6.

24 Interview with Arasaki, 3 December 2011.

25 *Hirogeru-kai* was founded by participants with diverse objectives, and therefore it is not easy to generalize the personal motivations that run underneath. Nonetheless, we could identify some similarities among the founding members' careers. For example, people such as Arakawa Akira, Irei Takashi and Okamoto Keitoku were originally students from Ryūkyū University who joined the literary circle *Ryūdai Bungaku* during the mid-1950s. Later, they supported anti-reversion campaign. Those critical local intellectuals were not only critical of Okinawan political elites who led the reversion movement but also considered that the CTS project was a product of Japanese economic incorporation of Okinawa backed by American expansionism in Asia. Therefore, the Kin Bay struggle was not only an environmental movement but also entailed the meaning as struggle against Okinawa's social integration by Japan and America.

26 Ken'ichi Yamakado, 'Sakishima no Shōhisha Undō: Taketomi, Ishigaki, Miyako kara', *Ryūkyū-ko no Jūmin Undō* 1 (1977): 8–9.

27 Moriteru Arasaki, 'Amami, Okinawa, Ryūkyū-ko: Gendai-shi kara no shiten', *Shin Okinawa Bungaku* 41 (1979): 94–5.

28 Moriteru Arasaki, *Okinawa Dōjidaishi 1978–1982: Ryūkyū-ko no shiten kara* (Tokyo: Gaifūsha, 2004), 193, 222.

29 Kozue Uehara, *Kyōdō no Chikara: 1970–80 Nendai no Kin Wan Tōsō to sono Seizon Shisō* (Tokyo: Seori Shobō, 2019), 159–61.

30 Akira Arakwa, *Tōgō to Hangyaku* (Tokyo: Chikuma Shobō, 2000), 94–5.

31 Moriteru Arasaki, *Okinawa Dōjidai-shi 1978–1982: Ryūkyū-ko no Shiten kara* (Tokyo, Gaifūsha, 2004), 68.

32 Ibid., 69–70.
33 For more detail of New Okinawa Forum, see, for example, Moriteru Arasaki, *Okinawa Dōjidaishi 1988–1990: Yawarakai Shakai wo Motomete* (Tokyo: Gaifūsha, 2004), 175–6.
34 Moriteru Arasaki, 'Chiiki Kenkyūjo no Kanōsei wo Saguru', *Okinawa Daigaku Chiiki Kenkyūjo Nenpō* 18 (2004): 195.
35 The original translation of 'Kyōdō no Chikara' is the 'power of commons'. 'Cooperation' is my own translation.

Chapter 4

1 Toshio Shimao, 'Amami and Japanesia', in *This Is Japan*, 13 (Tokyo: Asahi Shimbun-sha, 1965), 252.
2 Philip Gabriel, *Mad Wives and Island Dreams: Shimao Toshio and the Margins of Japanese Literature* (Honolulu: University of Hawai'i Press, 1999), 164.
3 Osamu Murai, *Nantōideologī no Hassei: Yanagita Kunio to Shokuminchi-shugi* (Tokyo: Fukutake Shoten, 1992), 14–15.
4 Kunio Terauchi, *Shimaoki: Shimao Toshio Bungaku no Ichi-haikei* (Osaka: Izumi Shoin, 2007).
5 Kaoru Kōsaka and Nobuaki Nishio, eds., *Nantō e Nantō kara* (Osaka: Izumi Shoten, 2005).
6 Shinzō Shimao and Kunihiro Shimamura, eds., *Kenshō Shimao Toshio no Sekai* (Tokyo: Bensei Shuppan, 2010).
7 Kunihiko Kudō, '"Bunjin-toshokanchō Shimao Toshio Korekushon" no Keiseikatei ni kansuru Ichikōsatsu', *Memoirs of Beppu Uiversity*, no. 57 (February 2016): 73–85.
8 Shuzen Hokama, *Okinawa no Rekishi to Bunka* (Tokyo: Iwanami Shoten, 1999), 2–8.
9 Anthony Reid, 'Indonesian Studies at the Australian National University: Why so Late?', *RIMA: Review of Indonesia and Malaysian Affairs* 43, no. 1 (June 2018): 52–3.
10 Toshio Shimao and Takeo Okuno, 'Shimao Toshio no Genfūkei', in *Uchi e Mukau Tabi*, ed. Shimao Toshio (Tokyo: Tairyūsha, 1976), 10.
11 Toshio Shimao, 'Nakamura Chihei-san no Koto', in *Shimao Toshio Zenshū 15*, ed. Shimao Toshio (Tokyo: Shōbunsha, 1982), 22–3.

12 Toshio Shimao, 'Saikin no Toshokan no Dōkō', in *Shimao Toshio Zenshū 16*, ed. Shimao Toshio (Tokyo: Shōbunsha, 1982), 92–3.
13 Ibid.
14 Toshio Shimao, *Naze Dayori* (Tokyo: Nōsan Gyoson Bunka Kyōkai, 1977), 21–2.
15 Torao Haraguchi, 'Atogaki', in *Kaitei Naze Shi-shi 3 Minzoku-hen*, ed. Yamashita Fumitake et al. (Naze: Naze Shi-shi Hensan Iinkai, 1973), 365.
16 Toshio Shimao, 'Watashi no Mita Amami', in *Yaponeshia Josetsu*, ed. Shimao Toshio (Tokyo: Sōjusha, 1977), 20–1.
17 Toshio Shimao, 'Kanashiki Nantō-chitai', in *Shimao Toshio Zenshū 16*, ed. Shimao Toshio (Tokyo: Shōbunsha, 1982), 131–2.
18 Toshio Shimao, 'Amami Taiken no Tojō de', in *Shimao Toshio Zenshū 16*, ed. Shimao Toshio (Tokyo: Shōbunsha, 1982), 238.
19 'Desert', *Cambridge English Dictionary*, s.v. https://dictionary.cambridge.org/ (accessed 29 September 2020).
20 Toshio Shimao, 'Kyūnen-me no Shima no Haru', in *Shimao Toshio Zenshū 16*, ed. Shimao Toshio (Tokyo: Shōbunsha, 1992), 168–9.
21 For the concept of presence, see, for example, Eelco Runia, *Moved by the Past* (New York: Columbia University Press, 2014).
22 Eva Domanska, 'The Material Presence of the Past', *History and Theory* 45 (2006): 337.
23 Keitoku Okamoto, *Yaponeshia no Rinkaku: Shimao Toshio no Manazashi* (Naha: Okinawa Taimusu-sha, 1990), 6.
24 Ken'ichi Tanigawa, 'Yaponeshia to ha Nani ka', in *Tanigawa Ken'ichi Chosakushū*, ed. Tanigawa Ken'ichi (Tokyo: San'ichi Shobō, 1984), 376–9.
25 Keitoku Okamoto, *Yaponeshia no Rinkaku* (Naha: Okinawa Taimusu-sha, 1990), 6.
26 Ibid., 7.
27 Prior to this, overseas travel was strictly regulated by the Overseas Travel Committee, which was the government committee under the Ministry of Finance and other relevant national government ministries and agencies. The committee assessed applications and decided whether to approve or refuse them. Their primary concern was to control the drain of foreign currencies to overseas.
28 Shinzō Shimao, 'Bunka Kaikan-jidai no Boku no Otōsan', in *Shimaoki: Shimao Toshio Bungaku no Ichi-haikei*, ed. Kunio Terauchi (Osaka: Izumi Shoin, 2007), 325–30; 'Kagoshima-kenritsu Toshokan Amami-bunkan to Otōsan', in *Kenshō Shimao Toshio no Sekai*, ed. Shimao Shinzō and Shimamura Kunihiro (Tokyo: Bensei Shuppan, 2010), 13–14. Charles and Iola both had worked for the

USIA in the city of Nakhorn Rachisma in Thailand for nine years prior to their relocation to Japan in 1957. In Japan, the couple first worked in the Nagasaki Office before they moved to Fukuoka upon the closure of Nagasaki Office. See Iola Lyttle Medd, *Sunshine and Shadows* (Lincoln: iUniverse, 2003).
29 Edwin O. Reischauer, 'The Broken Dialogue with Japan', *Foreign Affairs* 39, no. 1 (October 1960): 13.
30 Zen'ichi Nakamura, *Fukuoka Amerikan Sentā 40 Nen* (Fukuoka: Fukuoka Nichibei Kyōkai, 1993); Muku Hatojū, *Muku Hatojū no Hon 31: Tabi no Omoide Amerika Kikō, Shika-shū* (Tokyo: Riron-sha, 1989).
31 Toshio Shimao, 'Amerika no Ritō', in *Shimao Toshio Zenshū 14*, ed. Shimao Toshio (Tokyo: Shōbunsha, 1982), 344.
32 Toshio Shimao, 'San Fuan Antiguo nite', in *Shimao Toshio Zenshū 14*, ed. Shimao Toshio (Tokyo: Shōbunsha, 1982), 353.
33 Toshio Shimao, 'Okinawa Sakishima e no Tabi', in *Shinpen Ryūkyū-ko no Shiten kara* (Tokyo: Asahi Shimbun-sha, 1992), 205.
34 Ibid., 253.
35 In the Japanese text, which could be his original text, the term 'plantation' is translated as *satō jima* ('the sugar islands'). See, Toshio Shimao, 'Amami: Nihon no Nantō', in *Shimao Toshio Zenshū 17*, ed. Shimao Toshio (Tokyo: Shōbunsha, 1983), 44–53.
36 Shimao, 'Amami and Japanesia', 253.

Chapter 5

1 Kangjeong Village is located in the southern part of Cheju Island in South Korea. The South Korean government announced the plan to create a naval base in Cheju for the first time in 1993. After fifteen years of searching for a possible location for the naval base, the government eventually appointed Kangjeong Village in 2007. Since then, the concerned villagers and activists from Korea and the rest of the world have been conducting an anti-base construction campaign.
2 Moriteru Arasaki, Masahiro Tomiyama, Ichirō Nishio, Toshio Takahashi and Yusa Yo, 'Tomo ni Manabi, Tomo ni Kawaru, Okikan Minshu Rentai no Ayumi', *Keishi Kaji* 70 (March 2011): 6–25.
3 Moriteru Arasaki, *Okinawa Dōjidai-shi 1983–1987: Shōkoku-shugi no Tachiba de* (Tokyo: Gaifūsha, 2004), 107.

4   Fukiko Okimoto, 'A Study on the Drafted Koreans in the Battle of Okinawa: Focusing on the Special Water Service Unit', *Regional Studies* 20 (December 2017): 29–30.
5   Arasaki, *Okinawa Dōjidai-shi 1983–1987: Shōkoku-shugi no Tachiba de*, 102.
6   Komatsugawa Incident is the homicides of two Japanese schoolgirls by a young male, Ri Chin-u. The case became sensational partly due to the ethnic background of the culprit. Park exchanged a number of letters with Ri, who was sentenced to capital punishment. As a result of exchanges, she edited a book based on those letters titled: *Tsumi to Ai to Shi to* (*Guilt, Love and Death*) in 1963. Japanese progressive intellectuals were publicly criticizing the court decision in terms of Japan's historical relations with Korea. For more detail, see, for example, Simon Avenell, *Asia and Postwar Japan: Deimperialization, Civic Activism, and National Identity* (Cambridge: Harvard University Press, 2022), especially Chapter II.
7   Kurk Schock, *Unarmed Insurrections: People Power Movements in Nondemocracies* (Minneapolis: University of Minnesota Press, 2005), 146.
8   Ajia to Rentai suru Shūkai Jikkō Iinkai, ed. *Okinawa-Kankoku Hankichi Kōryūdan Hokokushū* (1997), 1.
9   Interview with Nishio Ichirō, 23 November 2011.
10 Arasaki et al., 'Tomo ni Manabi, Tomo ni Kawaru, Okikan Minshu Rentai no Ayumi', 7.
11 Interview with Nishio Ichirō and Tomiyama Masahiro, 23 November 2011.
12 Arasaki et al., 'Tomo ni Manabi, Tomo ni Kawaru, Okikan Minshu Rentai no Ayumi', 14.
13 Ibid., 15.
14 Ibid., 10.
15 Ibid., 14.
16 Interview with Nishio Ichirō and Tomiyama Masahiro, 23 November 2011.
17 Ibid.
18 Arasaki et al. 'Tomo ni Manabi, Tomo ni Kawaru, Okikan Minshu Rentai no Ayumi', 13.
19 Interview with Tomiyama Masahiro, 14 December 2011.
20 Arasaki et al., 'Tomo ni Manabi, Tomo ni Kawaru, Okikan Minshu Rentai no Ayumi', 18.
21 Interview with Tomiyama Masahiro, 21 November 2011.

Chapter 6

1. Tessa Morris-Suzuki, 'Civil Society across Frontiers: Three Japan-Based Grassroots Movements and Their Legacies', paper presented at The Seventeenth Conference of the Japanese Studies Association of Australia, the University of Melbourne, Melbourne, 4–7 July 2011.
2. Interview with Arasaki Moriteru, 20 December 2011.
3. Ibid.
4. Ibid.
5. Moriteru Arasaki, 'Watashi ga Ikita Okinawa-shi, soshite Sekai-shi 2'. *Keishikaji* 76 (October 2012): 56–65.
6. Ibid.
7. Ibid.
8. Ibid.
9. Interview with Arasaki Moriteru, 20 December 2011.
10. Ibid.
11. Arasaki, 'Watashi ga Ikita Okinawa-shi, soshite Sekai-shi 2', 58.
12. Ibid.
13. GENERAL HEAD QUARTERS UNITED STATES ARMY FORCES, PACIFIC Assistant Chief of Staff, G-2 Civil Censorship Detachment, *CODE FOR JAPANESE PRESS*, 21 September 1945. https://dl.ndl.go.jp/pid/9885095/1/1 (accessed 20 May 2023).
14. Moriteru Arasaki, 'Chīki to Tomoni Ikiru Daigaku', *Daigaku to Kyōiku* 31 (2002): 15–39.
15. Nakano's relationship to Okinawa began when he was a high school student. One of his close friends during that period was 'the last governor' of Okinawa before 1945, Shimada Akira, who died in the battle of Okinawa. See Yoshio Nakano, *Okinawa to Watashi* (Tokyo: Jijitsūshin-sha, 1972).
16. For more detail, see Okinawa Daigaku 50 Nen Shi Henshū Iinkai, ed. *Chiisana Daigaku no Ōkina Chōsen: Okinawa Daigaku 50 Nen no Kiseki* (Tokyo: Kōbunken Shuppan, 2008).
17. Moriteru Arasaki, *Okinawa Dōjidaishi 1988–1990: Yawarakai Shakai wo Motomete* (Tokyo: Gaifū-sha, 2004), 116–17.
18. Yoshirō Tamanoi, 'Ajia wo Miru Me', in *Tamanoi Yoshirō Chosaku-shū Volume 3: Chiiki-shugi kara no Shuppatsu*, ed. Kazuko Tsurumi and Moriteru Arasaki (Tokyo: Gakuyō-shobō, 1990), 175–98.

19 Yoshirō Tamanoi, 'Okinawa wo Omou', in *Tamanoi Yoshirō Chosaku-shū Volume 3: Chiiki-shugi kara no Shuppatsu*, ed. Kazuko Tsurumi and Moriteru Arasaki (Tokyo: Gakuyō-shobō 1990), 202–3.
20 In contrast to the economic profit-oriented growth model, Tamanoi calls it economy that is based on 'human scale'. (Yoshirō Tamanoi, 'Chiiki-shugi no Fukamari no Nakade', in *Tamanoi Yoshirō Chosaku-shū Volume 3*, 158.)
21 Moriteru Arasaki, 'Foreward', in *Tamanoi Yoshirō Chosaku-shū Volume 3*, 1.
22 Ibid.
23 Tamanoi, 'Ajia wo Miru Me', 196–7.
24 Keiko Itokazu, *Okinawasen to Heiwa Gaido* (Tokyo: Shiryō Sentā Hogō, 2008), 31–2.
25 Moriteru Arasaki, *Okinawa Dōjidaishi 1983–1987: Shōkokushugi no tachiba de* (Tokyo: Gaifūsha, 2004), 107.
26 Saburō Takahashi, Moriteru Arasaki and Chōsei Kabira, *Okinawa Mondai to Kirisuto-sha no Sekinin* (Tokyo: Seitō-sha, 1970), 22.
27 Ibid.
28 Arasaki, *Okinawa Dōjidaishi 1983–1987: Shōkokushugi no tachiba de*, 116.
29 Interview with Toshio Takahashi, 24 November 2011.
30 KPUJ or Mindan is one of two major organizations joined by ethnic Koreans in Japan together with GAKR. In contrast to GAKR, KPUJ is known for its support of the South Korean government.
31 Interview with Yeongja Yu, 2 March 2012. This interview was conducted at Café Rui in Naha.
32 Jeolla Province was one of the major provinces, along with Jeju Island and South Gyeongsan Province, from which Koreans migrated to mainland Japan during the 1920s and 1930s as a result of the land reform policy implemented by the Japanese authorities.
33 The fingerprinting system was introduced in 1955 as a part of the Alien Registration Act, which was enacted three years prior in 1952, with the aim to control and surveillance of non-Japanese residents within Japan. When foreign nationals need to live in Japan for more than ninety days, they are obliged to be issued with an official certificate of registration, the alien registration card, by the municipal governments in the area where they live. Until 2000, foreign nationals were supposed to have their fingerprints taken at the time of submitting the application form and of renewing the certificate.

Chapter 7

1 Tessa Morris-Suzuki, 'Civil Society across Frontiers: Three Japan-Based Grassroots Movements and Their Legacies', paper presented at The Seventeenth Conference of the Japanese Studies Association of Australia, the University of Melbourne, Melbourne, 4–7 July 2011.

Selected bibliography

Abe, Kosuzu. 'Re-thinking the Resistance and the Constellation of Minorities in Okinawan Politics.' *Seisakukagaku Kokusaikankei Ronshū* 10 (March 2008): 33–47.
Abe, Kosuzu. 'Repetition and Change: Direct Action in Okinawa.' *Seisakukagaku, Kokusaikankei Ronshū* 13 (March 2011): 61–90.
Abe, Kosuzu. 'Radikaru na Okinawa no "Tōjisha": Kussetsu suru Integiritī to Okinawa Sengo-shi Purojekuto.' *Okinawa Bunka Kenkyū* 28 (March 2012): 291–317.
Ahagon, Shōkō. *Beigun to Nōmin: Okinawaken Iejima*. Tokyo: Iwanami Shoten, 1973.
Arakwa, Akira. *Tōgō to Hangyaku*. Tokyo: Chikuma Shobō, 2000.
Arasaki, Moriteru. *Okinawa Gendaishi e no Shōgen*. Naha: Okinawa Times-sha, 1982.
Arasaki, Moriteru. *Okinawa Dōjidai-shi 1973–1977: Yogawari no uzu no nakade, Jiritsu e no Shikōsakugo*. Tokyo: Gaifūsha, 2004.
Arasaki, Moriteru. *Okinawa Dōjidai-shi 1978–1982: Yogawari no uzu no nakade, Jiritsu e no Shikōsakugo*. Tokyo: Gaifūsha, 2004.
Arasaki, Moriteru. *Okinawa Dōjidai-shi 1983–1987: Shōkoku-shugi no Tachiba de*. Tokyo: Gaifūsha, 2004.
Arasaki, Moriteru. *Okinawa Dōjidaishi 1988–1990: Yawarakai Shakai wo Motomete*. Tokyo: Gaifūsha, 2004.
Arasaki, Moriteru. *Okinawa Gendai-shi*. Tokyo: Iwanami Shoten, 2005.
Arasaki, Moriteru, ed. *Chiiki no Jiritsu Shima no Chikara* Vol. 2. Tokyo: Komonzu, 2006.
Arasaki, Moriteru, Masahiro Tomiyama, Ichirō Nishio, Toshio Takahashi and Yusa Yo. 'Tomo ni Manabi, Tomo ni Kawaru, Okikan Minshu Rentai no Ayumi.' *Keishi Kaji* 70 (March 2011): 6–25.
Avenell, Simon. 'Regional Egoism as the Public Good: Residents' Movements in Japan during the 1960s and 1970s.' *Japan Forum* 18 (August 2006): 89–113.
Avenell, Simon. *Making Japanese Citizens: Civil Society and the Mythology of the 'Shimin' in Postwar Japan*. Oakland: University of California Press, 2010.
Avenell, Simon. *Asia and Postwar Japan: Deimperialization, Civic Activism, and National Identity*. Cambridge, MA: Harvard University Press, 2022.
Dietz, Kelly. 'Transnationalism and Transition in the Ryūkyūs.' *Transnational Japan as History: Empire, Migration, and Social Movements*, edited by Pedro Iacobelli,

Danton Leary and Shinnosuke Takahashi. New York: Palgrave Macmillan, 2015, 211–42.

Domanska, Ewa. 'The Material Presence of the Past.' *History and Theory* 45, no. 3 (October 2006): 337–48.

Duara, Prasenjit. 'The New Imperialism and the Post-Colonial Developmental State: Manchukuo in Comparative Perspective.' *Japan Focus* 4, no. 1 (30 January 2006): 1–17. http://www.japanfocus.org/-Prasenjit-Duara/1715/article.html.

Foucault, Michel. *Security, Territory, Population*. Translated by Graham Burchell. New York: Palgrave Macmillan, 2007.

Gabriel, Philip. *Mad Wives and Island Dreams: Shimao Toshio and the Margins of Japanese Literature*. Honolulu: University of Hawai'i Press, 1999.

Hein, Laura, and Mark Selden, eds. *Islands of Discontent: Okinawan Responses to Japanese and American Power*. Lanham: Rowman and Littlefield, 2003.

Higa, Mikio. *Okinawa: Seitō to Seiji*. Tokyo: Chūkō Shinsho, 1965.

Hook, Glenn D., and Richard Siddle, eds. *Okinawa and Japan: Structure and Subjectivity*. London: Routledge Curzon, 2003.

Inoue, Masamichi S. *Okinawa and the U.S. Military: Identity Making in the Age of Globalization*. New York: Columbia University Press, 2007.

Kōsaka, Kaoru, and Nishio Nobuaki, eds. *Nantō e Nantō kara*. Osaka: Izumi Shoten, 2005.

Kwon, Heonik. *The Other Cold War*. New York: Columbia University Press, 2010.

Kwon, Heonik. 'Remembering the Cold War.' *Situations* 10, no. 1 (2017): 85–98.

McCormack, Gavan, and Satoko Oka Norimatsu. *Resistant Islands: Okinawa Confronts Japan and the United States*. Lanham: Rowman and Littlefield, 2012.

Medd, Iola Lyttle. *Sunshine and Shadows*. Lincoln: iUniverse, 2003.

Mori, Keisuke. 'Okinawa Shakaiundou wo 'Kiku'koto ni yoru Tagenteki Nashonarizumu-hihan ni Mukete: Okinawa-ken Higashi-son Takae no Beigun Heripaddo Kensetu ni Hantaisuru Suwarikomi wo Jirei ni.' *Okinawa Bunka Kenkyū* 39 (March 2013): 159–208.

Morris-Suzuki, Tessa. 'Civil Society across Frontiers: Three Japan-Based Grassroots Movements and Their Legacies.' Paper presented at The Seventeenth Conference of the Japanese Studies Association of Australia, The University of Melbourne, Melbourne, 4–7 July 2011.

Morris-Suzuki, Tessa. *Hihanteki Sōzōryoku no tame ni: Gurōbaruka Jidai no Nihon*. Tokyo: Heibonsha, 2013.

Morris-Suzuki, Tessa. 'Beyond Consumasia: The Neglected Challenges.' *The Social Sciences in the Asian Century*, edited by Carol Johnson, Vera Mackie and Tessa Morris-Suzuki. Canberra: ANU Press, 2015, 117–30.

Morris-Suzuki, Tessa. 'Liquid Area Studies: Northeast Asia in Motion as Viewed from Mount Geumgang.' *Positions: Asia Critique* 27, no. 1 (February 2019): 209–39.

Murai, Osamu. *Nantōideologī no Hassei: Yanagita Kunio to Shokuminchi-shugi*. Tokyo: Fukutake Shoten, 1992.

Nakano, Yoshio. *Okinawa to Watashi*. Tokyo: Jijitsūshin-sha, 1972.

Nakano, Yoshio, and Moriteru Arasaki. *Okinawa Mondai Nijyūnen*. Tokyo: Iwanami Shoten, 1965.

Nakano, Yoshio, and Moriteru Arasaki. *Okinawa Sengo-shi*. Tokyo: Iwanami Shoten, 1976.

Oguma, Eiji. *'Minshu' to 'Aikoku': Sengo Nihon No Nashonarizumu to Kōkyōsei*. Tokyo: Shinyōsha, 2002.

Okamoto, Keitoku. *Yaponeshia no Rinkaku: Shimao Toshio no Manazashi*. Naha: Okinawa Taimusu-sha, 1990.

Okimoto, Fukiko. 'A Study on the Drafted Koreans in the Battle of Okinawa: Focusing on the Special Water Service Unit.' *Regional Studies* 20 (December 2017): 29–53.

Onishi, Yuichiro. *Transpacific Antiracism: Afro-Asian Solidarity in 20th Century Black America, Okinawa, and Japan*. New York: New York University Press, 2013.

Ōta, Masahide. *Okinawa no Teiō Kotobenmukan*. Tokyo: Kume Shobō, 1984.

Reischauer, Edwin O. 'The Broken Dialogue with Japan.' *Foreign Affairs* 39, no. 1 (October 1960): 11–26.

Runia, Eelco. *Moved by the Past*. New York: Columbia University Press, 2014.

Sakurazawa, Makoto. *Okinawa no Fukki Undō to Hokaku Tairitsu*. Tokyo: Yūshisha, 2012.

Schock, Kurk. *Unarmed Insurrections: People Power Movements in Nondemocracies*. Minneapolis: University of Minnesota Press, 2005.

Shimabuku, Annmaria. 'Petitioning Subjects: Miscegenation in Okinawa from 1945–1952 and the Crisis of Sovereignty.' *Inter-Asia Cultural Studies* 11, no. 3 (August 2010): 355–74.

Shimao, Shinzō, and Shimamura Kunihiro, eds. *Kenshō Shimao Toshio no Sekai*. Tokyo: Bensei Shuppan, 2010.

Shimao, Toshio. 'Amami and Japanesia.' *This Is Japan* 13 (August 1965): 252–3.

Shimao, Toshio. *Naze Dayori*. Tokyo: Nōsan Gyoson Bunka Kyōkai, 1977.

Shimao, Toshio. *Yaponeshia Josetsu*. Tokyo: Sōjusha, 1977.

Shimao, Toshio, ed. *Shimao Toshio Zenshū* Vol. 14. Tokyo: Shōbunsha, 1982.

Shimao, Toshio, ed. *Shimao Toshio Zenshū* Vol. 15. Tokyo: Shōbunsha, 1982.

Shimao, Toshio, ed. *Shimao Toshio Zenshū* Vol. 16. Tokyo: Shōbunsha, 1982.

Shimao, Toshio, ed. *Shimao Toshio Zenshū* Vol. 17. Tokyo: Shōbunsha, 1983.

Shinjo, Ikuo. *Okinawa no Kizu toiu Kairo*. Tokyo: Iwanami Shoten, 2014.

Sun, Ge. 'Minshū no Shiten to Minshū no Rentai.' *Changbi* 151 (Spring 2011). https://magazine.changbi.com/jp/archives/89058?cat=2481.

Takahashi, Saburō, Moriteru Arasaki and Chōsei Kabira. *Okinawa Mondai to Kirisuto-sha no Sekinin*. Tokyo: Seitō-sha, 1970.

Tamanoi, Yoshirō. *Tamanoi Yoshirō Chosaku-shū* Vol. 3: *Chiiki-shugi kara no Shuppatsu*. Edited by Kazuko Tsurumi and Moriteru Arasaki. Tokyo: Gakuyō-shobō, 1990.

Tanaka, Yasuhiro. *Fūkei no Sakeme: Okinawa Senryō no Ima*. Tokyo: Serika Shobō, 2010.

Tanigawa, Ken'ichi. *Tanigawa Ken'ichi Chosakushū*. Tokyo: San'ichi Shobō, 1984.

Tanji, Miyume. *Myth, Struggle and Protest in Okinawa*. Abingdon: Routledge, 2006.

Terauchi, Kunio. *Shimaoki: Shimao Toshio Bungaku no Ichi-haikei*. Osaka: Izumi Shoin, 2007.

Tomiyama, Ichirō. *Ruchaku no Shiso: 'Okinawa Mondai' no Keifugaku*. Tokyo: Inpakuto Shuppankai, 2013.

Toriyama, Atsushi. *Okinawa: Kichi-shakai no Kigen to Sōkoku 1945–1956*. Tokyo: Keisō Shobō, 2013.

Uehara, Kozue. *Kyōdō no Chikara: 1970–80 Nendai no Kin Wan Tōsō to sono Seizon Shisō*. Tokyo: Seori Shobō, 2019.

Wakabayashi, Chiyo. 'Jīpu to Sajin: Senryō Shoki Okinawa Shakai No "Henyō" to "Hen'i".' *Okinawa Bunka Kenkyū* 29 (March 2003): 233–86.

Yanaihara, Tadao. *Shuchō to Zuisō: Sekai to Nihon to Okinawa ni tsuite*. Tokyo: Tokyo Daigashu Shuppankai, 1957.

Yara, Chōbyō. *Yara Chōbyō Kaikoroku*. Tokyo: Asahi Shuppan, 1977.

Yonetani, Julia. 'Appropriation and Resistance in a "Globalised" Village: Reconfiguring the Local/Global Dynamic from Okinawa.' *Asian Studies Review* 28, no. 4 (August 2004): 391–406.

Yoshiwara, Kōichirō, ed. *Okinawa: Hondo Fukki no Gensō*. Tokyo: San'ichi Shoten, 1968.

Index

Abe Kosuzu 9, 11, 14, 143
Action Committee for Solidarity with Asia (ACSA, *Ajia to Rentaisuru Shūkai Jikkō Īnkai*) 98–9, 101, 131
Activism by the Residents of the Ryūkyū Arc (ARC, *Ryūkyū-ko no Jūmin Undō*) 47–8, 58, 61–3, 156 n.25
Act on Special Measures for the Promotion and Development of Okinawa (*Okinawa Shinkō Kaihatsu Tokubetsu Sochi-hō*), 1971 46
Act to Establish the Okinawa Development Agency (*Okinawa Kaihatsu-chō Secchi-hō*) 46
Agent Orange 54, 153 n.50, 155 n.14
agriculture 25, 74
Ahagon Shōkō 26
Aka Island 94
Alien Registration Act 162 n.33
All-Base Workers Union (*Zengunrō*) 40
Allied Powers 13, 21, 25, 94, 118
Amami Kyōdo Kenkyū-kai (Amami Local Community Research Society) 75
Amami-Ōshima (Amami) island 2, 10, 13, 19, 21–2, 24, 31, 47–8, 58–9, 65, 67–8, 71–9, 83–6, 145–6, 147 n.2
Amami Shidan-kai (Amami History Discussion Group) 75
Ampo protest (1960) 82
anti-authoritarian movement 6, 20, 101
anti-base activism/movement 4–7, 11–12, 17–18, 21, 43, 54, 90, 92–3, 96, 98, 100, 104–7, 110, 113–15, 128, 137, 141
  social and political landscape before 26–32
anti-base politics 6–7, 9–10, 16, 20, 43, 53, 63, 97

anti-base solidarity movement 19, 96
anti-base struggle 4, 10, 12, 15, 21, 43, 93, 97, 104–5, 111, 137
anti-colonial struggles 7, 11, 15
anti-CTS struggle 18–19, 57, 155 n.18
anti-fingerprinting movement 133. *See also* fingerprinting system
anti-imperialism 7, 11, 15
anti-naval base construction movement 104
anti-racism 11, 15, 140
anti-reversion movement 40–2, 60, 80
anti-US base activism/movement 1, 99–100, 102, 104, 126
anti-Vietnam War movement 11, 15, 38–9, 42
ANZAS Treaty (Australia, New Zealand and the United States Security Treaty) 142
Arakaki Tokiko 97
Arakawa Akira 15, 19, 42, 57, 60, 67, 70, 84, 122, 156 n.25
  Okinawa: Antithesis to the Nation State (*Hankokka no Kyōku*) 41–2
  Shin Nantō Fudoki (*The New Culture and Geography of the Southern Islands*) 60
Arasaki Moriteru 7–8, 36, 57, 59–62, 65, 92, 96, 98, 100, 106, 113–16, 137, 151 n.22, 154 n.1
  'Can Okinawa Be a Catalyst for the Peace in East Asia?' 16
  The Contemporary History of Okinawa (*Okinawa Gendai-shi*) 16, 114
  early life and family 115–16
  finding Korea in Okinawa 124–6
  ill health during childhood 116
  impact on atomic bombing of Hiroshima 119
  and Nakano 120
  Okinawa That Became Japan (*Nihon ni Natta Okinawa*) 121

Okinawa: The Backlight of the Imperial System (*Okinawa: Tennōsei e no Gyakkō*) 121
patriotism (*aikokushin*) 116–19
The Postwar History of Okinawa (*Okinawa Sengo-shi*) 13, 114
postwar Japanese democracy 117
professional career 119–21
region/regionalism 122–4, 126
speech at graduation ceremony of Okinawa University 7
sphere of influence 17
sphere of living (*seikatsu-ken*) 17
The True Way to Japan's Independence 117
Arasaki Seibin 115
Arasaki Seichū 115–16
Arasaki Tawo 115–16
Article Three of the San Francisco Peace Treaty 24, 36–7
Asato Seishin 55–6
Asian Circle of Thought 2012 Shanghai Summit (2012) 16
Association of the Okinawan Landlords 32, 34
Association for Protection of Okinawan Children (APOC) 38
Association for the Return of Okinawa Islands to the Home Country (AROIHC, *Okinawa Shotō Sokoku Fukki Kisei-kai*) 37–8
Association for Solidarity with Asian People 20
Association for the Return of Okinawa to Japan (AROJ, *Nihon Fukki Sokushin Kisei-kai*) 36–7
Australia 9, 20, 51, 81, 141–4
 Darwin 20, 141–5
Australian National University (ANU) 71, 144
authoritarian regime 20, 97

B-29 *Superfortress* bomber 24
base-related crimes 37–8, 111. *See also* Yumiko-chan Incident
Base Watch group 143
Battle of Okinawa (1945) 1, 4, 13, 21, 25, 64, 94–5, 118–19, 124
Bayan (Bagong Alyasang Makabayan or the New Nationalist Alliance) 97–8

'becoming' model 10
the beggars' march (*kojiki kōshin*) 26–7
'being' model 10
Bonin Islands 24
borders/borderlands 9, 11, 14, 17, 60, 63, 72, 85–6, 90, 110, 117, 131, 139–41, 146
British Commonwealth 51
Buddhism/Buddhist 74–5, 131, 134–6

Cairo Communique. *See* Potsdam Declaration
Caltex firm 55
camp for civilians 22, 25, 42, 59, 151 n.11, 152 n.30
Camp Schwab 153 n.50
Canberra 142–4
Central Terminal Station (CTS) 55–9
Cheju Island 89–90, 159 n.1
Chibana Shōichi 136
Chibana Tatsumi 109
Chiba Prefecture 109
chiiki (location/region) 18–19
China 14, 16, 20, 24, 60, 142
Chisso Chemical company (mercury poisoning) 52–3
 case filed against 53
Chōshū Domain 3
The Citizens against the Noise from Futenma Airbase (*Futenma Bakuon Soshoudan*) 127
civic activism 1, 4, 19, 47, 52–4, 62–3, 129, 131
Clark Airbase 97–8
Cold War geopolitical reductionism 6–7, 11, 17
collective representation of base-politics 9
colonization 4, 12, 19
communication infrastructure 50
conservative coalition 39–40
Council for the Promotion for the Resolution of the Military Land Problem (*Gunyōchi Mondai Kaiketsu Sokushin Renraku Kyōgikai/Renkyō*) 34
Council for the Return of Okinawa to the Home Country (CROHC, *Fukki-kyō*) 38
criminal cases 29, 37–8

cultural homogeneity 61, 67, 79
customs (*kyūkan*) 3

The dancing cats disease 52. *See also* neurological disease
Dazai Osamu 72
Debating Club 117
decolonization 65, 70–1
deforestation 51–2, 54
Democratic Youth Student Association (DYSA) 130
democratization 93, 97, 99–103, 124, 140
Deoneum group 109
direct actions, activism 1, 5, 9, 101, 104, 132, 140
discrimination 2, 4, 15, 47, 63, 127
Domanska, Ewa, on presence 8, 78
Duara, Prasenjit 22

ecology/ecological system 54, 123–4
Edo period 75
Eisenhower, Dwight D. 22
environmental activism 47, 59, 63, 140
environmental pollution 52–4, 62, 81, 105, 155 n.14
Esso firm 55
ethnic Koreans 3, 20, 94, 103, 114, 129, 131–3, 135–6, 162 n.30
Europe 51

fingerprinting system 133, 162 n.33. *See also* anti-fingerprinting movement
First Promotion and Development Plan 53–4
Foucault, Michel, on population 6
Foundation for the Okinawa Oceanic Expo (*Okinawa Kaiyō Hakurankai*) 50
Freedom of Information Act 153 n.51
Fujimoto Yukihisa, *Marines Go Home: Henoko, Maehyang-ri, Yausubetsu* 148 n.23
fukkō (reconstruction) 28
Fukuchi Hiroaki 95
Fukuda Takeo 40
Fukuoka American Center 81
Futenma 25, 93, 97, 105, 107–8, 142, 155 n.14

General Association of Korean Residents in Japan (GAKR) 129–30, 162 n.30
geo-cultural 59, 66–8, 78, 145
geology/geological 5, 18, 58
geopolitics/geopolitical 7–9, 12, 24, 106, 140
Gillard, Julia 142
Government of Ryukyu Islands (GRI, *Ryūkyū Seifu*) 23, 32–3, 35
grassroots activism 5, 47, 52
grassroots land rights movement 1, 47
grassroots regionalism 12–17, 19, 61–2, 65, 91, 114–15, 139–40, 145–6
Gulf Oil Corporation 55–6

Hakuryūmaru ship 67
Han Jong-suk 133
Haraguchi Torao, *The History of Naze City* 74
Hashimoto Ryūtarou 99
Hawai'i 19, 22, 50, 81, 83–5, 145
Headquarters of the National Campaign for the Eradication of Crimes by US Troops (*Juhan Migun Beomjoe Geunjeor Undong Bonbu*/*Jumibun*) 99
Heian period (794–1185) 86
Heianza Island 55
Henoko 9–10, 54, 108, 136, 141–2
Hidaka Rokurō 119–20
Higa Shūhei 31–3
Himeji 134–5
Hirogeru-kai. *See* Activism by the Residents of the Ryūkyū Arc; Society for Promoting the Anti-CTS Struggle
Hitotsubo Hansen Jinushi-no-kai (*Hitotsubo* Anti-War Landowners Association) 64, 93, 100, 105, 121
Hokama Shuzen 70
Hokkaido 4, 59, 107
The House of the Red Tiles (*Akara no Ie*) 124
Human Pavilion, Osaka National Industrial Exhibition (1903) 3

Ie Island 1, 17, 26
    Maja community of 26–7

Ikeda Hayato 81
  aims of Ikeda's administration 49
  Income-doubling Plan 49
Ikemiyagi Shūi 30
Imperial Rule Assistance Association
  (*Taisei Yokusan-kai*) 30
independence (*dokuritsu*) 29, 62, 71, 117, 122, 126
India 16, 71, 142
indigenous activism 15, 59
Indonesia 16, 71
The Informed-Public Project 54
Inoue, Masamichi S., *Okinawa and the U.S. Military* 11
Institute of Regional Studies (IRS, *Chiiki Kenkyūjo*) 62-3
insularity (*kakuzetsu*) 60-1
International Union for Conservation of Nature (IUCN) 89
Irei Takashi 42, 57, 156 n.25
Ishigaki Island 54, 58, 60, 83-4
Ishihara Shintarō 40
Ishikawa Mao 95, 109-10
island-wide protest campaign 18, 34-5, 38, 42, 99

Japan 1-4, 6-7, 9-11, 13-14, 16, 18, 23-4, 35-6, 40-2, 49-51, 66-8, 78, 85, 98, 108, 113, 124, 142
  administration handover from United States to 45
    commemoration of Okinawa's administration to (*go ichi go* ceremony) 108-10
  anti-Vietnam War movement in 38-9
  Aqua-polis, aquarium (Motobu) 51
  Chiba 50
  economic growth in 13-14, 54-5
  internal colonialism of 69-70
  Japan Defense Bureau 64
  Japanese Communist Party 29, 42, 128
  Japanese Imperial Army 24, 94, 117
  Japanese Liberal Democratic Party (LDP) 39-40, 45
  Japan Socialist Party 42, 128
  mainland (*see* mainland Japan/Japanese)
  Minamata, Kumamoto 52-3
  Miyazaki 50
  Motobu 51
    deforestation 51-2
    land prices, rise in 52
  National Diet of Japan 41, 45, 128
  peace constitution 42
  postwar Japan 7, 15-16, 42, 49, 52-3, 65, 73, 87, 117, 119, 137
  refusal of nuclear weapon type 154 n.53
  restoration of independence 117
  reversion (*see* reversion-to-Japan movement)
  Self Defense Forces 10
  subtropical region in 49, 51
  Tokyo 15, 22, 38-9, 41, 46, 49-50, 66-8, 72, 109, 114-16, 120, 128, 133, 141, 144
  Toyama 53
  US-Japan Security Treaty 9, 82, 100, 128, 142
  Yokkaichi 53
Jeju Island 104, 162 n.32
Jeolla Province 162 n.32
Jeong Cho-myo (Jeong Sanae) 135
jichi (self-governance) 28, 34, 62, 122
Johnson, Lyndon B. 38, 66

Kadena Airbase 33, 54, 97, 105-7, 142, 155 n.14
  explosion of B-52 bomber in 41
Kadena Bakuon Soshō-dan group 54
Kagoshima Prefecture 18, 21, 58-9, 67, 72, 81-2, 115
Kakeroma Island 72
Kanagawa Prefecture 105, 127-8
Kaneshi Saichi 30-2
Kangjeong Village 159 n.1
Kawamıtsu Shin'ichi 19, 42, 60, 122
Kaya Okinori 153-4 n.51
Kazari Eikichi 75-6
Kerama Islands 21, 96
  forced suicide in 4
  Korean conscripted workers in 94-5
Kim Yong-han 99-100
Kin Bay 11, 47, 121
Kin Bay struggle 18, 47, 64, 123, 140, 156 n.25
Kinjō Minoru 134-6
Kin Town 54-7, 59
Kishi Nobusuke 128

Kkottaji group 109–10
kōgai (environmental pollution). *See* environmental pollution
Kojiki (Japanese myths) 50
Komatsugawa Incident 94, 160 n.6
Korean Peninsula 2, 106, 125
Korean Residents Union in Japan (KPUJ) 130, 133, 162 n.30
Korean War 13, 106–7, 125
Kōsaka Kaoru 70
Kubota Hikoho 72–3, 82
Kudo Kunihiko 70
Kumamoto 52, 59, 116
Kushi Fusako, 'Memoir of a Declining Ryūkyūan Woman' 4
Kyūshū Island 50, 72, 82, 116

Lanai Island 84
land acquisition 27, 152 n.26
land reclamation 55
land reform policy 162 n.32
land requisition policy 2, 27, 33–4
Lee Myung-bak 90
livelihood space 2, 8, 12, 54, 59
local activism 4, 6–7, 9–11, 17, 43, 53–4, 59, 63, 105, 114, 139, 146
locality/localities 5, 9–12, 17–18, 43, 61, 68, 113
local schools 28–9
lump-sum payment system 33–5

MacArthur, Douglas 118
Maehyang-ri 104–5
Maher, Kevin 5, 64
mainland Japan/Japanese (*naichi*) 2–4, 13–15, 25, 36–7, 46, 50–1, 55, 59, 72, 74–5, 80, 92–3, 95–6, 114–15, 121, 127, 145, 162 n.32
Maja community of Ie Island 26–7
Marcos, Ferdinando 97, 99
marure mission 94
mass protests 2, 5, 18, 34, 54, 82, 99–100, 128, 140. *See also* protest campaigns/movements
Master Plan of Land Development (*Dai-ichiji Zensō*) 49
Matsuoka Seiho 55
Medd, Charles 82
Meiji 3

Melanesia 66, 71
memories of wounds, Okinawa 8–9
Micronesia 59, 66, 71, 150 n.5
migrants 114–15, 126, 162 n.32
Miho Toshio 60, 67, 72
Miki Takeshi, *Okinesia* 60
military colony, Okinawa as 2, 15, 23–4
Ming China 2
Mitchel, Jon 153 n.50
Mitsubishi 56
Mitsui 56
Miyako Islands 22, 24, 31, 66, 83–4, 92
Miyanomori Elementary School, military plane crash 38. *See also* Yumiko-chan Incident
Miyazato Kiyogorō 95
Moon Se-gwang Incident 103
Muku Hatojū. *See* Kubota Hikoho
Murai Osamu 69–70

Naha 10, 16, 26, 32, 41, 47, 57, 67, 84, 90–1, 93, 100, 109, 120, 141
Nakamura Chihei 72–3
Nakano Yoshio 120, 161 n.15
Nakasone Genwa 29–30, 36
Nakasone Yasuhiro 56
Nansei Shotō (*Okinawa Shotō*) 58
nanyō (South Sea) 50, 68, 71
National Diet of Japan 41, 45, 128
National Library of America 64
National Security Act 103
Naze 67, 73–4
neurological disease 52
New Master Plan for the National Land Development (*Shin Zenkoku Sōgō Kaihatsu Keikaku/Dai-niji Shin Zensō*) 49
New Okinawa Forum (NOF, *Shin Okinawa Fōramu*) 62
News Joshi (News Girls) 6
New Tokyo International Airport (Narita Airport) 64
Nimitz, Chester 21
Nippon Decimal Classification system 73
Nishime Junji 39–40, 45, 97
Nishio Ichirō 91–2, 98, 100–1, 103–4, 108–9
Nishio Nobuaki 70, 129
Nixon, Richard 39–40

nōson bunko (village library) 73
nuclear power plant explosion 141

Obama, Barack 142
occupied territories (*gaichi*) 4
Oceanic Expo '75 51–3
The Oceanic Expo Shock (*kaiyōhaku shokku*) 52
Odaka Kunio 119
Ogata Matato 53
Ōhama Nobumoto 38, 46, 50
Oka Masao 68
Okamoto Keitoku 19, 42, 57, 60, 65, 79–80, 156 n.25
  Yapoesia no Rinkaku (*The Outline of Japanesia*) 80
Okinawa Advisory Council (*Okinawa shijun-kai*) 22
Okinawa Biodiversity 54
Okinawa Civilian Government (*Okinawa Minseifu*) 22, 29–31
Okinawa Communist Party 36
Okinawa Democratic Alliance (ODA, *Okinawa Minshu Dōmei*) 29–32
Okinawa Development Agency (*Okinawa Kaihatsu-chō*) 156 n. 19
Okinawa Education Consortium (*Okinawa Kyōiku Rengō-kai/Kyōren*). See Okinawa Teachers and General Staff Association (OTGSA)
Okinawa International University 62
Okinawa Korea People's Solidarity (OKPS) 19–20, 91–3, 96, 101–2, 104–11, 113–15, 127, 130–1, 136–7, 146
Okinawa Liberal Democratic Party (OLDP) 36, 38–9, 42, 45–6
Okinawa Mitsubishi Development 56
Okinawan identity 61–2
Okinawan Mayors' Association 32, 34
Okinawan problem (*Okinawa mondai*). See anti-base politics
Okinawa People's Party (OPP, *Okinawa Jinmin-tō*) 30–3, 36, 38–9
Okinawa Prefectural Government Employees Union (*Kenrōkyō*) 38
Okinawa Prefecture 3, 15, 21, 36, 45–6, 58, 62, 64, 92, 108, 147 n.2

Okinawa Socialist Party (OSP, *Okinawa Shakai-tō*) 30, 32, 39
Okinawa Social Mass Party (OSMP, *Okinawa Shakai Taishū-tō*) 31–3, 36, 38–9, 42
Okinawa Teachers and General Staff Association (OTGSA) 27–8, 34, 36–8, 40, 55–6, 63
Okinawa Women's Association 28, 38
Okinawa Youth Association 28, 38
Okinesia 60
Okuno Takeo 72
Orientalist/Orientalism 50, 69
Osaka National Industrial Exhibition (1903), Human Pavilion in 3
Ōta Kunio 92
Ōta Masahide 23, 97, 150 n.3
Overseas Travel Committee 158 n.27

'Pacific cultural space' (*Taiheiyō bunka-ken*) 70–1
Pacific Fellows Association (*Taiheiyō Dōshikai*) 94, 124–6
Parent and Teacher Association 36, 38
Park Sunam 130–1
  'Ariran no uta: Okinawa kara no shōgen' (*The Song of Arirang: Testimony from Okinawa*) 94
  Komatsugawa Incident 94, 160 n.6
  produced films on atomic bombs in Hiroshima and Nagasaki 95
patriotic boys (*aikoku shōnen*) 116–19
People Power Revolution 97
People's Republic of China 2, 24, 71, 125
petroleum storage plant, Kin Town 54–5
PFASs (per- and polyfluoroalkyl substances) 54
The Philippines 9, 13, 16, 20, 22, 39, 71, 84, 97–8, 140
  Luzon 69
  Okinawa-Philippine 97–9
  Tomiyama's visit to 97
philosophy of anti-reversion (*han-fukki no shisō*) 41
Pine Gap 142
political activism 30, 37, 69, 93, 129
pollution, environmental 52–4, 62, 81, 105, 155 n.14
Polynesia 66, 71

popular mobilization 34, 36
population, camp (northern region) 151 n.11
post-colonial nations 7, 14–15, 51, 71
post-reversion period 18, 40, 47, 53–4, 61, 63–4
postwar (*sengo*) period in Okinawa 7, 12–17
Potsdam Declaration 13, 24–5
Prefectural Government Workers' Union 56
Price, Charles Melvyn 33
The Price Report 33
principles to protect local land (Four Principles) 33–4
progressive coalition 39
progressive politics 18, 32, 38, 56, 62–3
pro-reversion movement 37, 41–2, 46
protest campaigns/movements 1, 6, 9, 10–11, 17, 21, 26, 27, 34–6, 40–1, 43, 47, 53–4, 56–9, 64, 82, 99–100, 104, 128. *See also* mass protests
Puerto Rico 19, 81, 83–5, 145
pungmur nori (traditional farmers' music) 109
punishment (*shobun*) 3, 37
Pyeongtaek 104–5

Qing China 3
Quemoy 16

racialization 3
radical subjectivity 10, 12, 18
Ramseyer, Mark 5, 64
Re-balance policy 142
regional government system 22–3, 31
regionalism 15, 18–19, 60, 63, 114, 123. *See also* grassroots regionalism
regionality 61–2
regional politics 15–16, 20, 23, 71, 113, 122
Republican Party (*Kyōwa-tō*) 32
Research School of Pacific Studies 71
residents' activism (*jūmin undō*) 52–3, 56
residents-centred economy 58
residents-oriented activism 53, 59
resistance 15, 27, 43, 53, 57–61, 67, 79
reversion-to-Japan movement 13–14, 28, 36–40, 45–6, 62
Revolutionary Workers Association 128
rinkai bunko (seaside library) 73

Roh Tae-Woo 102, 126
Roman Catholicism 75
Rosario, David 59
Royal Australian Airforce Base 142–3
Rūkyūan shamanism 74
Ryūdai Bungaku 156 n.25
Ryukyu-America Cultural Centers 81
Ryūkyū Arc (*Ryūkyū-ko*) 10, 18–19, 58–61, 65, 67–70, 77, 79, 84–7, 122–3
Ryūkyū Democratic Party (RDP, *Ryūkyū Minshu-tō*) 32–3
Ryūkyū Islands 3, 21–4, 26–7, 38, 47–8, 50, 54, 58–9, 62–3, 147 n.3
'The Ryukyu Islands and Their Significance' document 23
Ryūkyū Kingdom 2–3, 67
 abolishment of 3
 incorporation with military forces 4
Ryūkyū-ko no Jūmin Undō (the Residents Movements in the Ryūkyū Arc) 18
Ryūkyū Legislature 23, 32–5, 37
Ryūkyūnesia 60

Said, Edward 69
San Francisco Peace Treaty (1951) 24, 36, 117, 142
Satō Eisaku 38, 46, 48–50, 65–6, 81, 154 n.53
 visit to Okinawa in 1965 149 n.30
Satō-Nixon communique 40
Satsuma 2–3, 75, 83, 85
schooling system 28–9
Second World War 1, 12, 14, 16–17, 29, 35, 82, 115–17, 124–5, 134, 142
Segodon drama 72
Senaga Kamejirō 30
Shimada Akira 161 n.15
Shimao Shinzō 70, 82
Shimao Toshio 19, 59, 61, 65–72, 122, 145
 'Amami and *Japanesia*' 65–6, 85
 historical desert 75–7, 79
 Japanesia 59–60, 67–70, 79–86
 and Kazari 75–6
 and Kubota 72
 as librarian 73–4
 Murai's accusation against 69–70
 and Nakamura 73
 past of the community 78, 86
 reference to Indonesia 71

relocation from Tokyo to Amami 72
Sekai Kyōyō Zenshū (*The Complete Volumes of World Cultures*) 79
visit to Puerto Rico 83
visit to sugarcane islands 83, 85
visit to the United States 82–3
youth travel program 69
Shimazu clan 2–3, 67, 75, 85
Shimura Kunihiro 70
Shinjō Ikuo 8
Shin Nihon Bungaku-kai (The New Japanese Literature Association) 82
Shinran (Buddhist monk) 134–5
Shintoism 75, 134
Shirato Shin'ichi 124
social and political landscape of Okinawa (before anti-base movement) 26–32
Social Science Club 117
Society for Promoting the Anti-CTS Struggle (*CTS Soshi Tōsō wo Hirogeru-kai*) 18–19, 57
Society for the Promotion of the Kin Bay Struggle (*Kin-wan Tōsō wo Hirogeru-kai*). *See* Activism by the Residents of the Ryūkyū Arc
Society for the Protection of Kin Bay (SPKB, *Kin-wan wo Mamoru-kai*) 55–6, 58, 63
  lawsuit against Yara and Okinawa Mitsubishi Development 56–7
Society of One Feet (*Ichi-fito no Kai*) 64
socioeconomic 34, 46, 49, 51, 64, 85
solidarity movement 11, 15–16, 19, 42, 58, 60–1, 96–7, 100, 102–3, 105, 126
South Korea 6, 9, 14, 16, 19–20, 64, 89–93, 100, 114, 124–6, 129–31, 135, 140, 143, 146
  anti-US base struggles 100
  banning Okinawan activists to enter South Korea 89–90
  democratization of 97, 99–103
  Korean conscripted workers 15, 94–6
  and Okinawa (*see* Okinawa Korea People's Solidarity (OKPS))
  Seoul 103, 106–7, 130
  South Gyeongsan Province 162 n.32
  Status of Forces Agreement 99
sovereignty 15, 24. *See also* territorial sovereignty

Special Action Committee on Okinawa (SACO) 99
structural discrimination against Okinawa 2, 63
student activism 20, 92, 103, 128–9, 132
subjectivity 7, 10, 12, 18, 126
sugarcane plantation 3, 19, 75, 83, 85
Suh Sung 101
Supreme Commander of the Allied Powers (SCAP) 22, 24, 150 n.3

Taira Tatsuo 23, 31–2, 36
Taiwan/Taiwanese 3, 6, 14, 16, 58, 60, 69, 95, 125, 140
Takae (a village embraced by the forest) 1, 9–10, 54, 108, 141
Takahashi Saburō 125
Takahashi Toshio 89, 92, 98, 101–2, 108–9, 113, 126–8, 137
  as an anti-base activist 128–31
  declined by Korean Government to attend IUCN conference 89–90
  early life 127–8
  as social worker 129
  visit to Japanese Embassy in Seoul 130
takakura (thatch-roofed storehouse) 86
Takara Ben, *Ryūkyūnesia* 60
Takazato Suzuyo 96
Taketomi Island 58
Tamanoi Yoshirou 123–4, 162 n.20
Tanigawa Ken'ichi, 'What Is *Japanesia*' 80
Tanji, Miyume, *Myth, Struggle and Protest in Okinawa* 11
Tarama Island 58
targeted village (*hyōteki no mura*) 1
Terauchi Kunio, *Shimaoki* (*The Record of Shimao*) 70
territorial sovereignty 13, 24, 46, 117
Tessa Morris-Suzuki 8, 12
  invisible regionalisation 139
Thailand 13, 39
Third World movement 15, 140
Tokugawa Shogunate 3
Tomita Eiji 89–90
Tomiyama Masahiro 91–2, 96–8, 100–1, 103, 106, 146
  declined by Korean Government to attend IUCN conference 89–90
  visit to Philippines 97
Torishima 107

Toriyama Atsushi, decade of cooperation 34
To Yusa 92–3, 98, 101, 103, 107
trade 2–3, 22, 81, 98, 124
transnational/transnationalization 55, 67, 79, 84, 90–1, 100, 110, 113, 123, 137, 140
transpacific 11, 81, 84–5

Uehara Kozue 11, 59, 64, 155 n.18
Uemura Naoki 4
Ui Jun 62
The United States 10–11, 14, 24, 34, 45, 50, 66–7, 81, 83–5, 100, 142, 150 n.2, 154 n.1
    invasion of Okinawa Island 4, 8, 21, 24, 29, 43, 150 n.5
    military (*see* US military administration/government)
    public diplomacy policy 82
    Status of Forces Agreement 99
    United States Information Agency (USIA) 81–2, 159 n.28
    US Central Intelligence Agency 153 n.51
    US Far East Command 22
    US House of Representatives 33
    US-Japan bilateral security alliance system 2, 9, 18
    US-Japan Security Treaty 9, 82, 100, 128, 142
    US Marine Corps 1, 20
    US occupation authority 1, 13, 22–4, 27, 30, 34, 36, 67, 81, 84–5
    US Pacific Command 22
Urazoe 25, 93
US Civil Administration of the Ryukyus (USCAR) 2, 21–4, 27, 31–3, 37–9, 150 n.2, 151 n.22–3
    hardline approach 34–5
    Ordinance Number 109 27
    Proclamation No. 1 21
    Proclamation No. 13 31, 37
    Provisional Central Government 32
US military administration/government 13, 18, 21, 23, 26–7, 29–31, 37, 42, 45–6, 80–1, 84, 97–8, 102, 106–8, 147 n.3, 150 nn.1–2, 151 n.18, 151 n.22, 155 n.14

military facilities 2, 13, 24–5, 27, 46, 63
military personnel 25–6, 29, 35, 42, 46
military violence 2, 8–9
Special Proclamation Number 37 23
Yun Kuem-Yi case 99

Vietnam War 93, 97

wartime generation (*senchū-ha*) 116
Washington 2, 15, 22–4, 39, 41
Washington DC 32, 35, 66, 83
whole island struggle (*shimagurumi tōsō*) 2, 32–5, 119

Yaeyama Islands 22, 24, 31, 54, 58
Yakabi Osamu 9–10
Yamakado Ken'ichi 57–8
Yanagita Kunio 68–9
Yanaihara Tadao 2, 23
yanbaru (a mountainous field) 1, 51
Yara Chōbyō 36–40, 45–6, 56
    principles for the new Okinawa 45
    proposal of hosting '75 World Expo (October 1971) 50
Yokosuka 105
Yomitan Village 25, 63, 93
Yonaguni island 10, 48
Yonagusuku 55
Yoshino Genzaburō 120
Yumiko-chan Incident 37. *See also* Miyanomori Elementary School, military plane crash
Yun Kuem-Yi case 99
Yu Yeongja 113–14, 131–7
    Buddhism 134
    chima jeogori (traditional Korean women's dress) 135–6
    early life and family 132–3
    Jōdo Shinshū Buddhist School 134–5
    kesa (Buddhist gown) 135
    opposition from family 133
    Pīsu Pīpuru (*Peaceful People*) publication 133
    protest campaigns 133
    separate living without family 135

Zainichi Koreans 103
    arrest of 130
Zamami Island 94